MODERN ISSUES IN EUROPEAN LAW
Nordic perspectives

The Raoul Wallenberg Institute

Modern Issues in European Law

Nordic Perspectives

Essays in Honour of

Lennart Pålsson

Edited by

Göran Melander

KLUWER LAW INTERNATIONAL

Sold and distributed in the U.S.A. and Canada
by Kluwer Law International,
675 Massachusetts Avenue, Cambridge, MA 02139, U.S.A.

In all other countries, less the Nordic countries, sold and distributed
by Kluwer Law International,
Distribution Centre, P.O. Box 322, Dordrecht, The Netherlands.
Tel.: 31-78-654 64 54
Fax: 31-78-654 64 74

Norstedts Juridik AB
Kundtjänst
Box 6454
113 82 Stockholm/Sweden
Tel.: 08-690 96 96
Fax: 08-690 90 30

100124 1412

O

Modern Issues in European Law – Nordic Perspectives
Essays in Honour of Lennart Pålsson
Göran Melander (Ed.)
© 1997 Norstedts Juridik AB

Published by:
Kluwer Law International, holder of the World rights,
less the countries listed below.
Norstedts Juridik AB: Sweden, Norway and Finland

ISBN Kluwer International 90-411-0423-2

Printed in Sweden by Graphic Systems AB, Göteborg 1997

LENNART PÅLSSON

Lennart Pålsson was born in Halmstad, Sweden on 13 October, 1933. After matriculation he came to Lund and its university and he has been faithful to Lund since then.

Initially he studied classical languages – Latin and Greek. After having graduated as B.A. he declined to continue at the Department of Classical Studies within the Faculty of Humanities. He became registered at the Faculty of Law.

After graduation he received practical training as junior judge and was later accepted as a judge at the Court of Appeal. However, the attraction of the university and its law faculty became irresistable and he decided to devote his time to research.

In 1966 Lennart Pålsson published his thesis – Haltande äktenskap och skilsmässor – and he immediately became ass. professor (docent) at the Faculty of Law. In 1969 he was appointed professor in international law, which chair was newly established.

Lennart Pålsson's chair comprised both Public and Private International Law, but his main interests have always been focused on Conflicts of Law. His principal works in English on marriage, divorce and other family matters in comparative conflict of laws have become classical reading for conflict lawyers all over the world. Undergraduate students of law in Sweden, both in Lund and at the other Swedish law schools, have appreciated his case books, collections of statutes and collections of international treaties regarding conflicts of law, while his former and present doctoral students tell tales about his perfectionist demands and the exactitude of his legal thinking. To Swedish practicing lawyers, he is probably best known for his regular critical surveys of the decisions of Swedish courts in cases involving conflicts of law, and for his books and articles, in particular his detailed commentary on the Lugano Convention.

Lennart Pålsson was among the first Swedish legal writers who realized the importance of E.C. Law. His textbooks in this field (1970, 1976) have played a crucial role in spreading knowledge about the legal aspects of the European integration throughout Sweden. In connection with the referendum on Sweden's membership in the European Union, Lennart Pålsson made no secret of the fact that he was in favour of the European integration process and that he wished Sweden to plan an active role in it.

In addition to being an academic teacher and writer, Lennart Pålsson has made an important impact on Swedish legislation. His expert knowledge has been used by the Ministry of Justice, which commissioned him to investigate and propose new legislation on conflict of laws regarding family law issued. Some of his proposals have resulted in new Swedish statutes, while others are still being considered in connection with a legislative projekt which is presently being carried out at the Ministry.

For a number of years, Lennart Pålsson served on the Editorial Committee of the Nordic Journal of International Law, on the Board of the Raoul Wallenberg Institute of Human Rights and Humanitarian Law, and on the Board of the Emil Heijne's Foundation for Research in Legal Science.

Acting upon the advice of the publisher, the editor decided that all contributions to this book must be in the English language and deal with a subject within Lennart Pålsson's main fields of interests, namely Private International Law and E.C. Law. This policy has compelled the editor to decline, with regrets, some offers of contributions. I hope that the authors concerned understand my reasons and do not feel offended by my decision, which does not in any respect reflect any doubts about the quality of their work.

The editor wish to thank Emil Heijne's Foundation for Research in Legal Science (*Emil Heijnes Stiftelse för rättsvetenskaplig forskning*) for its financial support, without which this publication would not have been possible. It is my hope that this collection of essays will be a worthy tribute to Lennart Pålsson and constitute at the same time a valuable scientific contribution in the fields of law favoured by him. It is not intended to be a monument over Lennart Pålsson's scientific achievements, since these are not over yet. In spite of his retirement on 1 September, 1995, Lennart Pålsson remains active and hopefully will continue in good health to enrich Swedish legal writing for many years to come.

Göran Melander

CONTENTS

Michael Bogdan
Misleading Cross-Border TV Advertising in the EU   1

Ole Due
The Judicial System of the European Union in the perspective of the
1996 Intergovernmental Conference   17

Jens Fejø
Other Rules Aiming at Creating Competition in the European Union
– Inherent Contradictions   33

Ulf Göranson
A Swedish Centre of Gravity Test? – Law, Fact and Fiction on the
"Individualizing Method"   47

Maarit Jänterä-Jareborg
Application of Foreign Law in Swedish Courts – Recent Developments   79

Ole Lando
Being First. On Uses and Abuses of the Lis Pendens Under the
Brussels Convention   105

Hans Henrik Lidgard
Swedish Snus Confronts Basic EU Principles   123

Göran Melander
Human Rights and University Policy   155

Allan Philip
Scope of Application, Choice of Law and Jurisdiction in the New Nordic Law of Carriage of Goods By Sea   165

Carl Michael Quitzow
Some Brief Reflections About Federalism In the European Union and in the United States of America   183

Kurt Siehr
Comparative Law as a Yardstick for Academic Legal Education   199

Lotta Westerhäll
Social Assistance and Migrant Workers – Regulation No 1612/68 From a Swedish Perspective   211

List of Publications, 1960–1996, by Lennart Pålsson   235

Notes on the Contributors   243

MISLEADING CROSS-BORDER TV ADVERTISING IN THE EU

Michael Bogdan

1. Introduction

Cross-border television, i.e. television broadcasts where the state from which a TV programme is transmitted is not identical to the state where the programme is received by the public, is nowadays a common phenomenon throughout Europe due to, *inter alia*, satellite transmissions and cable TV networks. The cross-border programmes often contain substantial amounts of advertising.

Pursuant to the Council Directive of 10 September 1984, "relating to the approximation of the laws, regulations and administrative provisions of the Member States concerning misleading advertising",[1] all member states of the European Union are under the obligation to protect consumers, businesspeople and the public in general from misleading advertising and the unfair consequences thereof. The Directive defines misleading advertising in the following manner (in art. 2(2)):

> "Misleading advertising" means any advertising which in any way, including its presentation, deceives or is likely to deceive the persons to whom it is addressed or whom it reaches and which, by reason of its deceptive nature, is likely to affect their economic behaviour or which, for those reasons, injures or is likely to injure a competitor.

The Directive provides a number of additional guidelines for the determination of whether or not advertising is misleading (art. 3) and, most importantly, requires (in art. 4) member states to

---

1 Council Directive 84/450/EEC, O.J. 1984 L 250, p. 17.

ensure that adequate and effective means exist for the control of misleading advertising in the interests of consumers as well as competitors and the general public.

Pursuant to the same article, such adequate and effective means shall include legal provisions under which member states shall confer upon the courts or administrative authorities powers enabling them to order the cessation of misleading marketing practices, even without proof of actual loss or damage or of intention or negligence on the part of the advertiser. The Directive's rules are "minimal", i.e. they do not preclude member states from retaining or adopting provisions with a view to ensuring more extensive protection (art. 7). This means that the harmonisation achieved by the Directive is merely partial and that the relevant legal rules in the various member states may vary to some extent giving rise to questions of conflicts of law. For example, can/must the transmitting state apply its advertising rules to programmes that are directed to and receivable in other member states only? And, can the member state where the programme is received require that its advertising rules be respected and followed by programmes transmitted from another member state?

It is normally left to each state to decide on the geographical limits of application of its laws and on the applicability of foreign law, but this freedom may be restricted by the country's international commitments, in particular if the country in question is a member of the European Union.

The purpose of this essay is to examine the present state of EC law regarding the free movement of television advertising between member states. The first question to be asked is whether and to what extent cross-border television advertising can be subjected to restrictions under national law when it is used for the marketing of goods; another question is whether television advertising is a service within the meaning of art. 60 of the Rome Treaty and, as such, enjoys free movement within the Community pursuant to the Treaty's art. 59–66. The next issue to be discussed concerns the impact of Council Directive 89/552/EEC ("the TV Directive"). Finally, I shall deal briefly with the problem of evasion, i.e. those situations where the advertising is aimed at viewers in one member state but is transmitted from another in order to avoid the more stringent rules of the former country.

2. TV Advertising and the Free Movement of Goods and Services

To begin with, it is sometimes possible to regard television advertising as a mere accessory to the trade in goods that are being advertised.[2] Restrictions placed on advertising may, under certain circumstances, be considered to constitute measures having an effect equivalent to quantitative restrictions on imports of the advertised goods and thus violate the freedom of movement of goods stipulated in art. 30 of the Rome Treaty. The EC Court has consistently held that any measure capable of hindering, directly or indirectly, actually or potentially, intra-Community trade constitutes a measure having an effect equivalent to a quantitative restriction.[3]

Art. 36 of the Treaty provides that art. 30 shall not preclude prohibitions or restrictions on imports justified by certain enumerated considerations such as public morality or public policy, but these considerations will only exceptionally be relevant with regard to misleading advertising. The main principle of EC law regarding "measures having equivalent effect" follows instead the notorious decision of the EC Court in the case of Rewe-Zentral AG v. Bundesmonopolverwaltung für Branntwein, commonly referred to as Cassis de Dijon.[4]

Cassis de Dijon concerned a German law prohibiting the sale of fruit liqueurs containing less than 25 % alcohol, a law which prevented the export to Germany of a weaker liqueur manufactured and legally marketed in France. This gave rise to the question of whether the German regulation had an effect equivalent to a quantitative

---

[2] See Aragonesa de Publicidad Exterior v. Departemento de Sanidad y Seguridad Social de la Generalitat de Cataluna, joined cases C-1/90 and C-176/90, [1991] ECR I-4151.

[3] See Procureur du Roi v. Dassonville, case 8/74, [1974] ECR 837.

[4] Case 120/78, [1979] ECR 649.

restriction on imports contrary to art. 30 of the Rome Treaty. The EC Court held that "in the absence of common rules" the member states were free to regulate the production and marketing of alcohol in their own territory, provided that the obstacles to movement within the Community resulting from disparities between the national laws were necessary in order to satisfy mandatory requirements relating, in particular, to the effectiveness of fiscal supervision, the protection of public health, the fairness of commercial transactions and "the defence of the consumer" (the German rule in question was, however, found unacceptable since it was not deemed necessary for reaching these aims).

The standing of the Cassis de Dijon precedent in disputes concerning the national regulation of certain selling arrangements was somewhat weakened by the EC Court's judgment of 24 November 1993 in the joined cases of Keck and Mithouard.[5] Subsequent case–law indicates, however, that the Cassis rule is far from dead, at least as far as national rules on marketing and advertising are concerned.[6]

It can hardly be contested that restrictions imposed on television advertising may impair the free movement of goods, provided the restrictions affect marketing of goods imported from other member states.[7] If an advertisement which is considered legal in the member state from which it is transmitted is forbidden as being misleading in one or several other member states, the advertising undertaking will be forced to bear additional costs for adapting its TV advertisement to the various national requirements. Such adaptation may sometimes be technically impossible, especially if satellite transmission is being used, which may force the undertaking to cease its advertising altogether. Despite this fact, national restrictions may be permitted if they are necessary to satisfy the requirements of, *inter alia*, consumer protection, but only to the extent that there are no common EC rules in the field. As far as misleading advertising is concerned, the above-

---

[5] Joined cases C-267/91 and C-268/91; [1993] ECR I-6097.

[6] See, for example, Verband Sozialer Wettbewerb eV v. Clinique Laboratories SNC and Estée Lauder Cosmetics GmbH, case C-315/92, [1994] ECR I-317.

[7] Cf., for example, Oosthoek's Uitgeversmaatschappij BV, case 286/81, [1982] ECR 4575; SARP v. Chambre syndicale des raffineurs, case C-241/89, [1990] ECR I-4695.

mentioned Council Directive 84/450/EEC of 1984 was designed to protect consumers, competitors and the public in general from misleading advertising. Although this Directive confines itself to a partial harmonisation of the national laws on misleading advertising by establishing minimum objective criteria for determining whether advertising is misleading and minimum protection against such advertising, it does establish a common threshold to be respected by all member states. It must be assumed that the member state from which the television advertising is transmitted has adapted its law on misleading advertising to the minimum EC rules. Due to the TV Directive of 1989 (see infra), the transmitting state is obliged to apply its national rules even to outgoing television advertisements intended for viewers in other member states. It is therefore submitted that the existence of such minimum common rules makes it unlawful for an individual member state to stop television advertising coming from another member state, provided that the advertisement concerns goods imported from a member state other than the receiving country.[8]

Television advertising is, however, normally considered to be an independent service, not connected to the free movement of the advertised goods.[9] The EC Court has held in several judgments that the transmission of advertisements by means of television signals is a service within the meaning of EC law.[10] It is, in the first place, a service provided by the broadcaster to the advertising undertakings that wish to have their message "delivered" to the public. Pursuant to art. 59 of the Rome Treaty, there is freedom to provide services within the Community. Furthermore, although there is no explicit stipulation to that effect in the Treaty, the principles behind art. 30 and 36 are applied to the free movement of services as well.[11] The

---

[8] Questions regarding the status of minimum protection rules in a directive vis-à-vis art. 30 and 36 of the Rome Treaty arose in Gourmetterie Van den Burg, case C-169/89, [1990] ECR I-2143, but they were not conclusively answered there.

[9] See Sacchi, case 155/73, [1974] ECR 409.

[10] See, e.g., Bond van Adverteerders v. The Netherlands, case 352/85, [1988] ECR 2085; Stichting Collectieve Antennevoorziening Gouda v. Commissariaat voor de Media, case 288/89, [1991] ECR 4007; TV10 SA v. Commissariaat voor de Media, case C-23/93.

[11] Cf., for example, Her Majesty's Customs and Excise v. Schindler, case C-275/92, [1994] ECR I-1039.

freedom of movement for services is thus subject to limitations similar to those mentioned above in connection with the free movement of goods, i.e. member states may impose restrictions in the interest of general good, provided that the restriction applies equally to national and cross-border services and that it is necessary in order to safeguard a legitimate public interest. In the Debauve case,[12] the EC Court stated the following:

> In view of the particular nature of certain services such as the broadcasting and transmission of television signals, specific requirements imposed upon providers of services which are founded upon the application of rules regulating certain types of activity and which are justified by the general interest and apply to all persons and undertakings established within the territory of the said Member State cannot be said to be incompatible with the Treaty to the extent to which a provider of services established in another Member State is not subject to similar regulation there...
>
> In the absence of any harmonisation of the relevant rules, a prohibition of this type falls within the residual power of each Member State to regulate, restrict or even totally prohibit television advertising on its territory on grounds of general interest.

As indicated by this quotation, restrictions imposed by national law are not allowed in a field where there are common or harmonised rules prescribed by Community legislation, such as Council Directive 84/450/EEC on the approximation of national rules on misleading advertising. In fact, the EC Court seems to consider it sufficient that the transmitting state has a "similar regulation", which needs not result from any harmonisation on the Community level. In any case, the existence of Directive 84/450/EEC leads to the conclusion that a member state would not normally be justified in restricting cross-border television advertising for reasons of its misleading character.[13]

---

[12] Procureur du Roi v. Debauve, case 52/79, [1980] ECR 833.

[13] This was the reasoning and conclusion reached by the EFTA Surveillance Authority in its observations of 6 December 1994 to the EFTA Court in case E-5/94 Konsumentombudsmannen v. TV Shop i Sverige AB (request for an advisory opinion by the Market Court in Sweden). The Market Court withdrew its request after Sweden's accession to the European Union and requested a preliminary ruling from the EC Court instead. The case is still pending, see joint cases C-34/95, C-35/95 and C-36/95.

3. The Impact of the TV Directive

The next question to be dealt with is whether the Council Directive of 3 October 1989 "on the coordination of certain provisions laid down by law, regulation or administrative action in Member States concerning the pursuit of television broadcasting activities"[14] (the TV Directive) has brought about any change with regard to the right of member states to impose restrictions on allegedly misleading advertising in incoming television programmes transmitted from and lawful according to the laws of another member state.

The Preamble of the TV Directive mentions among its aims the adoption of measures to permit and ensure the transition from national markets to a common programme production and distribution market in the field of television broadcasting. The Preamble also states that the Directive is specifically confined to television broadcasting rules and that it is without prejudice to existing or future Community acts of harmonisation, in particular to satisfy mandatory requirements concerning the protection of consumers and the fairness of commercial transactions and competition. The Preamble also points out that television broadcasting constitutes, in normal circumstances, a service within the meaning of the Rome Treaty. In order to ensure that the interests of consumers as television viewers are fully and properly protected, the Preamble declares that it is essential for television advertising to be subject to a certain number of minimum rules and standards, while the member states must maintain the right to set more detailed or stricter rules for television broadcasters under their jurisdiction.

The substantive rules of the TV Directive do not deal directly with the problem of misleading advertising, although some closely-related issues are covered, such as the art. 10 requirement that television advertising be readily recognizable as such and kept quite separate from other programmes and that subliminal and surreptitious advertising be prohibited. Also of interest is art. 12, pursuant to which television advertising shall not prejudice respect for human dignity, include any discrimination on grounds of race, sex or nationality, be

---

[14] Council Directive 89/552/EEC, O.J. 1989 L 298, p. 23.

offensive to religious or political beliefs, or encourage behaviour prejudicial to health or to safety. Other articles restrict or require the prohibition of, *inter alia*, television advertising for tobacco products, alcoholic beverages and certain medicinal products, forbid television advertising causing moral or physical detriment to minors, etc.

Art. 3(2) stipulates that member states shall, by appropriate means within the framework of their legislation, ensure that television broadcasters under their jurisdiction comply with the Directive's provisions. Member states remain free, pursuant to art. 3(1), to require television broadcasters under their jurisdiction to follow more detailed or stricter rules in the areas covered by the Directive. However, art. 2 requires each member state to ensure that all television broadcasts transmitted by broadcasters under its jurisdiction[15] comply with the laws applicable to broadcasts intended for the public in that member state, i.e. no member state is allowed to apply less stringent rules to transmissions intended for viewers in other member states than the rules which it applies to transmissions intended for its own national public. These obligations imposed on the transmitting state are interconnected to the obligations of the receiving member states, in particular the freedom of reception enacted in the first sentence of art. 2(2) :

> Member States shall ensure freedom of reception and shall not restrict retransmission on their territory of television broadcasts from other Member States for reasons which fall within the fields coordinated by this Directive.

Member states are, nevertheless, permitted to provisionally suspend retransmissions of television broadcasts coming from another member state in some rather extreme situations, such as when the broadcast manifestly, seriously and gravely infringes the Directive's art. 12 (see supra).

It is disputed whether the Directive's so-called "transmitting state principle", i.e. the principle that the transmitting state is obliged to ensure that its laws are respected by cross-border transmissions ema-

---

[15] The same applies to broadcasts transmitted by broadcasters who, while not being under the jurisdiction of any member state, make use of a frequency or a satellite capacity granted by, or a satellite up-link situated in, the member state in question.

nating from its territory while other member states are obliged to ensure the freedom of reception, is relevant in the field of misleading advertising.

A preliminary proposal of a Directive concerning the pursuit of broadcasting activities, submitted by the EC Commission on 29 April, 1986,[16] stated that national regulations on advertising in general, applicable indiscriminately to internal and cross-border broadcasters and necessary in the general interest, would be permitted even after the entry into force of the Directive. However, no such statement is found in the final version of the TV Directive. Statements in travaux préparatoires are in any case given limited weight in the interpretation of EC law.

The prevailing view in, for example, German legal writing is that the transmitting state principle does not restrict the receiving state's freedom to take action pursuant to its own law against misleading television advertising transmitted from other member states.[17] It has, for instance, been argued that the said principle pertains exclusively to broadcasters and not to advertisers, and that the principle merely concerns "radio-law" matters covered by the Directive and, consequently, not misleading advertising as such.

Similarly, Sweden's observations of 6 December 1994 to the EFTA Court[18] stated that the transmitting state principle applies only for reasons which explicitly fall within the fields coordinated by the TV Directive, which contains no provisions concerning misleading trade practices; the observations quoted the Directive's Preamble in this connection, in particular the words "this directive, being confined specifically to television broadcasting rules, is without prejudice to existing or future community acts of harmonisation, in particular to satisfy mandatory requirements concerning the protection of consumers and the fairness of commercial transactions". Furthermore, Sweden's observations interpreted the freedom of reception, as stip-

---

[16] Com(86) 146.

[17] See, e.g., G. Schricker, UWG Grosskommentar, 1994, sections F369–F374, with further references.

[18] In case E-5/94, Konsumentombudsmannen v. TV Shop i Sverige AB (request for an advisory opinion by the Market Court in Sweden).

ulated in the TV Directive, as merely forbidding actual interference with reception and retransmission (an action against the broadcaster), while not preventing action against advertisers.

On the other hand, it is interesting to note that the official Swedish investigation committee, which had been set up to elaborate new Swedish legislation on marketing practices, interpreted the TV Directive to mean that Swedish rules against misleading advertising could no longer be applied to TV advertisements transmitted from another member state.[19] In the Government Bill introducing legislative amendments necessary to adapt Swedish law to the Directive, the Swedish Government expressed, however, a different opinion, namely that the Directive does not prevent intervention on the part of the receiving state against cross-border misleading advertising.[20] Nevertheless, the Government Bill was careful enough to add that it was up to the Market Court, when exercising its judicial function, to pay due account to "international rules" restricting the field of application of the Swedish rules on marketing practices.[21]

It might seem that the problem had been solved by the EFTA Court in its recent judgement Forbrukerombudet v. Mattel Scandinavia A/S and Lego Norge A/S,[22] when the Court made an obiter dictum to the effect that the TV Directive "was not intended to preclude a State from taking action under Directive 84/450/EEC with regard to an advertisement that must be considered to be misleading under the terms of the latter Directive". However, the opinion of the EFTA Court is not binding on the EC Court; the precedential value of a statement made obiter, without any proper discussion and argument, about a point that did not arise in the actual case (it was not asserted that the advertisements under scrutiny were misleading), is in any case questionable.

True, the TV Directive is not quite clear and easy to interpret regarding, for instance, its relation to the 1984 Directive on misleading advertising. The lack of coordination may be due to the fact that

---

[19] See Statens Offentliga Utredningar 1992:49, pp. 76–80.

[20] See prop. 1992/93:75, p. 35.

[21] Ibid.

[22] Joined cases E-8/94 and E-9/94.

the two directives had been prepared by different Directorates General and that one is five years older than the other. It is nevertheless submitted that the TV Directive normally prevents member states from applying their rules on misleading advertising to TV advertisements transmitted from another member state.

It would, first of all, be incorrect to draw far-reaching conclusions from the mention in the TV Directive's Preamble that the Directive is confined specifically to "television broadcasting rules". That mention was obviously not intended to restrict the field of application of the Directive to the more-or-less technical rules of "radio law" since the Directive contains numerous provisions of substantive law concerning the contents of the transmitted advertisements: for example the rules that television advertising shall be readily recognizable as such; that subliminal and surreptitious advertising shall be prohibited; that television advertising shall not be discriminatory or offensive to religious or political beliefs; and that all forms of television advertising for cigarettes and other tobacco products shall be prohibited. It is very difficult to argue that these prohibitions are covered by the Directive's transmitting state principle while misleading advertising is not. The only reasonable explanation at hand appears to be that the authors of the TV Directive did not find it necessary to deal with misleading television advertising since they were aware of the existence of the 1984 Directive specially designed to combat misleading advertising in general. The formulation in art. 2(2) of the TV Directive, requiring member states to ensure freedom of reception and to refrain from restricting retransmission on their territory of television broadcasts from other member states for reasons which "fall within the fields coordinated by this Directive" should not, therefore, be interpreted literally but should rather be understood to comprise all fields coordinated by Community legislation, regardless of whether that legislation is found in the TV Directive or elsewhere. A literal, restrictive interpretation would lead to the failure of the TV Directive's main aim, i.e. the creation of a common programme production and distribution market.

Furthermore, the wording of the reference in art. 2(2) to reasons "which fall within the fields coordinated by this Directive" seems to merely concern restrictions on retransmissions, while the main duty of the receiving state to ensure "freedom of reception" appears to be unconditional.

It can be mentioned that the Swedish Government, which argued that the transmitting state principle did not cover misleading advertising from abroad since such advertising had not been coordinated by the TV Directive, invoked the same Directive and the same principle in order to extend the application of the Swedish rules on, *inter alia*, misleading advertising to television transmissions from Sweden. It is hardly the Directive's purpose to subject cross-border advertising to a double control, forcing the advertisers to comply with the advertising rules of both the transmitting and the receiving state. Such double control would naturally mean the application of the legal system which is more strict and would place cross-border television advertisers at a competitive disadvantage in comparison with advertisers in purely national, domestic TV channels since the latter would have only the laws of one country with which to comply. Such a model, forcing advertisers to tailor television advertisements to the different national legislations in the various receiving member states, would clearly be incompatible with the TV Directive's vision of "a common programme and distribution market" in Europe.

It must be noted that art. 3(1) of the TV Directive permits member states to impose more detailed or stricter rules on television broadcasters "under their jurisdiction". This provision obviously concerns the transmitting state's right to regulate, in accordance with the transmitting state principle, outgoing television advertisements transmitted to other member states, while not even mentioning the receiving state's right to regulate incoming advertising from another member state.

It is true that the Preamble declares that the Directive is without prejudice to existing or future Community acts of harmonisation, in particular ones to satisfy mandatory requirements concerning the protection of consumers and the fairness of commercial transactions and competition, but it must be stressed that this refers to Community acts of harmonisation only, not to purely autonomous provisions of national law. Harmonised rules are, at the same time, in no way exempted from the transmitting state principle. In fact, the contrary is true: the harmonised rules, constituting parts of or duly transformed into the law of the transmitting member state, are upheld by the operation of the transmitting state principle within the whole common market.

As was pointed out by the EFTA Court in the case of Forbrukerom-budet v. Mattel Scandinavia A/S and Lego Norge A/S,[23] it would be incorrect to interpret the receiving state's duty of non-interference, which forms an essential part of the transmitting state principle embodied in the TV Directive, to function solely for the benefit of broadcasters and not of the advertisers. It seems rather artificial to argue that the Directive does not prevent a receiving state from taking action in respect of an advertisement broadcast from another member state as long as the action is directed against the advertiser without also being aimed against the broadcaster. By attacking and imposing penal or administrative sanctions on the advertisers whose advertisements are considered misleading by the receiving state but not by the transmitting state, the receiving state makes it in fact impossible for the broadcaster to sell his cross-border services to the advertisers or forces him to limit his transmissions to only a part of the common market (something that may sometimes be technically difficult or even impossible to do). In a common market it is crucial that undertakings have clear and easily accessible rules to follow. If the transmitting state principle is not upheld in the field of misleading advertising, the undertakings will have to study the contents of and tailor their broadcasts to the varying (and sometimes mutually incompatible) advertising rules prevailing in all member states where the broadcast can be received. It is obvious that this would be a serious obstacle to the creation of a truly common market in the area of television advertising. As was put by the EFTA Court in the above-mentioned judgement, the receiving state cannot escape its obligation to ensure freedom of reception, as embodied in the TV Directive, by taking action against the advertiser and not against the broadcaster.

---

[23] Joined cases E-8/94 and E-9/94.

4. The Problem of Evasion

The final issue to be addressed in this essay is whether the conclusions reached above apply even when the advertisement is transmitted from another member state for the purpose of avoiding the stricter rules against misleading marketing practices in the member state to which the advertising is directed.

The problem of evasion has been discussed in a number of decisions rendered by the EC Court of Justice.[24] These decisions, which dealt with events and situations occurring before the entry into force of the TV Directive, indicate that a member state is free to apply its rules in order to combat attempts to circumvent its law. Thus, in Veronica,[25] the Court upheld a Dutch rule prohibiting national broadcasting organizations from setting up a commercial radio transmitter in Luxembourg for the purpose of transmitting programs to the Netherlands in circumvention of Dutch law.

It must, however, be pointed out that although the phenomenon was well-known when the Directive was adopted, the TV Directive contains no special rule about broadcasts transmitted from one member state and directed exclusively to a particular other member state. In this respect, the Directive differs from the European Convention on Transfrontier Television of the same year (the Convention was opened for signature on 5 May 1989).[26] The Convention is based on a transmitting state principle similar to that of the Directive, but art. 16 of the Convention makes it possible to stop circumventions of the rules of the receiving country if the programme is transmitted from abroad but directed to viewers in one particular contracting state ("advertisements which are specifically and with some frequency directed to audiences in a single Party other than the transmitting Party"). The Convention and the TV Directive were formulated almost simultaneously and they obviously influenced each other. The

---

[24] See, e.g., van Binsbergen, case 33/74, [1974] ECR 1299; Vereniging Veronica Omroep Organisatie v. Commissariaat voor de Media, case C-148/91; TV10 SA v. Commissariaat voor de Media, case C-23/93.

[25] Case C-148/91, [1993] ECR I-487.

[26] The text of the Convention is found, inter alia, in Statens Offentliga Utredningar 1990:7, pp. 305–327.

fact that the Directive clearly differs from the Convention on this point seems to indicate that the difference was intentional and that the member states of the Community, having in mind the harmonisation of their rules on misleading advertising by means of the 1984 Directive, considered it unnecessary to introduce an exception for directed broadcasts. This conclusion finds support in the recent judgement of the EFTA Court in Forbrukerombudet v. Mattel Scandinavia A/S and Lego Norge A/S[27] in which the Court stated that "advertising specifically aimed and directed at the receiving State only" was not exempted from the scope of the fields coordinated by the TV Directive.

5. Conclusion

The analysis above results in the conclusion that an attempt by a receiving member state to apply its national rules on misleading advertising in order to take action against a cross-border television advertisement transmitted from another member state is normally incompatible with the Rome Treaty as such, as well as with the TV Directive.

This article was completed in 1995.

---

[27] Joined cases E-8/94 and E-9/94.

THE JUDICIAL SYSTEM OF THE EUROPEAN UNION IN THE PERSPECTIVE OF THE 1996 INTERGOVERNMENTAL CONFERENCE

Ole Due

1.

Article N (2) of the Treaty on European Union prescribes the convocation in 1996 of a conference of representatives of the governments of Member States "to examine those Treaty provisions for which revision is provided, in accordance with the objectives set out in Articles A and B".

This wording may create the impression that the revision will have some specific and limited objectives. In fact, there are specific references to Art. N (2) in some of the treaty's other provisions. This is the case in Art. J (4) concerning "the eventual framing of a common defence policy" and relations with the Western European Union. Furthermore, Art. 189 b of the EC treaty on the so-called "codecision procedure", introduced by the Treaty on European Union and under which the European Parliament adopts acts "acting jointly with the Council", provides in its paragraph 8 that the scope of this procedure may be widened in accordance with Art. N (2); moreover, Declaration No. 1 to the Final Act of the Treaty on European Union declares that the question of introducing treaty titles relating to civil protection, energy and tourism into the EC will be examined in accordance with the procedure laid down in Art. N (2).

However, the reference to Art. N (2) contained in Art. B of the Treaty on European Union clearly envisages a much more general review when it speaks of considering "to what extent the policies and forms of cooperation introduced by this Treaty may need to be revised with the aim of ensuring the effectiveness of the mechanisms and the institutions of the Community".

Thus, the masters of the Treaty left the agenda for the next intergovernmental conference very open-ended. One major objective of a general character, can nevertheless be identified, although it is not expressly stated. It appears in the word "effectiveness" and in the extremely short time-limit for the convocation of a new conference, and it was very much present in the minds of the Member States at the conclusion of the Treaty on European Union in Maastricht: the Union must prepare to receive a significant number of new Member States, in particular from Central and Eastern Europe, without losing its ability to cope with economic, social and political problems in accordance with its general objectives.

The open-ended character of the agenda calls for a thorough preparation for the Conference. To this end, a Study Group with representation from the Member States, the Commission and the European Parliament has been established. Before starting its work on the first of June 1995, this group invited the institutions to submit reports on the operation of the Treaty on European Union.

The Court of Justice presented its report in May 1995 and the Court of First Instance submitted a separate contribution. Both documents have been made public and I shall, in the following, refer to them and even quote some passages. The Report of the Court of Justice, in particular, contains in a condensed, but carefully drafted and well-balanced form, the general views of the Court concerning the tasks and functioning of the judicial system within the Union; I strongly recommend reading the full text.

I shall not follow the order of problems used in the Report of the Court of Justice, nor that followed in the Contribution of the Court of First Instance. In 2 I shall indicate the limited experiences gained under the operation of the Treaty on European Union and reported by the Court of Justice. The one and only problem facing the courts which has a direct link to the adhesion of several new Member States will be mentioned under 3. I shall, under 4, examine some ideas concerning the courts which have been voiced during the public debate while 5 treats some proposals put forward by the European Parliament. 6 contains some proposals and questions raised by the two courts themselves, 7 treats other aspects of the work of the Conference that may have repercussions on the judicial system and *8* touches upon problems of transparency and legal certainty caused by present treaty texts.

2.

The entry into force of the Treaty on European Union was delayed nearly one year: first by the negative outcome of the first Danish referendum and later by the action brought before the German Constitutional Court directed against the German ratification bill. Thus, by the first of June 1995 the Treaty had only been in force for 19 months, a period much too short to really evaluate the experiences gained under its operation. This is particularly true as far as the Court of Justice and the Court of First Instance are concerned. It normally takes longer before changes in the written law are reflected in case-law. The only clear tendency revealed in the Report of the Court of Justice concerns the operation of Art. 165 (3) as amended by the Treaty on European Union, which permitted all kinds of cases to be assigned to a Chamber unless a Member State or an institution, being a party to the proceedings, requests that the case be heard in plenary session. Such requests have in practice only been exceptionally made and the Court has therefore been able to profit from this procedural reform.

3.

As already mentioned, a main objective of the Conference will be to prepare the Union to receive a considerable number of new Member States, many of them being relatively small. This objective undoubtedly calls for a review of the rules on the Council of Ministers, especially as to the presidency and the way in which a qualified majority and a blocking minority may be formed, as well as of the rules on the composition of the European Parliament. It may also give rise to a discussion on the composition of the Commission and maybe that of the Court of Auditors, partly because there are natural limits to the size of collegiate executive and controlling bodies and partly since difficulties will be caused by the distribution of internal responsibility for the activities of these institutions between an increased number of members without the creation of artificial boundaries. The last-mentioned problem does not arise within the two Community Courts. However, in the Court of Justice where cases involving important questions of principle are still heard in plenary sessions, an increased number of judges may create a problem similar to that faced by the Commission.

In point 16 of its report, the Court points to this problem without indicating a definite solution. In deciding whether the link between the number of judges and the number of Member States hitherto maintained by the Treaty (without prescribing the nationality of the judges) should be upheld, the Court considers that two factors must be balanced:

- the existence of an "invisible boundary between a collegiate court and a deliberative assembly";

- the fact that "the presence of members from all the national legal systems on the Court is... conducive to harmonious development of Community case-law" and that "the presence of a judge from each Member State enhances the legitimacy of the Court".

Here, the Court touches upon an extremely difficult issue. In cases where interests of a Member State having no permanent judge on the Court are at stake, it is no answer to provide for the presence of an *ad hoc* judge from that Member State. On the contrary, such a system would violate one of the fundamental procedural principles of the judicial system of the Community. Art. 16, last paragraph, of the EC Statute of the Court expressly provides that:

> "A party may not apply for a change in the composition of the Court or of one of its Chambers on the grounds of either the nationality of a judge or the absence from the Court or from the Chamber of a judge of the nationality of that party".

Thus, the practice of choosing a judge from each of the Member States must never be seen as a guarantee that the interests of each Member State are represented on the bench. National law is nonetheless an important source when the Court develops general principles of Community law not expressed in the treaty texts; the absence of a judge with an intimate knowledge of the concepts, fundamental principles and traditions of one of the legal systems within the Union will therefore, at least in the long run, create a problem for the legitimacy of the future development of this important part of Community law.

The proper solution to this problem may be to maintain the present practice of appointing judges, but to assign even very important cases to big Chambers with well-balanced compositions representing all the main "legal families" in the Union and to reserve plenary sessions for situations where a real risk for the consistency of the case-law has appeared.

4.

It should be expected that institutional problems other than these, linked with future adhesions of new Member States, will be discussed during the Intergovernmental Conference. Such discussions will at least concern Parliament's participation in the legislative procedure, cf. Art. 189 b mentioned above under 1. The two preceding conferences resulting, respectively, in the Single European Act and the Treaty on European Union have only marginally touched upon the jurisdiction and functioning of the Community Courts, and amendments on this point have normally followed proposals put forward by these courts. The public debates in the Member States since the signing of the last-mentioned treaty indicate, nonetheless, that the 1996 Conference may well submit the judicial system of the Union to closer scrutiny. Some ideas have already been advanced. As most of these ideas have not been presented as official proposals, the Court took care not to mention them nor to comment directly on them in its report. However, it is easy to find in the Report discreet but nevertheless clear answers to these ideas.

4.1

In the Preamble to the Treaty on European Union, the Member States have confirmed "their attachment to the principles of liberty, democracy and respect for human rights and fundamental freedoms and of the rule of law". These principles include the requirement of an independent judiciary. According to Art. F (2) of the Treaty "The Union shall respect fundamental rights as guaranteed by the European Convention for the Protection of Human Rights and Fundamental Freedoms signed in Rome on 4 November 1950 and as they result from the constitutional traditions common to the Member States, as general principles of Community Law". This wording, which is an almost literal transcription of the case-law of the Court of Justice since the Nold-judgment (Case 4/73 [1974] ECR 491), also presupposes the existence of an independent judiciary.

With this background, it is surprising that one of the ideas put forward with a certain force during the public debates has been to confer power on the Council of Ministers to override certain decisions of the Community Courts.

In this respect, it is interesting to note the judgment of the European Court of Human Rights in the Van de Hurk case (judgment of 18 April 1994, case 9/1993/404/482, published as A 288). The case concerned a Dutch administrative tribunal, the decisions of which could in principle be set aside by the government. The Human Right's Court ruled that although the Dutch government had never made use of this power, such a body could not be considered an independent court or tribunal in the sense of Art. 6 of the Human Right's Convention.

It is in fact difficult to disagree with the Court of Justice when, in point 4 of its report, it states that:

> "Any decision affecting the structure of the judicial system must ensure that the courts remain independent and their judgments binding. Were that not to be the case, the very foundation of the Community legal order would be undermined".

4.2

One of the earliest ideas voiced in the debate on a possible restructuring of the judicial system of the Union concerned the creation of a specific Constitutional Court. At first, such a court may seem to be a natural counterpart to the national constitutional courts in some of the Member States. However, the situation of the Community is very different from that of a national State. Separate national constitutional courts are intimately linked with the existence of a constitution, the provisions of which are of another character than those of normal legislation. Although the EC treaty is often referred to as the "Constitution of the Community" (The first Court opinion 1/91 on the EEA agreement, [1991] ECR I-6079, calls the EC treaty a "constitutional charter"), its structure differs greatly from that of a national constitution. So do many of its provisions and it is not easy, if at all possible, to draw a clear line of distinction between treaty provisions which may be said to have constitutional character in the normal sense of the word and those having no such character. At the same time, many of the fundamental principles expressed in national constitutions are not to be found in the Treaty texts. A clear distinction between the jurisdiction of a new constitutional court and that of the present Court of Justice can be founded neither on the substantive provisions of the Treaty nor on the different kinds of action provided for by this treaty. In fact, the same legal problem may present itself in practically any of these actions. Further, without such a clear line of distinction, the existence of two courts would necessarily create problems for the cohesion of the Community case-law. As stated in point 5 of the Report of the Court of Justice:

> "... the need to ensure uniform interpretation and application of Community law... presupposes the existence of a single judicial body, such as the Court of Justice....That requirement is essential in any case which is constitutional in character or which otherwise raises a question of importance for the development of the law."

To the extent that the idea of a separate constitutional court was intended to avoid the same judicial body having to rule on general questions of legal principles and having to examine, in depth, the often extremely complicated questions of fact presented by cases in the fields such as competition and anti-dumping measures, this objective has already been attained by the establishment of the Court of First Instance, provided for by the Single European Act. The creation of this two-tier system, which now applies to practically all actions brought by natural or legal persons, has permitted the Court of Justice to concentrate on questions of law and the distinction based on the nature of the applicant has provided a clear-cut delimitation of the jurisdictions of the two existing Community Courts. There are a few areas where, in practice, actions are brought by Member States as well as by legal persons directly and individually concerned by the measures in question, but this problem may (if experiences gained so require) be solved on the basis of the present wording of Art. 168 a of the EC treaty as amended by the Treaty on European Union.

4.3

The existence of the two-tier system has, particularly in the legal literature, given rise to a discussion of the possibility of establishing regional or specialized courts of first instance. The idea of regional courts is supported neither by the Court of Justice nor by the Court of First Instance. The Court of Justice points to the fact that "the national courts are called upon to play a central role as the courts with general jurisdiction for Community law". At least within the area of jurisdiction of the Court of Justice, it is in fact difficult to find a proper role for regional courts of a "federal" nature. The Court of First Instance finds that the "juxtaposition of several parallel courts would be likely to jeopardize the unity and consistency of Community case-law and would necessarily entail a considerable increase in the cost of the administration of justice". As to eventual needs for specialization, the Court of First Instance prefers the setting up of specialized chambers, a solution which does in fact present obvious advantages of not only an administrative and financial nature but also in relation to the coherence of case-law within the different fields of Community law, even though appeals may also be brought before the Court of Justice in the case of specialized courts.

4.4

An idea which for some time played a considerable role in the public debate on eventual reforms of the Community judiciary was to abolish the possibility for national courts and tribunals of first instance to request preliminary rulings from the Court of Justice. Since the establishment of the Court of First Instance, preliminary rulings count for more than half of the entire case-load of the Court of Justice and a reduction of the number of preliminary questions would certainly be an efficient measure in order to avoid overburdening this jurisdiction. However, cooperation between the Court of Justice and national courts and tribunals of all levels has proved the most efficient means to ensure the uniform interpretation and application of Community law in all parts of the Union and the rights of natural persons – in particular migrant workers – have to a large extent been safeguarded by preliminary questions put by national courts and tribunals of first instance.

It may well be that the last-mentioned circumstance lies at the roots of this proposal. If this is the case, it is totally misconceived. National jurisdictions of first instance would still have the obligation to apply Community law – if need be by setting aside a national rule or decision (See, for example, case 106/77, Simmenthal [1978] ECR 629). They would simply be deprived of their possibility to seek the guidance of the Court of Justice as to the proper interpretation of the Community law to be applied. Such an amendment would thus increase the risk of erroneous judgements and the work load of the national courts of appeal.

Furthermore, the proposed modification of the present system of preliminary rulings would seriously restrict the judicial protection of natural and legal persons against acts adopted by the Community institutions. No national court may itself declare such an act invalid (See, for example, case 314/85, Foto-Frost [1987] ECR 4199). To take away the possibility of presenting a preliminary question on the validity of the act would therefore exclude any judicial review of Community acts before national courts or tribunals of first instance.

As stated in point 11 of the Report of the Court of Justice:

"To limit access to the court would have the effect of jeopardizing the uniform application and interpretation of Community law throughout the Union and could deprive individuals of effective judicial protection and undermine the unity of the case-law".

It may be added that to limit this access would fly in the face of the principles to which the Member States have confirmed their attachment in the passage of the Preamble to the Treaty on European Union, quoted above (4.1), and of the introduction by the same treaty of the concept of Union Citizenship.

5.

If, in its report, the Court of Justice has been discreet in commenting on the ideas put forward in the public debate, there are some ideas that have been formally advanced in resolutions adopted by the European Parliament and which, for this reason, are the objects of specific comments in the Report of the Court of Justice and in the Contribution of the Court of First Instance. The proposal of interest to both courts concerns the procedure for the appointment of members to the courts.

5.1

Taking as a model the provisions of the EC treaty on the Court of Auditors in Art. 188 b (3), the European Parliament has proposed that the members which are presently appointed by common accord of the governments of the Member States should in the future be appointed by the Council, acting unanimously after consulting with the Parliament. Following the pattern known from national constitutional courts, such a modification might, in the view of the Parliament, be combined with the introduction of a non-renewable term of office which might be longer than the present 6-year period.

In point 17 of its report, the Court of Justice, having stressed that the present procedure and the practice generally followed in renewing the terms of office of its members have satisfactorily ensured the independence of the Court and the continuity of its case-law, indicates that it "would not, however, object to a reform which would involve an extension of the term of office with a concomitant condition that the appointment be non-renewable". It considers that such a reform "would provide an even firmer basis for the independence of its members and would strengthen the continuity of its case-law". It also considers that it would be an advantage for the continuous functioning of the Court if the system were adopted in such a way that the present simultaneous replacement of a number of Judges and Advocates General every third year could be avoided.

As to the procedure, however, the Court of Justice considers that "a reform involving a hearing of each nominee by a parliamentary committee would be unacceptable". The Court especially mentions the risk that prospective nominees would be unable to adequately answer questions without betraying the discretion incumbent on a judge and without prejudging positions they may have to adopt with regard to future contentious issues.

On these points, the position of the Court of First Instance differs somewhat from that of the Court of Justice. The Court of First Instance considers a system of renewable appointments best suited to the specific requirements of the way in which it operates, but it also stresses the need for continuity in the exercise of the judicial function and its desire to avoid replacement of several of its judges every third year. As to the procedure, the position of the Court of First Instance is less absolute than that of the Court of Justice. However, it draws the attention of the Conference "to the fact that any projected intervention of the Parliament should be confined to the initial appointment, for the obvious reason that it cannot extend to a review of the manner in which judicial functions have actually been carried out. Any such intervention by the Parliament should be solely for the purpose of ascertaining whether the prospective nominees possess the qualifications required by the Treaty...".

This difference of opinion between the two courts is fully understandable in light of their different jurisdictions and of the differences in their compositions and functioning. Experiences from the appointment procedure to the Court of Auditors have, however, shown how difficult it is to restrict a parliamentary hearing to a pure examination of professional qualifications which, by the way, could just as well be judged on the basis of written documents as is done by the representatives of the governments. At least as regards the Court of Justice, it is very important to avoid anything that may involve the slightest risk to its independence in relation to an institution which appears more and more often as party before it.

5.2

In point 14 of its report, the Court of Justice also comments on two other proposals made by the Parliament. One concerns an extension of the standing of this institution in actions for annulment. In accordance with previous case-law, the Treaty on European Union acknowledged the right of the Parliament to bring such an action "for the purpose of protecting [its] prerogatives" (See Art. 173, third paragraph of the EC treaty). The Parliament proposes the abolition of this limitation. The other proposal is to give Parliament the right to request the Court's opinion on international agreements envisaged by the Community (Art. 228 (6) of the EC treaty). The Court simply points out that there should be no technical objection to such amendments and that it has already admitted observations from the Parliament in cases pursuant to Art. 228, but it does, on the other hand, express doubts as to "whether it would be appropriate to remove to the judicial arena disputes which could just as satisfactorily be settled at a political level, given the mechanisms provided for that purpose".

6.

The Report of the Court of Justice and the Contribution of the Court of First Instance show that, in general, neither of the two jurisdictions finds it necessary for the Conference to modify the treaty rules on their jurisdiction, composition and functioning.

6.1

Some amendments to the existing rules, wished for especially by the Court of First Instance, may be adopted by special procedures including the unanimous approval by the Council (See Articles 168 a and 188 (3) of the EC treaty). However, in its report the Court of Justice proposes to simplify the procedure prescribed as regards the Rules of Procedure of the two courts. Either the requirement for the Council's approval could be abolished or it could be deemed, in the absence of amendments by the Council to the proposals forwarded, to have been given on expiry of a specified period. To one who has witnessed the lengthy examination by a working group under the Council of proposals elaborated by the Court after thorough debates among all its members, this proposal is indeed welcome.

6.2

The present judicial system of the Union does, however, present one important problem which the Court of Justice had to address in its report. According to Art. L of the Treaty on European Union, the Court has no jurisdiction in relation to the two new pillars of the Union: the common foreign and security policy and cooperation in the fields of justice and home affairs. The only exception is the possibility for Member States, in conventions drawn up pursuant to Art. K 3 (2) (c) and thus concerning the third pillar, to stipulate that the Court shall have jurisdiction to interpret the provisions of such convention and to rule on any disputes regarding their application. In point 4 of its report, the Court draws the attention of the Conference to "the legal problems which may arise in the long, or even the short, term" as a result of this judicial *lacuna*. In particular, the Court considers it "obvious that judicial protection of individuals affected by the activities of the Union, especially in the context of cooperation in the fields of justice and home affairs, must be guaranteed and structured in such a way as to ensure consistent interpretation and application both of Community law and of the provisions adopted within the framework of such cooperation". Yet the Court also mentions the delimitation of powers between the Union and the Member States and between the institutions of the Union, as well as the implementation of the decisions taken. Unfortunately, even as regards conventions under Art. K 3 (2) (c), it seems difficult to obtain unanimity among the Member States on the attribution of jurisdiction to the Court of Justice, as the recent discussions on the Europol agreement have shown.

6.3

Compared to this problem, the last two proposals put forward by the two courts may seem to be of minor importance. The Court of Justice once again proposes to allow the Advocates General to take part in the election of the President of the Court; the Court of First Instance raises the question whether its name and the way in which the Treaty refers to it are compatible with its present tasks and place within the judicial system of the Union.

7.

Both courts have concentrated their remarks on the problems of the present judicial system. However, in a last chapter of its report, the Court mentions certain other aspects of the work of the Conference which may have repercussions on this system.

7.1

Thus, the introduction into the Treaty of a catalogue of fundamental rights may, according to point 20 of the Report, although not creating a new role for the Court, raise the question "whether the right to bring an action for annulment under [the existing Articles of the Treaties], which individuals enjoy only in regard to acts of direct and individual concern to them, is sufficient to guarantee for them effec-tive judicial protection against possible infringements of their fundamental rights arising from the legislative activity of the institutions".

Such access for individuals to a supreme court in all cases where the unconstitutionality of a legislative act is alleged is known in some Member States as well as in third countries like the United States and has often been discussed in the literature on Community law. In order to avoid overburdening the Court, it would have to be combined with a filtering system much stricter than that already provided for in respect of "clearly unfounded" appeals from the Court of First Instance. (See Art. 119 of the Rules of Procedure of the Court of Justice.)

7.2

In case the Conference adopts the idea, put forward but not adopted during the elaboration of the Treaty on European Union, to establish a hierarchy amongst the acts of the institutions, it would be essential, so the Court says in point 21, to take account of the consequences for the system of remedies, in particular the right of individuals to bring actions for annulment.

8.

Finally, the Court in point 23 of its report expresses the hope that "the forthcoming process of revision may provide an opportunity for codifying and streamlining the constitutive Treaties". The Court vividly describes the structural and logical inconsistencies of the present texts which "all run counter to the need for transparency and put citizens of the Union in an unsatisfactory position from the point of view of legal certainty".

It will certainly be difficult to find anyone ready to disagree with the Court on this point. No doubt the result of the latest Intergovernmental Conference was a great diplomatic achievement, but the way in which it was drafted was easy to criticize from a legal point of view and politically it was nearly a catastrophe. It was incomprehensible to the peoples of Europe and even to the national politicians and media. This certainly contributed to the negative outcome of the first Danish referendum, to the very narrow acceptance of the Treaty in the French referendum, to the equally narrow parliamentary approval in the United Kingdom and to the widespread resistance and skepticism in some of the other Member States. To restructure and simplify the Treaty and to redraft a number of its titles must be a priority objective of the 1996 Conference. Whether it is called a constitutional document or not, the Treaty is of major importance not only to governments, public authorities and companies involved in business transactions across the borders but also to other undertakings and to the populations in general. Many of its provisions confer rights and directly impose obligations on the Community citizens. It is legally and politically unacceptable if, to understand such a document, they need the assistance of a specialized lawyer.

To fully join in the hope thus expressed by the Court of Justice seems to me to be the best way to conclude this essay.

OTHER RULES AIMING AT CREATING COMPETITION IN THE EUROPEAN UNION – INHERENT CONTRADICTIONS

Jens Fejø

1. Presentation of the Problem

It is widely accepted that one of the *purposes of competition law/anti-trust law* should be the maximization of *consumer welfare*.[1] The philosophy behind this includes an acknowledgement of the fact that the consumers are themselves the very best at deciding what is good for them and how they prefer to be served. At the same time, the competition system is faster than any other system to adapt to consumer needs and is especially faster than the political system. For that reason, the traditional systems in the Western countries – and now also in the former socialist countries – are moving in the direction of increasing competition in many areas of importance for modern society at the expence of political solutions. This goes for the private as well as for the public sector.

When we look at the *European Union* in particular, it is also remarkable how the competitive trend is nowadays clearcut and extending to new areas such as transportation, telecommunications, postal services, etc. On the other hand, there can be no doubt that *another purpose* besides consumer welfare is also of special importance here, that is to say the *creation of an integrated Internal Market*. The in-

---

[1] See *e.g.* R.A. Bork, *The Antitrust Paradox: A Policy at War With Itself*, 1978, 50ff. But other writers disagree; see *e.g.* D. Dewey, "Antitrust and Economic Theory: An Uneasy Friendship" 87 Yale Law Journal [1978] 1516, 1523.

For a more detailed discussion on this, see J. Fejø, *Monopoly Law and Market*, 1990, Chapter II.

creasing application of anti-trust rules within the European Union[2] is part of this development. Yet, in addition to those rules, the whole range of provisions aiming at promoting competition is supporting the trend. The provisions prescribing the application of specific procedures for *public procurement* of goods and public works contracts as well as of services is one example out of many of different sets of rules aimed at promoting competition. Another example can be found in the Treaty provisions on *state aid*[3] and its increasing application by the Commission and the Court.

When, however, we look at competition law, one of the striking facts seems to be an apparent *contradiction* built into the co-ordination of the various fields of competition rules (in the broadest sense). Whereas one set of rules aiming at promoting competition might prohibit or allow a certain form of behaviour, another set of provisions apparently endorses the opposite behaviour.

As an illustrative example one could think of the Commission's Decision of 21st December, 1993 concerning aid to be provided by the Irish government to the *Aer Lingus Group*.[4] Here, the United Kingdom government and a number of Aer Lingus's competitors on the United Kingdom/Ireland routes and other interested parties responded to the invitation by the Commission to comment on the case. They specifically pointed to the fact that the state aid would enable Aer Lingus to maintain the same level of capacity on several routes or increase the present capacity at uneconomic fares. With the aid Aer Lingus was said to be able to operate new routes or re-enter routes previously abandoned. The creation of overcapacity would then harm the competitors' position by reducing their loadfactors, obliging them to offer uneconomically low fares or forcing them out of business. The Commission, despite these comments, found that the restructuring aid to Aer Lingus could be considered compatible with the Common Market pursuant to Article 92(3) (c) of the Treaty, provided that the Irish government undertook some conditions specified in the Decision. At the same time as this state aid case was under the Commission's scrutiny, however, the Commission was also dealing with a complaint from another competitor alleging that Aer Lingus had infringed

---

[2] Articles 85 to 90 of the Treaty on the European Community and the Merger control rules in Council Regulation 4064/89.

[3] EC Treaty Articles 92–94 and supplementing secondary legislation such as the specific rules on state aid to the shipbuilding industry.

[4] OJ 1994 L 54/30.

Article 86 of the Treaty by engaging in *predatory pricing* on the London Heathrow-Dublin route.[5]

So, when the state aid provisions of the Treaty aiming at avoiding distortion of the competitive conditions within the European Union are being administered by the Commission, situations may often occur where the Commission is inclined to accept the state aid measure as compatible with the Common Market, though at the same time there may be competitive hesitations linked to the acceptance. Plus, the very same company that is the recipient of lawful state aid may be accused of infringement of, or may actually infringe, the antitrust/competition rules.

In this contribution I intend to draw attention to these apparent inherent contradictions in various regulations which all aim to promote competition within the European Union. I have chosen to illustrate the subject with examples from two fields, namely where anti-dumping measures may contradict the purpose of anti-trust law and where agreements on industrial property rights – more specifically trademarks – may counteract the competition rules.[6]

2. Antitrust Rules and the Anti-Dumping Rules

A. Protection through Agreements against Dumping

It has from time to time been argued by companies accused of *cartellising* or otherwise acting in *collusion* that this kind of behaviour was necessary – and thus legal – in order for them to live up to the international standards in relation to *dumping* prohibitions. At other times the dumping rules have been invoked in order to justify cartellisation thus reacting against prices and other conditions resulting from the alleged exercise of dumping by companies from third countries.

---

[5] It could also be noted that a few years earlier in *British Midland v. Aer Lingus*, 26th February, 1992, OJ 1992 L 96/34, Aer Lingus had been found guilty of infringement of Articles 85 and 86 in relation to various anti-competitive measures. Fines had been imposed on Aer Lingus.

[6] Normally I use the phrase "competition law" as synonymous with "antitrust law".

Both arguments based on dumping legislation were presented by the parties to some agreements being assessed by the Commission in its Decision of 15th July, 1975 relating to a proceeding under Article 85 of the IFTRA Rules for *Producers of Virgin Aluminium*.[7]

> Under the IFTRA Rules, the parties to the agreements had undertaken an obligation to refrain from *dumping*. They argued that dumping was condemned under GATT Article VI as an unfair trade practice for which reason they were allowed to undertake the obligation in question. The Commission rejected this argument, finding it obvious that reference was made to the concept of dumping as contained in, and the principle formulated by, GATT Article VI, and no reference was made in the IFTRA Rules to the *territories* to which this GATT provision was or was not applicable. Consequently, the clause in its natural sense would require the parties to refrain from dumping not only in relation to third countries but also in each other's territory. The clause hereby applied to trade *within the Community*. In so doing, the parties to the agreements had undertaken an obligation to refrain from dumping, at least in each other's respective territory.
>
> By directly looking into the obligation undertaken to refrain from "dumping", the Commission found that the object or effect was the prevention of acts which were in fact quite compatible with the EEC rules of competition. Within the EEC, the rules on dumping had ceased to be applicable for which reason a low-price sale from one Member State to another would no more be subject to such rules than such a sale from one zone to another within the same Member State. For that reason it was clear that the sole object and effect of the IFTRA Rules relating to dumping, as far as sales from one Member State to another were concerned, was to prevent the type of inconvenient competitive offer which was no longer prevented by any Community legal provision.

On the basis of this it is clear that the parties to restrictive agreements cannot rely on dumping rules when agreeing on prices *within* the *European Union*, but the Commission apparently made the distinction whether there was an agreement prohibiting dumping within the Community or towards third countries. There would probably have been a problem, as a matter of principle, had the Commission intervened against restrictive agreements solely effective outside the Community. One might have questioned whether the applicability of Articles 85 and 86 extends to such situations, at least if that behaviour

---

[7] OJ 1975 L 228/3.

would have had no influence on the parties' interrelationship in the Community market.

A *"dumping defence"* – meaning a defence from dumping by third countries – was simultaniously relied on in the same case by both parties.

> The Commission, however, found – when presented with an argument that the agreements were a defence against alleged dumping on the part of third countries in 1970 and 1971, which the parties insisted had occurred – that not only was the information submitted to the Commission insufficient to establish that any act of dumping had taken place, but it was furthermore inadequate to justify the opening of proceedings under the relevant Council regulation on dumping by third countries.

By rejecting this argument on the grounds of *evidence*, the Commission avoided responding directly to the question which might have been put regarding whether substantiated dumping by a third country might have been an acceptable excuse for a cartel arrangement. Yet the Commission, moreover, found it necessary to stress that, as far as sales between the Common Market and third countries were concerned, the appraisal of whether acts could be considered as dumping and the imposition of defensive measures under the existing rules relating to dumping were matters which could only be undertaken by a competent authority, viz. a national authority or the Commission. Any other method would be open to the risk of abuse. Such an authority, the Commission went on, was the only entity entitled to assess, after a necessarily complicated and lengthy examiniation, whether the imposition of anti-dumping measures interfering with the free movement of goods could be justified. It was therefore often difficult to predict whether a proposed sale would constitute unlawful dumping. As a consequence, a reciprocal undertaking to refrain from dumping would necessarily discourage the parties from sales which might inconvenience other parties in their national markets, but which would not ultimately be found contrary to the rules concerning dumping.

In its Decision of 29th November, 1974 relating to the *Franco-*

Japanese Ball-bearings Agreement[8] the Commission had found basis for describing in greater detail the applicability of Article 85 to situations where trade policy (anti-dumping measures) and anti-trust meet. In relation to the actual case, the Commission pointed out that four types of measures could be distinguished and should be assessed differently:

(a) Measures taken in pursuance of trade agreements between the Community and Japan. These were acts of external commercial policy which were as such outside the scope of Article 85 of the EEC Treaty;

(b) Measures imposed on Japanese undertakings by the Japanese authorities. These measures were also outside the scope of Article 85;[9]

(c) Measures resulting from agreements or concerted practices between undertakings which were merely authorized by the Japanese authorities under Japanese law. Such an authorization, while required for the measures to be lawful in Japan, would not necessarily mean that Article 85 could not apply since it would in no way alter the fact that the undertakings concerned were free to refrain from entering into an agreement or engaging in concerted practices; and

(d) Measures resulting solely from agreements, concerted practices or decisions by associations of undertakings, entered into or engaged in either unilaterally by Japanese undertakings or in concert with the appropriate European undertakings. These measures of a private nature might also fall within the scope of Article 85. The Commission had expressly drawn the attention of undertakings to this point by an opinion which had been published in the Official Journal.[10]

It is clear from this statement, especially point (d), that when undertakings themselves take to measures which might violate Article 85, they are on dangerous ground even when such measures might be contrary to the trade policy pursued by the Community. This is well in accordance with the Commission's Decision of 8th January, 1975 relating to *Preserved Mushrooms*[11] where the opinion was expressed

---

[8] OJ 1974 L 343/19.

[9] However, in both situations (a) and (b) Article 85 could be applicable to any agreements or concerted practices additional to such measures.

[10] "Opinion relating to imports of Japanese products in the Community falling under the Treaty of Rome", OJ 1974 C 111/13.

[11] OJ 1975 L 29/26.

that even if the producers concerned had had good reason to believe that there would be a serious disturbance of the market, such as was recognized in a Commission Regulation,[12] it was not permissible for them, in order to alleviate this situation, to take the initiative by infringing the Treaty or even to participate in an infringement thereof.

In subsequent cases, the Commission has found reason for expanding its hostility towards the "dumping defence", especially in its Decision of 6th August, 1984 on the *Zinc Producer Group*[13] relating to a proceeding under Article 85 of the EEC Treaty.

> The undertakings concerned argued in their defence, i.a., that an agreement on the producer price and price support measures was a reaction to dumping by centrally planned economies.
>
> However, the Commission reacted in reply to these arguments by pointing out that in attempting to cope with difficult market conditions or extreme falls in demand, firms must use only means which are consistent with competition. The fixing of purchase or selling prices by competitors is not a legitimate means of combating alleged difficult market conditions. Even the prevention of alleged dumping practices did not justify attempts to regulate prices and markets through private agreements.

B. Undertakings by the Exporting Company as to Price Conditions

Another aspect of dumping which could be discussed in relation to competition law involves when an exporting company has committed itself to an undertaking. This situation is, e.g., present in anti-dumping cases when an exporting company signs a declaration to the Commission regarding its willingness to increase prices when exporting to the European Union. One might wonder here whether this undertaking is an "agreement" or other act which could violate the competition rules of the Treaty in Article 85(1). On the one hand one could argue that this is a *unilateral act* and for that reason not contrary to Article 85(1) dealing with "agreements between under-

---

[12] Commission Regulation (EEC) 2107/74 of 8th August, 1974.
[13] OJ 1984 L 220/27.

takings, decisions by associations of undertakings and concerted practices". On the other hand it has been established by the Commission and the Court that unilateral behaviour can also be contrary not only to Article 86 but also to Article 85(1) when it is part of a broader scheme.[14]

Despite the obvious possibility for the European companies within the particular business to profit from an undertaking by one or more exporting companies from third countries by way of undercutting the price undertaken or otherwise harmonizing price levels, no antitrust case has arisen concerning the adjustment to price revision undertakings. However, in Council Regulation No 2322/85 of 12th August, 1985 which imposes a definitive anti-dumping duty on imports of *Glycine* originating in Japan,[15] two Japanese companies offered undertakings concerning their exports of glycine to the Community. These undertakings were not accepted by the Commission.

> The grounds for this rejection were mainly that the Commission had noted a disparity between the average export prices charged by the two Japanese companies during the period under investigation. This disparity had been created by the companies themselves. Imposing the same amount of anti-dumping duty with regard to the product manufactured by both companies would mean that the difference between the prices at which the two exporters' goods would be sold in the Community would remain essentially the same, unless the companies decided to alter their pricing policy. *It was not considered in the interest of the Community to take protective measures which would tend to reduce competition in the Community market.* It was not an objective of the anti-dumping rules to bring about an alignment of export prices to the Community.
>
> The Commission added that, in a market where only a limited number of companies are competing, an alignment of prices resulting from undertakings of the kind offered by the Japanese companies, *i.e.* to respect the same minimum price, would reduce competition. So, it was considered not to be in the Community's interest to accept the undertakings offered because of *the*

---

[14] See *e.g.* Judgment of the Court of Justice of 16th June, 1994, *Automobiles Peugeot SA and Peugeot SA* v. Commission, case C-322/93 P, ECR 1994 p I-2727, where the Commission had found in its Decision that the dispatch of a circular by Peugeot to its dealers in France, Belgium and Luxembourg and its implementation by them – which brought to a halt supplies of Peugeot vehicles to a third company – constituted an agreement or at least a concerted practice prohibited by Article 85(1) of the EEC Treaty. The Court upheld the Decision and the Judgment of the Court of First Instance.

[15] OJ 1985 L 218/1.

effect these price undertakings could have in this case *on the competitive situation* and structure of the glycine market.

Since the Commission is to a great extent in charge of enforcing both the anti-dumping rules and the competition rules, this may be the reason why no cases in relation to undertakings have come up on the part of the exporters. Notwithstanding, the Commission's attention is undoubtedly focused on the problem.

> In Council Regulation No 3687/87 of 8th December, 1987 imposing a definitive anti-dumping duty on imports of *Mercury* originating in the Soviet Union,[16] the Soviet exporter had made certain submissions, *i.a.* referring to an investigation being carried out under Regulation No 17[17] concerning possible price agreements between producers established in the Community and in third countries. The Soviet exporter claimed that such an investigation indicated that the Community mercury producer was not competitive and that the price on the Community market was artificially high. However, the Soviet exporter submitted no evidence in support of its allegations. The Commission rejected this point of view by referring to the fact that the present dumping proceeding had no bearing on the investigations under Regulation No 17 concerning possible price agreements between producers established in the Community and in third countries. The object of an anti-dumping proceeding was not, and could not be, to condone or encourage restrictive commercial practices, and the initiation of such proceedings in no way restricted a firm's right to invoke the provisions of Articles 85 and 86 of the Treaty. Moreover, if an infringement of Articles 85 and 86 was discovered and proceedings initiated under Regulation No 17, the Commission might review the present proceedings in accordance with the Regulation on anti-dumping.

It can thus be seen from the above that anti-dumping proceedings may include various elements which may seem to be in conflict with antitrust rules. While the Commission is to a large extent in charge of the enforcement of the anti-dumping as well as of competition rules, there seem to have been no problems so far in connection with the administration of the two sets of legislation which have been unsolvable.

---

[16] OJ 1987 L 346/27.

[17] Council Regulation No 17: First Regulation Implementing Articles 85 and 86 of the Treaty, OJ 1962 no 13, p. 204.

3. The Anti-trust Rules and Agreements on Trademark Delimitations

Agreements on industrial property rights such as patents or trademarks, may be extremely dangerous for competition and for that reason clearly be prohibited by Article 85. This could be the situation for many patent licensing agreements if they created powerful patent pools or reciprocal patent protection. Or, it could be the result of trademark agreements whereby the parties refrain on a reciprocal basis from attacking each others' trademark or undertake obligations unduly extending the lawful scope of such trademarks. It is, on the other hand, generally accepted that some trademark agreements – even if they include a partitioning of markets – may or should be acceptable, at least to some extent. Moreover, many patent licensing agreements will undoubtedly have very pro-competitive effects by spreading the possible application of the invention to the licensees. The acceptability of some of the agreements dealing with industrial property rights is recognized under the impression of the normal ground for the acceptance of the monopolistic position that will usually be part of the industrial property right. Broadly speaking, legislation on industrial property rights is based on the assumption that when special protection of the right in question is conferred upon the owner of the right – thereby conferring the possible monopolistic position to the owner – is, at least in the long run, in favour of promoting the competition as an encouragement for the inventor or entrepreneur. As a consequence, societal welfare will increase. There are, however, situations where the welfare trade-off may be difficult to make and where the intersection between competition rules and the rules on industrial property rights may be difficult to harmonize. One area is agreements on the delimitations of trademarks.

It seems as if the Commission has been rather hostile towards *"delimitation agreements"* in which the parties agree not to invade each others' territory with a specific trademark. The Court has taken a more favorable attitude.

Thus, in its Decision of 5th March, 1975 concerning the *Sirdar-Phildar* agreement,[18] the Commission was faced with a United Kingdom company called Sirdar Ltd. Its main line of business was the manufacture and sale of knitting yarn and carpet wool. The company, or its predecessor in title, had been using the trademark SIRDAR since 1898, and the SIRDAR trademark had been registered on behalf of Sirdar Ltd. in all Member States of the Community, including France.

In France, Les Fils de Louis Mulliez S.A. was the largest manufacturer of knitting yarn. In 1943 it registered the descriptive trademark LE FIL D'ART in the French trademark register for, i.a., knitting yarn and clothing which became registered internationally in 1945. Meanwhile, its phonetic abbreviation PHILDAR had been registered in France and was entered into the international register in 1946.

Although Les Fils de Louis Mulliez S.A. contested the view that the PHILDAR and SIRDAR trademarks were likely to be confused, in 1964 it entered into an agreement with Sirdar Ltd. because it feared for the continued existence of its French trademark PHILDAR over which the French trademark SIRDAR of Sirdar Ltd. had priority in class 23.

In the agreement, an obligation was put on Les Fils de Louis Mulliez S.A. not to use its trademark PHILDAR for knitting yarns in the United Kingdom while Sirdar Ltd. agreed not to use its trademark SIRDAR for knitting yarns in France. Furthermore, Les Fils de Louis Mulliez S.A. undertook to use in the United Kingdom, as their trademark for knitting yarns, a mark which would not be in any way confused with the trademark SIRDAR and which would not include the suffix "DAR" or any other suffix likely to be confused with the suffix "DAR". Sirdar Ltd. gave a similar undertaking for the protection of the PHILDAR trademark in France.

The Commission made a preliminary examination under Article 85(1) of the agreement. It found, i.a., that the existence of a restriction of competition could not be denied on the ground that the trademarks SIRDAR and PHIL-DAR were similar and therefore likely to be confused. Even if this were the case, it would not justify market sharing between the parties. As the agreement raised barriers to trade between France and the United Kingdom, it was liable to affect trade between Member States.

One might question whether this solution by the Commission was based on good reason. As can be seen, it was the opinion of the Commission that the agreement was in violation of Article 85(1). This solution, however, was reached without going into the question of whether either party would have had the possibility, on the grounds of its respective trademark legislations, to prevent the sale from the

---

18 OJ 1975 L 125/27.

other party into its own terrirory without the agreement. If that was so, one must raise doubt as to the reasonableness of the Decision since a delimitation agreement does not, in that situation, restrict any of the parties in their possible action. Through their respective trademark legislations, in combination with their ownership of the trademarks, they could have already prevented the sale in their own territory by the other party. An agreement to the same effect does not therefore restrict competition.

A few years later, in its *Penneys*[19] decision of 23rd December, 1977, the Commission presented a somewhat more flexible attitude than it had in the Sirdar-Phildar case.

> In connection with an assessment of a settlement agreement, the Commission pointed out that prior to the settlement the parties had conflicting trade names and trademarks for the name "Penneys" and various other names in a number of Member States. The ensuing controversy between the parties could have been decided in different ways in various Member States. If the controversy between the parties had not been settled, and Penneys Ireland had prevailed in Ireland and France where it claimed to have the greater right to the word "Penney" while the other company, Penney America, prevailed in other Member States as it already had on a provisional basis in England and Wales, the result under national trademark laws would have been the prevention of Penney America from making any trademark or trade name use of the word "Penneys" in Ireland and France, while Penneys Ireland would have been prevented from making any trademark or trade name use of the word Penneys in the other Member States. As a consequence, each party would have been effectively prevented by the operation of national law from exporting its goods marked "Penneys", or the other trademarks, into the territories legally reserved for the other party.
>
> In addition, the Commission found it relevant to note that both parties remained competitors trading in the same articles, in particular the same types of clothing and household furnishing, under different names and even to a limited extent under the same name "Penneys", *i.e.* so far as Ireland was concerned and for so long as the former Penneys Ltd. desired to continue the use of "Penneys". Even so, this restriction was not appreciable in the present case for several reasons.

So, despite the fact that the Commission, in its assessment here, was careful to describe that enterprises involved in a situation such as the

---

[19] *Penneys*, OJ 1978 L 60/19.

present one must normally seek the least restrictive solution possible – such as incorporating distinguishing marks, shapes or colours to differentiate the products of the two enterprises which bear identical or confusingly similar marks – it did not find that the agreement was necessarily a restriction to competition. A contractual obligation for the parties to assign or waive their trademark and trade name rights, which would make it necessary for them to re-establish goodwill under other names, might, the Court held, under certain circumstances have restrictive effects. Nonetheless, this case was unusual because although the name "Penneys" was at one time used by both parties both as a trade name and as a trademark, it was to a great extent replaced in the EEC by one of the parties, except in Ireland, with another name independent of the agreement with the other party, following the injunction of the British High Court. Therefore it was not the party's assignment of its trademark rights that made it necessary for that party to re-establish goodwill under another name. For mainly these reasons the Commission did not find the delimitation agreement contrary to Article 85(1).

The Court of Justice has contributed to the shedding of light on the subject with its Judgment of 30th January, 1985 in the case *BAT Cigaretten-Fabriken* GmbH v. Commission, Case 35/83.[20]

> Dealing with an application by BAT Cigaretten-Fabriken GmbH for a declaration that a Commission Decision relating to a proceeding under Article 85 was void, the Court had to deal with trademark *"delimitation agreements"* in which the parties had agreed to a no-challenge clause contained in a disputed agreement.
>
> The Court pointed out that it had already stated in its Grundig-judgment[21] that the Community system of competition does not allow the improper use of rights under any national trademark law in order to frustrate the community's law on cartels. The Court, however, acknowledged that agreements known as *"delimitation agreements"* are lawful and useful *if they serve to delimit*, in the mutual interest of the parties, the spheres within which their respective trademarks may be used, and are intended to avoid confusion or conflict between them. That was not to say, however, that such agreements were excluded from the application of Article 85 of the Treaty if they also had the

---

[20] ECR 1985, p 363ff.

[21] Joined cases 56 and 58/64, Consten and Grundig v. Commission [1966] ECR 299, 346.

aim of dividing up the market or restricting competition in other ways. In the present case such a division had taken place.

So, the Court apparently expresses more favorable opinions on delimitation agreements than the Commission. At least under certain circumstances, the Court will find such agreements not to be restrictive to competition and for that reason to be acceptable.

4. Concluding Remarks

It is interesting to compare the anti-dumping situations with the delimitation agreements. The attitude of the Court of Justice towards delimitation agreements seems to be that the parties may, to a large extent, be able to avoid the application of the judicial system – for instance an injunction – and replace that procedure with an agreement, even when such an agreement may come close to a restrictive agreement that would normally fall under Article 85. It thus seems as if the Court is inclined to indicate that only when such an agreement is directly restricting competition contrary to the provisions of Article 85(1) may it be prohibited. The attitude of the Commission in cases dealing with the "dumping defence", however, paints the picture that the Commission is rather hostile towards self-defence through restrictive agreements in situations when, as in the dumping cases, there exists a formal administrative system built up to make the economic and legal assessments. This also seems to be case with delimitation agreements.

It should be noted that the attitude of the Court appears to be more in favour of leaving it to the parties to avoid the (costly and uncertain) administrative and judicial procedures by substituting them with agreements, which is certainly a cost saving alternative.

In the future we shall see whether the Court will follow this road and further develop the possibility of defensive agreements when blatant violations of Article 85(1) are not at hand.

A SWEDISH CENTRE OF GRAVITY TEST?
– LAW, FACT AND FICTION ON THE
"INDIVIDUALIZING METHOD"

Ulf Göranson

1. Introduction

Sweden, having just entered the European Union, is at present preparing to follow suit with the twelve old Member States by acceding to the 1980 Rome Convention on choice of law in contract.[1] When the Rome Convention is ratified, Sweden will, for the first time, receive comprehensive statutory conflict rules in this vast field of law. Until recently, only the sale of goods had attracted the interest of the conflct legislator, then as a consequence of the Swedish ratification of the 1955 Hague Convention.[2] As a result of the EEA co-operation, Sweden, by Act (1993:645), implemented EC directives on the choice of law in certain insurance matters. In addition to this sparse legislation, a few provisions relating to private international law have appeared in acts on substantive contractual matters.[3]

Anyone not familiar with current Swedish international contract law may well believe that we, lacking legislation, have a full body of case-law where the specific rules of this area are to be found. With the

---

[1] Convention on the Law Applicable to Contractual Obligations, Rome 1980.

[2] Act (1964:528) on the Law Applicable to Contracts for the International Sale of Goods. Before that, Sweden had, in 1932, entered into co-operation under the Geneva Conventions on bills of exchange and cheques with enactments containing choice of law rules; they have had no influence on the general rules of Swedish contractual conflict law.

[3] The technique of mixing substantive and conflict law in the same act may lead to confusion, not always clarified by the *traveaux préparatoires*. For a critical analysis, see M. Jänterä-Jareborg, "Internationellt tvingande civilrättsregler, fastighetsförmedling och konsumenter – några reflexioner", *Svensk Juristtidning* 80 (1995), pp. 374–384, and M. Bogdan, "Fastighetsmäklare och svensk internationell konsumenträtt", *Svensk Juristtidning* 80 (1995), pp. 1–6.

Rome Convention in force, it would then be only for the commentators in the legal literature to single out which precedents are still valid under the Convention and which are not. The situation is, however, a bit more complicated.

Until the first years of the 1990s, the Swedish Supreme Court had not dealt with general questions on the conflict of laws in contract for almost 50 years. When the Court, in the 1930s and 1940s, ruled on such matters, only two important cases emerged, both possible to construct in various ways. In the Swedish literature from that period onwards, these cases are said to constitute what is called the "individualizing method",[4] a Swedish centre of gravity test. This "method" is supposed to contain the main rule on how to decide the contractual choice of law in the absence of an agreement by the parties.

How does the "individualizing method" operate? The only current Swedish textbook on private international law[5] gives the following presentation:

> When choosing the law applicable to the contract, regard is to be had for "all individual connections of the contract to various countries, *inter alia* the parties' nationality and domicile (perhaps the place of business responsible for the conclusion of the contract), place of conclusion, place of performance, currency and language of contract, etc. The choice of law applicable is dependent on the individual intensity and intercourse of the various connecting factors. Certain factors, e.g. domicile, are given considerably greater relevance than others, e.g. language. By weighing the connecting factors against each other, a total picture as to the closest connection to one country is sought. The individualizing method gives the courts considerable discretion and the result can be difficult to predict." Further is stated that the legal literature and case-law have developed a number of *in dubio* rules to be used when the free weighing of factors does not give a result. It is immaterial whether these rules are used as presumptions *prima facie*, as some writers have suggested, or *in dubio*, only after an ineffective free weighing. In every individual case the strength of the connecting factors must be examined. The rules are not binding but rather to be regarded as recommendations.

---

[4] We will use this expression throughout the article in order not to give a false impression that the "individualizing method" has any deep similarities with common law doctrines on "proper law" or "centre of gravity".

[5] M. Bogdan, *Svensk internationell privat- och processrätt*, 4th ed., 1992, pp. 241–244, quotations at p. 242; in substance the presentation is unchanged since the first edition in 1980.

We will trace the origins of this method and examine the merits of its extremely flexible approach in comparison with presumptions and fixed rules on choice of law in contract. We will also ask if there exists, as suggested, a unanimous appreciation of the method in courts and among commentators.

Now that Swedish international contract law is in a state of transition, it may seem slightly out of touch to study a 60 year-old doctrine which will soon be superseded by modern legislation. Had it not been for seemingly widespread views, *inter alia* that the "individualizing method" is an excellent way to decide questions on choice of law, that it reflects modern trends in private international law, that it is still upheld by the Supreme Court and that it does not deviate from the rules of the Rome Convention, it would probably have been best to let it be forgotten and peacefully put to rest. Since, however, our esteemed colleague Lennart Pålsson has not, to our knowledge, been one of the ardent advocates of the "individualizing method",[6] he will, hopefully, find some pleasure in our critical views on it.

We will first approach the *origins* of the Swedish "individualizing method" in case-law and follow its reception in the early domestic legal literature, *section 2*. The *recent development* will be studied in *section 3* in order to find out whether or not the Swedish Supreme Court still abides by it. A short *section 4* will comment on the compatibility of the "individualizing method" with Article 4 of the Rome Convention, followed by some concluding remarks, *section 5*.

2. The Origins of the "Individualizing Method"

2.1 Swedish Case-Law

2.1.1 The General Legal Environment

The need to solve a rather particular legal question in relation to the universal recession of the early 1930s led Swedish contractual conflict law to adopt an "individualizing method". As has been evidently shown by *Lando*, a similar development took place in the other

---

6 See, *i.a.*, critical remarks by *Pålsson* in case-law notes, especially on Labour Court cases which are not considered in this article, *Svensk Juristtidning* 67 (1982), pp. 231–235.

Scandinavian countries at the same time.[7] The immediate cause was the abrogation by the United States of gold clauses in bonds. In the 1920s, many states had issued gold dollar bonds intended for the American market. A Congressional Joint Resolution in 1933 abrogated all such clauses in bonds payable in the United States. Litigation started in several jurisdictions over the world by creditors to whom substantial loss was caused when they suddenly were paid in depreciated paper currency. Was, according to the private international law rules of the issuing state, United States law or debtor's law applicable to the obligation of the bond debtor?

In Sweden, the question was brought to court in late 1933. The judgment of the Supreme Court appeared in early 1937 and is reported as *NJA 1937 p. 1*. The case attracted wide attention and a full report of all written materials was published simultaneously and separately by the defendant, Riksgäldskontoret, i.e. the National Debt Office.[8] It is in the argumentation of the defendant that we find the first traces of an "individualizing method".

The standpoints of the parties were, of course, that according to the bond debtor the laws of the United States should govern the obligations, whereas the bond buying plaintiff, a major Swedish insurance company, demanded the application of Swedish law.[9]

The case was brilliantly argued on both sides. We must bear in mind the deplorable state of Swedish international contract law in the early 1930s. We lacked a usable textbook. Other forms of discussion in the legal literature were practically nonexistent. In matters related to the contractual choice of law, only one fairly modern precedent existed to give guidance: *NJA 1912 p. 231*. In that case, probably under the influence of the ideas put forward by the great authority on

---

[7] O. Lando, *Kontraktstatuttet. Hovedpunkter af den internationale kontraktsrets almindelige del*, 1962, pp. 266–271, 274–279, 282–285, 287–291.

[8] *Guldklausulmålet*, (three volumes in all 648 pp.), 1935–1937. This unique mode of publication had as a consequence that the report in *Nytt Juridiskt Arkiv (NJA)* is extremely digested and lacks the argumentation of the parties.

[9] In addition to the contractual choice of law, the case contains a number of important private international law questions, *inter alia*, party autonomy, the application of foreign public law, *dépeçage*, and *ordre public*. They will not be dealt with here. For a full reference to these matters, see L.A.E. Hjerner, *Främmande valutalag och internationell privaträtt*, 1956; on this particular case, see pp. 167–169.

the Swedish Sale of Goods Act 1905, Tore Almén, the Supreme Court had applied *lex debitoris* in a mode that is close to the use of a fixed conflict rule.[10] This supported the position of the plaintiff in the gold bond case. The Court of Appeal, without much ado, ruled in favour of the plaintiff on this point and declared Swedish law (*lex debitoris*) applicable to the contractual relation between the bond debtor and creditor.

We must also remember that in the early 1930s there was still a vivid discussion in many leading jurisdictions on, *inter alia*, two important issues appearing in the case: where should the limits of party autonomy be drawn and what type of conflict rules was preferable – fixed or flexible?[11] The counsel for the defendant was able to take advantage of this general situation. On the tabula rasa, in Sweden, of the conflict of laws in contract, numerous foreign cases, references to foreign literature and legal opinions from important foreign academics were presented.[12]

Of immediate interest is the then-current international discussion on *fixed or flexible choice of law rules*. The fixed rule doctrine was, to a considerable extent, discredited by the fact that there had been a tendency to single out one connecting factor to decide the choice of law in the whole variable sphere of contract law. In particular, the *lex patriae/domicilii debitoris* rule had the easily-recognized negative result that, in most contractual relations, two laws would govern since the

---

[10] The opinion in *NJA 1912 p. 231* states that the debtors (sureties) were Swedish nationals residing here. The Court also made an implied intention test which showed that the debtors neither had the intention nor had reason to foresee that the law of a foreign country would be applicable. However, in the "Heading" of the case – an indistinct supplementary instrument for the interpretation of old Swedish cases – the legal question is presented in a way which lies closer to a flexible than a fixed rule method. The "Heading" does not simply say that the obligation of the debtor is to be governed by his law. Instead, five connecting factors are mentioned, i.e., residence and nationality of debtor and, additionally in the same direction, *locus contractus* against which are contrasted language of contract and its place of performance, both German.

[11] A comprehensive overview and analysis of the case-law and literature in several countries is found in Lando, *op. cit.* (note 7).

[12] Also the counsel for the plaintiff made similar efforts in favour of the *lex debitoris* rule and even found a firm believer in a Swiss academic who wrote an elegant opinion.

performances of both parties had to be considered.[13] To favour, instead, *lex loci solutionis* could give similar "multi-law" results. At a time of more speedy communications and wider possibilities to conclude a contract without the simultaneous presence of both parties, *locus contractus* became less attractive as a comprehensive connecting factor.

A need for more flexible rules was certainly felt. Tendencies in that direction were also supported by the continuous development of new contract types. To find the "proper law of the contract" without coming to the sometimes artificial solutions found by the use of fixed choice of law rules had its early heralds in the United States. The doctrine soon spread to England and was also taken up by some continental European lawyers. The methods on how to find the "proper law" were, however, widely divergent. Some used the test of objective presumed intention, others preferred the free weighing of numerous objective connecting factors, only to mention the two dominating streams.

2.1.2 NJA 1937 p. 1 and Nussbaum's "Individualizing Method"

What happened in the Swedish gold bond case of the mid 1930s was, according to the present author, that the tendencies in leading foreign jurisdictions towards very flexible choice of law rules were highly exaggerated by the bond debtor. The counsel for the National Debt Office advanced, particularly, one German author, *Arthur Nussbaum*, and his in 1932 published textbook on German private international law.[14] Instead of being introduced as the most radical proponent, at least among German conflict lawyers, of a flexible method, Nussbaum was presented as an example and even a leading authority of the mainstream. From this source was deduced what the counsel, in literal translation, called the "individualizing method" with its free

---

13 For example, in a sales contract the seller's law would apply to questions concerning his obligation to deliver the goods in accordance with the contract, whereas the buyer's law would apply to his obligation to pay the price. – The idea of preferring the debtor who was to effect the characteristic performance was not yet developed as a general rule, see *infra* n. 54.

14 A. Nussbaum, *Deutsches internationales Privatrecht. Unter besonderer Berücksichtigung des österreichischen und schweizerischen Rechts*, 1932.

weighing of all objective connecting factors in order to find the centre of gravity of the contractual relation.[15]

Without mentioning it explicitly the majority of the Supreme Court in *NJA 1937 p. 1*[16] was strongly influenced by Nussbaum's "individualizing method" when ruling in favour of the bond debtor and applying US law:[17]

> The Court recognized party autonomy but found that no explicit or tacit intention of the debtor could be traced by studying the printed bonds. Without searching for a presumed intention, the Court went on and formulated the rule that in the absence of an agreement the choice of law "decision must be arrived at by weighing against one another the objective factors in the legal relationship that are calculated to turn the scales in favour of one side or the other".
>
> In favour of Swedish law were the facts that the obligation was unilateral and performed by the sovereign Swedish State as debtor. The main factors connecting the contract with the United States were the place of performance and the currency. Other factors, of lesser weight and rather a consequence of the two main ones, i.e. place of issue, use of American Fiscal agent, language, wording and appearance of the bonds, place of publication of notices concerning the bonds, all served "to strengthen the impression that the bonds in reality belong[ed] to the American market". After declaring the connecting factors decisive not only as to the modes of payment but also as to the substantive parts of the obligation, the Court concluded that "the debt has a

---

[15] Nussbaum's authority on the general conflict of laws in contract was probably raised by his eminent knowledge of international currency matters, the second main legal problem in the case. – For defendant's references to Nussbaum's textbook, see *Guldklausulmålet* vol. I, 1935, pp. 186–189. – After Nussbaum had had to leave his chair in Berlin and emigrated to the United States, he was called upon to deliver an opinion in which he is methodologically rather indistinct. According to Nussbaum in the opinion, published *ibid.*, pp. 134–141 (German version pp. 295–303), the contractual relationship of the case has a definite centre of gravity in New York (i.a., *locus solutionis*) but at the same time he recognizes the fixed *lex debitoris* rule used by the Hague Permanent Court of International Justice in a gold bond case decided in 1929. In order to exclude the *lex debitoris* rule, Nussbaum gives particular weight to the fact that the Swedish National Debt Office deliberately refrained from stating the place of issue (Stockholm) on the printed bonds. To support his view that US law governs the contract, Nussbaum also adds the tacit intention of the issuing debtor.

[16] An English translation of the judgment including dissenting opinions is found in *Guldklausulmålet*, vol. III, 1937, pp. 147–153. This translation has been followed in the quotations made below.

[17] To be more exact: The law of the State of New York was applied to the contractual relationship and, consequently, the Federal Joint Resolution was considered to relieve the debtor of the obligation to pay the bond creditor in gold currency.

more natural connection [*naturligare anknytning*] with the law of the place of payment than with the law of the debtor's country'.

Since New York law was, for these reasons, applicable to the contractual relationship between debtor and creditor, the Court had to decide the question whether US currency legislation as such was applicable in a Swedish court. This, however, is a matter beyond the scope of this article. It may briefly be said that the Court reversed the question and asked whether a connection to Sweden was enough to disregard such provisions. The answer could not always be in the affirmative. Regard must be had both to the scope and purpose of such legislation and to the connections of the underlying contract to the country of currency. The equal and general effects of the US currency reform and the close connection already found of the contractual obligation to the State of New York both spoke for the recognition of the monetary legislation. Subsequently, the creditor's demands to be compensated for the depreciation losses were rejected.[18]

The case, no doubt, represents an important development in the Swedish laws of conflict in contract. The full recognition of party autonomy, the rejection of a presumed intention test and the abolition of a fixed choice of law rule (*lex debitoris*) are of a general character. In the absence of an agreement by the parties, a test based on objective factors shall guide the search for a "natural" connection. All these results are appreciated by the present author. However, one major problem remains and was not satisfactorily solved by the Supreme Court in 1937. How shall the close or natural connection be decided? Did the Court create an "individualizing method" and, if so, with what instruments was it supposed to operate?

It is obvious from the published documents of the case that the Court was well informed of *Nussbaum's* "individualizing method" or at least of its first part, the free weighing of connecting factors. Cleverly, the counsel for the bond debtor excluded Nussbaum's detailed discussion, in his textbook, on the presumptions necessary to make the method functional in a litigation context.[19] Unless any of the judges had, on his own motion, studied the full text of Nussbaum, the Court had a simplified view of his theoretical foundations.

---

[18] The dissenting minority did not find it necessary to decide which law governed the contractual relationship. Instead, immediate effect was given to the US currency legislation, thus reaching the same result, in favour of the debtor, as the majority.

[19] *Guldklausulmålet*, vol. I, 1935, pp. 186–188.

It must, however, be admitted that Nussbaum is not always easy to follow. In the absence of an explicit or tacit agreement by the parties, the choice of law procedure should be started with an evaluation of the many objective connecting factors of the contract. His main criticism of the German case-law was, first, the blurred mixture of presumed party intention with objective factors and, second, a too quick-and-easy "escape" to the solution by isolating one connecting factor, primarily the place of performance, and making it decisive.[20]

Having said that, Nussbaum continues to elaborate on the individual weight and application of the objective connecting factors. His analysis is divided into two parts. First, he examines a few basic types of factors, related primarily to the parties or to the object of the contract. The approach here is the general use of the factors in contractual conflict law as weak presumptions, "Indizien".[21] In a later part, Nussbaum treats the choice of law question in view of a limited number of contract types or contractual matters. Both the basic and additional individual connecting factors are tried as to suitability and certain weight.[22] Throughout, Nussbaum confronts his theories with an astonishing amount of published German cases from the late 1800s and the early 1900s.

Nussbaum's systematic approach is far from clear – he admits its novelty[23] – and the reader is left without a firm grip as to the strength of these presumptions, neither in general nor in the many specific contracts discussed. Nussbaum's criticism of the role played by presumptions in the case-law leads us to conclude that he was in favour of a much weaker presumption than what is generally meant when using this term. According to our view, a presumption means that the burden of proof is placed on the party who seeks a solution other than that of the presumption rule. He must produce enough evidence to rebut it. This, in turn, demands a discussion of procedural law which is not done by Nussbaum. As we will see, few others speaking in favour of the "individualizing method" do.

We will now return to the gold bond case *NJA 1937 p. 1* and try to analyse the Court's choice of law method. It has been said that the Swedish Court, contrary to a widespread tendency in the adjudi-

---

[20] Nussbaum, *op. cit.* (note 14), pp. 216–223. – *Nussbaum* speaks of "Eventuallösung", i.e., the decisive connecting factor which, according to him, may be used after the free weighing has shown no result. The courts, on the other hand, seem to have used the "Eventuallösung" as a very strong presumption, on the border of a fixed rule, instead of exhaustively weighing all the connecting factors, or at least the suitable ones, against each other.

[21] *Ibid.*, pp. 226–234.

[22] *Ibid.*, pp. 263–294.

[23] *Ibid.*, p. 226.

cation of conflict cases, did not limit itself to the individual case but
formed a general rule for the choice of law in contract.[24] It may be so,
but there is nothing in the text – nor in the "Heading" – of the
judgment to confirm it. The rule on the free weighing follows immediately from the conclusion that nothing is to be found in the bond
documents as to the intention of the issuing debtor. In favour of a
more general bearing speaks that the method chosen is in contrast
with the fixed rule used by the Court of Appeal and, perhaps, by the
Court in *NJA 1912 p. 231*, discussed above. However, as will soon be
shown, the Court did not apply the same clear method when given
the chance a few years later. We should also remember the very
specific legal issue of the case. There is some cause to say that the
more general the underlying substantive legal question, the more
reason to interpret the choice of law rule generally and with effect on
the whole area of contracts. Such a line must not be stretched too far.
The Swedes have to make the most out of the few conflict cases there
are.

Further, it is interesting to note that the Court did not say anything
as to what specific purpose the weighing of the factors had. It should
"turn the scales" [giva utslag]. *Nussbaum*, the probable inspirer, was
more outspoken when saying that the goal of the operation was to
find the jurisdiction with which the contract was most closely connected.[25] The closest connection test is, however, not omitted by the
Court. It appears in the end of the Court's reasoning, but in a rather
peculiar form. After having noted the main connecting factors and
the directions in which they pointed, the ones with certain weight are
generalized as "the American market". From there the Court makes
the ultimate weighing, no longer between the objective factors but
between what looks like two old *fixed* choice of law rules, i.e. *lex
debitoris* and *lex loci solutionis*. It is to the *law* of the place of perform-

---

[24] Practically all commentators share this view, even those not totally in favour of the
"individualizing method", see, e.g., O. Lando, *op. cit.* (note 7), pp. 287–289; H. Nial,
Internationell förmögenhetsrätt, 1944, pp. 36–37; Hj. Karlgren, *Kortfattad lärobok i internationell
privaträtt*, 1945, p. 96. See even Hult, *infra* note 41.

[25] Nussbaum, *op. cit.* (note 14), p. 222: "[Z]u entscheiden, mit welchem Rechtsgebiet das
streitige Rechtsverhältnis am stärksten verknüpft ist".

ance, not to the place itself, that the contract is said to have "a more natural connection" than to the debtor's law.

To connect, as the Court did, the contract to a legal system and not to a certain place the legal system of which shall govern, is considered to be a slightly erroneous line of thought. It may be a slip of the pen, but it shows that the judges were not fully in line with private international law theory. Perhaps it is mostly the view of an academic to reduce the value of the Court's method on this ground.

Going back to *Nussbaum's* rather difficult theory on the weak presumptions, there is not much connection between the theory and the Court's opinion. This is not strange since the weighing itself gave a clear result. What has been said in the Swedish literature on this second stage of the "individualizing method" has, thus, no foundation in this or any other Supreme Court case.[26]

There is yet another, albeit different, reason to be emphasised. By whatever method or rule the Court had chosen the law applicable to the contract, it was in any case necessary at a later stage of its reasoning to weigh in an individual manner the connections with Sweden and the United States. In order to solve the question of whether or not to apply foreign currency legislation, the Court found it imperative to estimate the degree of connection the underlying contractual relation had with that foreign country. If such a procedure had to be used once, it could as well, for economic reasons, found the conclusions of the first issue under consideration.

A final but perhaps too devious remark would be that the Court found it necessary to apply whatever way possible to reach a fair and reasonable result. Had the Swedish State been obliged to pay the gold value of the bonds in this case, a number of foreign creditors would have followed the example and, in spite of acting on the American market, received an unjust favour in comparison with those buying bonds issued by American debtors. In this particular case it was crucial to circumvent the old *lex debitoris* rule. However, that does not

---

[26] *Lando* also makes similar observations for the other Scandinavian countries, *op. cit.* (note 7), p. 289.

say much for the Court's wish to establish a new general and totally different method for the choice of law in contract.[27]

There can be no doubt that the factors connecting the case with "the American market" were extremely strong. Perhaps they would have sufficed to rebut even strong modern presumptions in favour of *lex debitoris*. If so, there is no need to let one single case rule out all other approaches for a more predictable way of solving a conflict situation.

2.1.3 The "Individualizing Method" and NJA 1941 p. 350

The analysis above has tried to show that there is cause to distinguish *NJA 1937 p. 1* on several grounds. We will regard the very few later cases to see if the Supreme Court has not done so itself. A new contractual conflict case appeared before the Supreme Court after only four years, *NJA 1941 p. 350*:

> Three Swedish nationals had agreed that one of them, a masseur who then, contrary to the others, resided in Sweden, should perform health care services in a massage parlour, owned by the two others, in South Africa. The masseur had accepted to pay a fine if he, after terminating his association with the owners, started within a certain time limit a similar practice in the vicinity of their establishment. Such a clause was permissible according to Swedish law but void according to South African law. Which law should apply?[28]

The Court's decision defies an infallible interpretation. The rare thing happened that the judgment of the first instance court was upheld "blankly", as the Swedish expression goes, by the Court of Appeal and the Supreme Court. Thus, there was only the opinion of a single local judge and assisting laymen to evaluate the question whether this case is an expression of the "individualizing method" or something else.[29]

The judgment is, according to the present author, a complicated

---

[27] Cf. the Norwegian development, *infra* note 38.

[28] The reason for the case to be tried in Sweden was that two Swedes, residing here, stood surety and were the defendants.

[29] One dissenting Court of Appeal judge used *lex loci solutionis* as a fixed choice of law rule.

mixture of the imperfect use of a presumption (*lex loci solutionis* =South African law), the free weighing against this of other connecting factors (nationality of all three parties=Swedish; debtor's place of residence at time of concluding the contract and place of his acceptance of contractual terms=Sweden), presumed intention of creditors and debtor to apply the law which allowed the fine clause and finally, as an addition to the presumed intention test, the application of a rule in Swedish substantive law on the interpretation of contracts, i.e. an *a contrario* construction of Section 32(1) Contracts Act 1915 (party in bad faith bound by the other party's corrective interpretation of a contract clause which due to a mistake by that other party has a false or misleading content).[30] In an additional sentence the Court declared that it weighs the grounds which "thus and for other [not mentioned] reasons" speak in favour of either law. It concluded that decisive weight should be given to the circumstances speaking in favour of applying Swedish law to the contract.

Is all this an example of the "individualizing method"? Hardly. If, as the Supreme Court said in *NJA 1937 p. 1*, the conclusion should be reached by "weighing against one another the objective factors in the legal relationship", then the Court already took, four years later, another course. Naturally, the Court found factors connecting the contract with both South Africa and Sweden. On that stage the balance seems to have been considered even. Then the Court embarked on a different course and used a combination of the suitable contract construction in substantive law and the presumed intention test of conflict law. There is little resemblance between this procedure and Nussbaum's refined "individualizing method".

The starting point of the Court looks more like the establishment of a presumption: *lex loci solutionis*. Then it is examined whether it was rebutted. Nussbaum, as we have seen, starts with the connecting factors and uses the presumptions as decisive only if the factors themselves do not show a centre of gravity. Since the Court probably

---

[30] This rule is a typically Swedish way of substantive contract law construction. In the case, the court may be interpreted as having stated that the offerors made their "mistake" by not explicitly demanding the application of Swedish law, had they known that South African law did not permit the fine clause. Of this the offeree must have been aware and was, thus, in bad faith regarding their mistake.

did not find the connecting factors for a country different than the one pointed out by the presumption heavy enough to rebut the presumption, a totally different method was used to find a solution.

Already, the contract construction procedure would have sufficed to solve the case. It looks as if the Court did not fully trust it and, therefore, added the presumed intentions and the evenly balanced connecting factors.[31] To weigh against each other objective factors, a presumed intention test and a contract construction is far beyond the Court's 1937 standpoint that only the objective factors should be weighed. It is simply too much in one operation. If not altogether fair to use against Nussbaum's theoretical construction, *Kahn's* often quoted judgment, the "Prinzip der Prinziplosigkeit", may be passed on the method used in *NJA 1941 p. 350*.[32]

From these two cases, the natural conclusion would be that the Supreme Court had no interest in creating one comprehensive "individualizing method" for the whole area of contracts.[33] The Court remained silent for almost fifty years on general questions on the

---

[31] *Nial* distinguishes this part of the Court's opinion on similar grounds: "normal contract construction", *op. cit.* (note 24), p. 29 note 2. When speaking explicitly on labour contracts, *Nial* refers to the case in detail and holds it as an example of the use of the "individualizing method", *ibid.*, pp. 56–57, cf., also p. 36. – *Karlgren* uses the case as an example of a remaining presumed intention test, *op. cit.* (note 24), pp. 95–96. – *Dennemark*, in *Svensk Juristtidning* 35 (1950), pp. 42–44, recognizes the case as proof of the "individualizing method" although he repeats his earlier pronounced criticism of it, see text *infra* at note 37.

[32] *Nussbaum* himself *op. cit.* (note 14), p. 222 drew the reader's attention to *Kahn's* characteristic, but it should be noted that it was coined more than 40 years earlier and not directed towards Nussbaum; see F. Kahn, "Gesetzeskollisionen" first published in 1891 and reprinted posthumously in *Abhandlungen zum internationalen Privatrecht*, 1928. The short and no further commented remark "Prinzip der Prinziplosigkeit" (1928, p. 84) is directed towards *L. von Bar's* efforts to reach more reasonable results in certain cases than those afforded by a strict application of a fixed and comprehensive *lex domicilii debitoris* rule, see L. von Bar, *Theorie und Praxis des internationalen Privatrechts*, vol. II, 1889, pp. 17–30.

[33] In the literature *NJA 1942 p. 389* has also been mentioned as an example of the Supreme Court using the "individualizing method". It is difficult to agree. The conflict question – which law governed an assignment of debts and the transfer of ownership to movables – was solved by a combination of the *lex loci contractus* and *lex rei sitae* rules, which according to both was Swedish law. There is nothing in the wording of the Court to speak for another construction than that the Court used fixed choice of law rules, happily coinciding. Connecting factors in favour of another location were not even mentioned. (The assignor was a German company represented by a German national residing in England; the assignee was also a German with residence in England, both having left Germany due to the persecution of Jews.) – The main question of the case was whether or not to apply a German act prohibiting Germans to dispose of assets abroad. The legal issue concerns more

choice of law in contract.[34] The gold bond case *NJA 1937 p. 1* stands out as an isolated example with no clear successor in the same direction. For the theories behind the case, one may say that though it be incoherency, yet there is Nussbaum in it. It was Swedish legal writers who grabbed the torch, advanced Nussbaum's ideas and quickly labeled the "individualizing method" universal.

2.2 The Swedish Legal Literature

The gold bond case of 1937 and its richly published materials drew the attention of an enlarged set of lawyers to exciting private international law questions.[35] The first commentator, *Malmar*, in a case-law review, did not interpret the Supreme Court as having created a new choice of law rule, but said that "no clear rule was given".[36] By this he must have meant that no fixed rule was established. More "awake" as to the novelties of the case was *Dennemark*, in an article on the contractual choice of law.[37] Dennemark opposed the great amount of flexibility pronounced by the Supreme Court in 1937 when applying, according to Dennemark, an "individualistic principle". He also contradicted an influential Norwegian academic, *Knoph*, whose "individualistic" ideas were rejected on the basis of their lack of predictability.[38] Dennemark also noted the difference between presumptions and the lesser weight given to the "orientation rules" for

---

proprietary than contractual law. Thus, the case involves interesting questions on characterization.

[34] For the recent development in Swedish case-law, see *infra section 3.2.1*.

[35] As *Lando*, (see *supra* at note 7), has shown, a similar development took place in the other Nordic countries. For a presentation of the discussion in the literature we have to restrict ourselves, in this article, mostly to Swedish examples. The close Nordic co-operation in other fields of private international law has been said to give Nordic authorities an increased influence on contractual matters as well. This, however, is difficult to measure and the case law is not coherent.

[36] F. Malmar, *Svensk Juristtidning* 27 (1942), p. 402.

[37] S. Dennemark, "Om avtalsstatutet", *Svensk Juristtidning* 28 (1943), pp. 675–697.

[38] R. Knoph, "Omkring guldklausuldommen", *Tidsskrift for rettsvidenskap* 51 (1938), pp. 46–58. Knoph comments on the Norwegian gold bond judgment, also from 1937, and states explicitly the secondary character of any presumptions in relation to the free weighing of all connecting factors. – In Norway, a flexible centre of gravity test was applied by the Supreme Court already in 1923 but there were also later examples of the Court using fixed choice of law rules, Knoph, *ibid.*, pp. 48–51.

certain contracts, according to the Nordic literature. To speak, by that time, of "the Nordic literature" seems slightly exaggerated. Only Knoph could by then have been counted as a supporter of the "individualizing method".[39] Dennemark preferred the formulation of more precise choice of law rules for certain contracts and hoped that, after the on-going war, the leading jurisdictions in international co-operation would agree on a harmonious set of such rules. However, Dennemark did not specify if these rules should be fixed or comprise strong presumptions possible to rebut.[40] Also, *Hult* spoke very sceptically of the individualistic approach.[41]

In 1944 and 1945, the first two "modern" Swedish textbooks on our subject appeared, both by well renowned professors. *Nial* (1944) was much in favour of the "individualizing method";[42] *Karlgren* (1945) was very sceptical.[43]

On what grounds did *Nial* place himself as the herald of the "individualizing method"? It is difficult to believe that the two re-ferred cases were sufficient to form his quite elaborate theory which was presented with both general and detailed provisions. He rejected the presumed intention test and fixed choice of law rules, advocated the free weighing of connecting factors and reduced the weight of any presumptions while stressing their subsidiary role for situations when the centre of gravity could not be founded on its own. He also discussed a number of contract types and the special weight given to certain connecting factors for each of them. This cannot be a positivist analysis of Swedish law. Already by looking at the footnotes which mostly give references to foreign literature (Batiffol, Cheshire, Le-

---

[39] Other writers are disregarded here since they addressed other p.i.l. questions attended to in *NJA 1937 p. 1*, i.a., party autonomy, *dépeçage*, application of foreign currency regulations and *ordre public*.

[40] Dennemark, *loc. cit.* (note 37), pp. 683–687.

[41] In a short exemplifying note in a general "anti-standards" article, *Hult* finds the "individualizing method" no more than a reformulation of the question which law to apply, giving full discretion to the judge, see Ph. Hult, "'Regel, standard och skön", in: *Festskrift- ....Stjernberg*, 1940, p. 140. In a later monograph Hult seems to have accepted a discretionary method for the search of the closest connection, *Föräldrar och barn*, 1943, p. 19.

[42] Nial, *op. cit.* (note 24), pp. 36–71.

[43] Karlgren, *op. cit.* (note 24), pp. 95–105.

wald, Nussbaum, Schnitzer, and a few others), it is obvious that Nial's sources were to be found outside Sweden.

Nial, however, did not explicitly say that his purpose was to give a general comparative overview of contractual conflict law. Sometimes he labeled his rules, statements and suggestions "generally accepted", "often applied" and similarly. The not-so-careful reader might, however, get the impression that Nial was describing the position of Swedish private international law. Such glidings between positive and comparative law may be justified, perhaps even more so in a typically international field like ours. When the rules of his own country are less developed, in need of reform and lacking legislation and case-law, a legal writer must be methodologically clear and present the reader with sufficient information as to which sources he has used. Nial did not do so in a satisfactory manner.

Nial's systematic presentation started with the general rule, the "individualizing method", for the choice of law in the absence of a party agreement and presented some general subsidiary presumptions. Then he studied which areas of contract law were covered by the chosen law, *inter alia*, capacity, form and modes of payment. Finally, he addressed a number of specific contracts. Only one earlier author had arranged his account in the same way: *Nussbaum*. A detailed comparison between Nial and Nussbaum shows extremely close conformity with the German master. Important passages, such as the purpose of finding subsidiary presumptions, are almost literal translations – without reference.[44] Nial's concealed but extreme dependence on Nussbaum is all the more astonishing since Nial declared his "individualizing method" in accordance with the English proper law of the contract doctrine.[45] It is one thing to be influenced

---

[44] Nial, op. cit. *supra* note 24 p. 43; A. Nussbaum, op. cit. *supra* note 14 p. 226.

[45] Nial, *op. cit.* (note 24), p. 36. – Nial does not refer to any authorities on the accordance between the "individualizing method" and common law conflict solutions. Any similarity is only on the surface, i.e., the search itself for the closest connection.

by important authorities,[46] but another to be totally dependent on them, especially without revealing it.[47]

According to the present author, the fact that Nial, in his textbook, so closely adopted the doctrine not of a universally acknowledged standing but of a quite radical German proponent of a new method which was only partly founded in German case-law and never raised to a "herrschende Meinung", strongly reduces the authority of Nial's teaching. Nial nevertheless received followers in the literature to which we will now return. However, he was not followed by the Supreme Court and he was faced by a powerful opponent in *Karlgren*.[48]

In his short but sharp textbook, appearing one year after Nial's book, *Karlgren* recognized with approval that the Supreme Court in *NJA 1937 p. 1* had weighed objective connecting factors against one another without the interference of a presumed party intention. He also found the method able to give satisfactory results in individual cases. He was, however, highly critical of its lack of predictability and directive functions. Karlgren understood that courts are sympathetic

---

[46] *Lando* has rightly drawn attention to Nussbaum as influential on Swedish literature and case law, *op. cit.* (note 7), pp. 78–79, but has not continued the investigation to the extent that he has shown Nussbaum's decisive connection with the opinion of the Supreme Court in *NJA 1937 p. 1* or Nial's total reliance on Nussbaum in *Internationell förmögenhetsrätt*. *Lando's* opinion, *ibid.*, on Nussbaum's influence on German literature and case-law seems slightly exaggerated in view of Lando's own presentation of the later German development, pp. 79–97. Indirectly, a contrary opinion on Nussbaum's position in the development of German private international law can be understood by the fact that *Zweigert* does not even mention Nussbaum in his review of the most important masters of the subject, see K. Zweigert, "'Die dritte Schule im internationalen Privatrecht. Zur neueren Wissenschaftsgeschichte des Kollisionsrechts" in: *Festschrift....Raape*, 1948, pp. 35–52. *Schnitzer* notes in his bibliography that Nussbaum is a "praktisches Werk, bes. Währungsfragen", *Handbuch* vol. I, 1944. Modern German writers, as far as our knowledge goes, pay no particular attention to Nussbaum.

[47] We have found Nussbaum's elaboration of the presumptions vague in various ways, *supra* at notes 21–22. This is even more so when studying Nial's version since it lacks the broad case-law material which accompanies Nussbaum's account.

[48] Karlgren, *op. cit.* (note 24), pp. 95–98. However, Karlgren has also read Nussbaum and, astonishingly, praises the book as an "unusually profound and instructive work, probably the best of all existing books of comparable size", *ibid.*, p. 44. Exactly the same comment remained in all later editions for almost thirty years which shows that Karlgren had ceased to follow the international development.

towards rules which enable them to give each case the "substantively most attractive solution". Similar trends prevailed in wide areas of substantive private and penal law. They had, however, no admirer in Karlgren.[49]

A suitable solution, according to Karlgren,[50] and a compromise between the "individualizing method" and fixed choice of law rules was a set of *presumptions* applicable to *certain types of contracts*. Although Karlgren called them *"in dubio* rules", they should operate as presumptions possible to rebut only if there was "particular support [särskilt stöd]" for other connecting factors to decide the choice of law. He gave a few such rules, *inter alia, lex domicilii* of the seller for the sale of goods, *lex rei sitae* for contractual matters concerning immovables, *lex loci solutionis* for labour contracts and *lex domicilii debitoris* for unilateral (money) obligations.[51] By "partially abandoning the individualizing method", its "disadvantages" would be "highly reduced". Consequently, Karlgren did not recommend the free weighing of connecting factors as the starting point for the choice of law procedure when a choice is to be made for a contract of the type to which such a presumption is attached.

With reference to the private international law of European continental countries, Karlgren, finally, gave an alternative approach if, as he preferred and had been done abroad, the courts restricted them-

---

[49] Karlgren, *op. cit.* (note 24), pp. 97–99. – *Karlgren* is in a more spirited mode of criticism towards the "individualizing method" in a review of Nial's book, appearing in *Tidsskrift for Rettsvidenskap* 59 (1946), pp. 336–340. Nial has, according to Karlgren, "fallen victim to the captivating power of the 'individualizing method'. The high esteem with which he regards this method is, to me [Karlgren], hard to digest". The practical difference between Nial's approach and Karlgren's favouring of a more fixed subsidiary rule will be shown by the courts in their conflict of laws proceedings: will the courts – if there should be a subsidiary rule – use the free weighing of connecting factors only in very specific cases or will they, nevertheless, do so "cheerfully and without great hesitation". Karlgren's acidity may have been increased by Nial's short and not very appreciating review of his book in an earlier issue of the same publication, see H. Nial, *Tidsskrift for Rettsvidenskap* 59 (1946), p. 232.

[50] Karlgren, *op. cit.* (note 24), pp. 99–101.

[51] Karlgren does not present any authorities for each particular presumption suggested. He favours further development of such rules in case-law and legal literature.

selves in the use of the "individualizing method".[52] He returned to the old question if it was possible to find one comprehensive connecting factor to decide the whole area of choice of law in contract. Such a *subsidiary rule* should apply when the weighing of connecting factors did not give an expedient and immediate answer to where the centre of gravity is situated. After having rejected *lex loci contractus* and *lex loci solutionis*, Karlgren suggested *lex loci debitoris* as a subsidiary basic rule. The *lex loci debitoris* rule had been greatly criticised for reasons stated above.[53] To overcome the risk of having to apply two laws and to find only one law applicable to all parts of a bilateral contract, Karlgren suggested that the obligation which consisted of only the payment of money should be opted out. Here we have, quite interestingly, an early attempt to generalize the *characteristic performance* test. Much later it would constitute the prevailing rule according to Article 4 of the Rome Convention and several autonomous national statutes, *inter alia* in Finland and Switzerland.

> Karlgren did not mention a source of inspiration for this ingenious solution, but he referred to the preparatory materials, from the 1920s, of a draft Hague Convention on the international sale of goods in which it was suggested to apply the law of the seller as the general rule. It is, otherwise, universally held that the origins of giving decisive weight as connecting factor to the domicile of the characteristic performer are Swiss case-law and literature. According to *Schnitzer*, he himself was the inventor of the rule in the second edition of his handbook on Swiss private international law,[54] published one year before Karlgren's book. It has not been possible to trace any immediate connection, i.e. a direct but not admitted loan by Karlgren.[55] Had he written in one of the great languages and elaborated his theory, Karlgren may have been considered to be at least the co-inventor.

---

[52] Karlgren, *op. cit* (note 24), p. 102. With a reference to Nussbaum, *Karlgren* admits that the "individualizing method" together with the suggested presumptions is able to solve all choice of law problems, if "the weighing of the significance of different connecting factors is made with extreme intensity and if the demands for a convincing answer are not too great", *ibid*.

[53] See at and in note 13.

[54] A. Schnitzer, "Les contrats internationaux...", *Recueil des Cours* I 123 (1968–I), pp. 562–577.

[55] *Karlgren* states a few foreign p.i.l. books in his bibliography, the German ones being von Bar, Kahn, Nussbaum (cf., *supra* note 48) and Wolff, but none from Switzerland. A consultation of the consolidated acquisition catalogue of the Swedish scientific libraries shows that Schnitzer's book, in 1944 or 1945, was bought in Uppsala and Stockholm but not in Lund

There were few modifications to these basic standpoints by *Nial* and *Karlgren* in successive editions of their books. Nial produced only one additional edition, in 1953, with some mild counter-attacks. Karlgren's book became the standard study book at the law faculties through its fifth and final edition in 1974. For almost thirty years the text of the parts of interest here received no significant changes besides for a section on the 1964 legislation implementing the 1955 Hague Convention on the international sale of goods.

Subsequent writers on the choice of law in contract have associated themselves with Nial's ideas. *Eek* and *Bogdan* are probably the most influential ones due to the wide circulation of their books in practice and at universities.[56] There is, however, no exhaustive discussion of the foundation and merits of the theory to be found in the Swedish literature.[57] Both Eek and Bogdan give a very short account of Nial's method. Bogdan does not even take a clear stand on the strength of the presumptions – *prima facie* or *in dubio* rules – since he prefers to regard them rather as recommendations. When it is said that the presumptions are developed not only in the literature but

---

where Karlgren, then, had his place of performance. A striking but probably coincidental likeness between Schnitzer and Karlgren is their bibliographies. After each entry they give a short evaluation, e.g., "influential", "sharp", "excellent".

[56] W. Michaeli, *Internationales Privatrecht*, 1948, pp. 285–287; H. Eek, *The Swedish Conflict of Laws*, 1965, pp. 267–268 (decisively not in favour of strong presumptions); *idem*, "'Svensk eller utländsk lag?"*, in: *Exporträtt* 4, 1970, pp. 56–59, (admits that the "individualizing method" is debated); *idem, Lagkonflikter i tvistemål II*, 1978, pp. 92–93, where his favouring of the weak *in dubio* rules is, wrongly, supported by a reference to Karlgren; Bogdan, *op. cit.* (note 5), pp. 241–244 in the latest edition and practically unchanged since the first edition, for details see *supra* at note 5; *idem.*, "'Tillämplig lag på handelsagentur"*, *Juridisk Tidskrift vid Stockholms universitet* 4 (1992–93) p. 60; K. Hobér, "'In Search for the Centre of Gravity"*, in: *Swedish and International Arbitration 1994*, pp. 8–11.

[57] Of a different depth is *Lando's* comparative study of the contractual choice of law (*Kontraktsstatuttet*, 1962 and later editions; note 7). On our review's limitation to the Swedish literature, see *supra* n. 35. – Lando does not agree with Karlgren's general appreciation of strong presumptions but acknowledges the greater need thereof in the contractual relations which include a need to observe mandatory substantive law, see *ibid.*, pp. 346–347. This rather vague general position must be read in contrast to the very detailed and analytic discussion of the individual weight of numerous connecting factors in different specific contracts, *ibid.* § 18, pp. 291–324. For reasons given, I have not regarded Lando's further prolific and influential writing. – Also *Hjerner's* deep analysis of the interaction between the law applicable to the contract and foreign legislation on exchange restrictions is of great interest. Since he abstains from general views on the contractual choice of law in the absence of a party agreement, it is not easy to find a definite standpoint towards the "individualizing method". However, he underlines the importance of a com-

also in case-law,[58] it must be cases other than those forming precedents according to the Swedish source of law doctrine. No such Supreme Court cases exist. We have, earlier, been able to establish that the case-law which supports the views of advocates of the "individualizing method" is that of Germany at the latest turn of the century and used by Nussbaum for his in Sweden through Nial implemented teaching.

The scepticism towards the "individualizing method" shown before and by Karlgren was not repeated in the Swedish literature.[59] However, Karlgren's ideas seem finally to have received the appreciation of the Supreme Court.

3.2 Recent Case–Law

3.2.1 The Swedish Supreme Court

In 1992 the Supreme Court was faced with an international case on the law applicable to the relation between principal and agent, *NJA 1992 p. 823.*[60] The choice of law question was addressed by the Court in a very clear and straightforward way. The Court started by declaring a presumption in favour of the law of the agent's principal place of business.[61] Such a rule was supported by the fact that the agent often has a weak position in relation to his principal. However, in the

---

parative approach in forming conflict rules, see *Främmande valutalag och internationell privaträtt*, 1956, pp. 169, 216–224.

[58] Bogdan, *op. cit.* (note 5), p. 242.

[59] In the study materials for the law students at Uppsala, the present author has strongly recommended a deviation from the "individualizing method" already before the Rome Convention comes into force, see Göranson in: *Internationell privaträtt. Studiematerial och rättsfall för Terminskurs 6*, 1995, Uppsatser pp. 135–137. – To the sceptics, after Karlgren, *Gihl* may be counted. In "'Till frågan om skuldstatutet", in: *Festskrift....Nial*, 1966, pp. 170–203, Gihl treats the contractual choice of law from a historical point of view and does not take part in the then current debate; he briefly calls the method of the Supreme Court in *NJA 1937 p. 1* "juridicial impressionism" and finds a development in that direction "far from reassuring", Gihl, *ibid.*, p. 201.

[60] No agreement existed between the parties on the choice of law; no doctrine of tacit or presumed intentions was discussed by the Court.

[61] The expression by the Court indicates, on obscure grounds, both that the presumption as such was established in Swedish private international law and that the method had good standing. On favouring the agent's law, the Court was supported by a statement in the *traveaux préparatoires* of the recent Commercial Agents Act (1991:351) to which a citation was made (Regeringens proposition [Government Bill] 1990/91:63, p. 24–25). The Act

"interest of a simple and clear choice of law rule", the same will apply even in cases between principals and agents of equal commercial strength. The presumption, the Court continued, may be rebutted if the contract "has a clearly closer connection with another country". After having discussed connecting factors in favour of the principal's law and the agent's law, the Court found that the connection with the principal's country was not "weighty enough" to rebut the presumption.

According to the present author, extreme importance must be given to *NJA 1992 p. 823*. The case was on a general issue in contract law. It lacks the very particular character of the gold bond case *NJA 1937 p. 1* to which no reference was made by the Court. Had it considered the "individualizing method" used in 1937 as a rule of law, the Court could not have changed that rule sitting in a chamber of only five judges.[62]

Methodologically, the Court itself spoke up for "simple and clear" rules on choice of law. The statement is, admittedly, directed towards the scope of the presumption in favour of the agent's law. However, it is open to generalization: The Supreme Court's judgment as a whole must be read in contrast to the opinions of the two courts below. They had come to divergent conclusions, both using the "individualizing method".[63] The Supreme Court did not have to say explicitly that it used a totally different method. It is evident from the way the Court proceeded in its opinion: first the presumption, then the question whether it should be rebutted. This has no similarity to any form of

---

itself, however, does not contain a clear choice of law provision. The Minister's statement should, therefore, be regarded merely as an *obiter dictum*.

[62] To change an established rule all judges of the Court – or in certain situation at least twelve judges – must convene, see 3:5 Code of Procedure.

[63] The District Court found that the free weighing of all connecting factors did not give a clear result and, then, followed the Nial–Eek–Bogdan line and resorted to an *in dubio* rule in favour of the agent's law. According to the Court of Appeal, when weighing the same connecting factors, there was a centre of gravity in the country of the principal's place of business. Thus, like the Supreme Court had done in *NJA 1937 p. 1*, no assistance was necessary from any guiding or "presuming" choice of law rules. – The divergent results of these two instances' evaluation of the same connecting factors show, according to our view, the drawbacks, dangers and unpredictability of the "individualizing method".

the "individualizing method" so far presented in the Swedish litera-ture.[64]

If the Supreme Court did not follow the principles of the "individ-ualizing method", what then was the guide? To let a strong and clear presumption be the starting point for the choice of law is, as we have seen, the method favoured by *Karlgren*.[65] Although not explicitly mentioned, there can be no doubt that Article 4 of the Rome Conven-tion was also before the eyes of the Court.[66]

3.2.2 Swedish Arbitral Practice

Hobér has given an interesting entry to an otherwise concealed world of case-law by reporting and commenting on four arbitral awards dealing with the contractual choice of law.[67] We can not go into the details of these cases, but it is of importance to note that there is no coherent principle or method followed in all four of them.

The first case shows a tendency towards a characteristic perform-ance test, similar to that of Article 4(2) of the Rome Convention.[68] The outcome of the second case – on exclusive rights to market and sell a

---

[64] *Bogdan*, however, *loc. cit.*(note 56), p. 915 manages to construe *NJA 1992 p. 823* in a way that he finds the judgments of all three instances to be in harmony, not only with each other and with the prevailing views in Swedish private international law, i.e. the "individuali-zing method", but also with Article 4 of the Rome Convention. – *Hobér loc. cit.* (note 56), p. 13 distinguishes the case as relating only to agency situations.

[65] No specific legal writer is cited in the judgment, but to the printed report is, unusually, added a reference list containing both Karlgren and supporters of the "individualizing method".

[66] In an earlier case, *NJA 1990 p. 734*, the Court actually mentioned that its decision was in accordance with a rule in the Rome Convention. The 1990 case, however, was on the question which law should govern in a subrogation situation: A German insurer had satisfied a German who was injured in a car accident in Sweden. The German insurer's recovery claims against the tortfeasor's Swedish insurer was governed by the law which governed the German insurer's duties towards the injured German, i.e. the same rule as appears in Article 13 of the Rome Convention. – The case is interesting in showing the application by the Supreme Court of a comparative method to find suitable choice of law rules and the rejection of an "individualizing method" also in this special situation. For the more general question on how to find the law applicable to a contract, the case is of no help: There was no doubt that the underlying insurance contract was an internal German obligation. – For further comments on *NJA 1990 p. 743*, see L. Pålsson, *Svensk Juristtidning* 67 (1992), p. 490; Hobér, *loc. cit.* (note 56), p. 13.

[67] Hobér, *loc. cit.* (note 56), pp. 13–32.

[68] Cf., *ibid.*, pp. 18–19, *Case No. 1*, which also seems to include some reference to a presumed intention test.

foreign product – shows, perhaps, a centre of gravity test focussing on the market concerned. Since that market was North America, the law of a particular state must be chosen. The arbitrators applied the law of the state where the characteristic performer was incorporated.[69] The third case seems to have been rather bluntly solved by an analogous application of the fixed rule in the Swedish International Sale of Goods (Applicable Law) Act 1964, thus applying the law of the seller's domicile to the contract.[70] In the fourth case, the tribunal does not even discuss connecting factors contrary to the place of contract and performance, both in the same country. The short report gives a flavour of the application of fixed choice of law rules, in this case the coinciding *leges loci contractus* and *loci solutionis*.[71]

In order to speak of the adherence to a juridical method, it must be necessary to show that the elements and practices of the method have been observed or applied. The dissimilarity between the usages in the four reported arbitral awards tells us that either the same method has not been applied throughout or that the "individualizing method", according to arbitrators, has such a limitless and diffuse content that it also allows an analogous or even immediate use of fixed choice of law rules, which it was originally invented to avoid. The expressions met earlier, "Prinzip der Prinziplosigkeit" and "juridical impressionism", are close at hand.

4. Article 4 of the Rome Convention

It was argued above that the Swedish Supreme Court in the case *NJA 1992 p. 823* used, as a model for the contractual choice of law in the absence of an agreement by the parties, the method laid out in Article

---

[69] *Ibid.*, pp. 23–24. It is not clear if the state of incorporation was also the principal place of business of the characteristic performer, the latter being the more modern connecting factor than the "nationality".

[70] *Ibid.*, p. 29.

[71] *Ibid.*, p. 32.

4 of the Rome Convention. Only a few words will be said about the construction of that provision.[72]

Article 4 contains five paragraphs and, at least to a Swedish reader, it would seem natural for the main rule to be found in the first paragraph. This is only partly so. Article 4(1) tells us that "the contract shall be governed by the law of the country with which it is most closely connected". This general statement may give an impression that an "individualizing method" is intended. However, the three following paragraphs consist of presumptions: one general and two for specific contracts on immovables and the carriage of goods.[73] According to the general rule in Article 4(2), "it shall be presumed that the contract is most closely connected with the country where the party who is to effect the performance which is characteristic of the contract has....his habitual residence...." For legal persons and parties acting in the course of their trade or profession, more detailed provisions are given as to their "domicile".

To clarify what is already evident by the use of the word "presume", a special provision is included in the Article, on the scope of the presumption and when it may be rebutted, in paragraph 5: The presumption in paragraph 2 "shall not apply if the characteristic performance cannot be determined".[74] Here we find the single instance when an "individualizing method" may be used under Article 4. If there is a contract with no characteristic performance, a free weighing of the connecting factors must take place to fulfil the provision of paragraph 1, i.e. to find the country with which the contract is most closely connected. Then, and only then, does this rule become substantive. In all other choice of law situations, paragraph 1 is merely ornamental. No doubt a skilled legislator should have been

---

[72] The following passages on the construction of Article 4 have support in the leading European commentaries on the Rome Convention; suffice it to mention Ch. von Bar, *Internationales Privatrecht*, vol. II, 1991, pp. 360–363; Dicey & Morris on *The Conflict of Laws*, vol. II, 12th ed., 1993, pp. 1233–1238 (by L. Collins); G. Kegel, *Internationales Privatrecht*, 6. Aufl., 1988, pp. 425–430; A. Phillip, *EU/IP*, 2nd ed., 1994, pp. 144–148; See also Giuliano & Lagarde, "Report on the [Rome] Convention", *Official Journal of the European Communities* 31 October 1980, C 282, pp. 20–23.

[73] For the purpose of this presentation we may disregard the specific presumptions for *lex rei sitae* and the law of the carrier in a restricted set of situations.

[74] Barter is the typical example.

able to make that more clear by rearranging the provisions of Article 4 in a more rational order, thus causing less confusion to the speedy reader.

The presumption in favour of the characteristic performer shall, according to the second rule in Article 4(5), "be disregarded if it appears from the circumstances as a whole that the contract is more closely connected with another country". What is demanded to rebut the presumption? There is as of yet no clear answer to the question. No consistent case-law has developed in the leading jurisdictions. The Protocols conferring jurisdiction on the European Court of Justice to give preliminary rulings on the interpretation of the Rome Convention – similar to its powers in regard to the Brussels Judgment Convention – have not come into force. A division line like that between Nial and Karlgren may easily be seen in the comments on the Rome Convention. Those in favour of an individualistic approach reduce the strength of the presumption. Those in favour of clear choice of law rules – easy to apply and of a type which reduces unnecessary litigation but at the same time allows for the taking into account of special peculiarities in a unique situation – put greater demands on the weight of the "counter-connecting" factors. It could be no mystery to the reader on which side the present author stands.

Only two further comments – probably important in the Swedish conflict environment – will be given on the possibilities to disregard the presumption for the law of the characteristic performer. One thing is clear from the wording of Article 4(5) : The mere fact that there is little weight in the characteristic performer's residence as connecting factor is not enough to rebut the presumption. There must always be stronger connections to another country. In situations where attention is drawn to the place of performance, the place where the contract was concluded, the language of the contract, a prorogation clause and whatever, they all, or at least a sufficient number of them, must point in the same direction, i.e. to one country other than that of the characteristic performer's geographical base. It is of no avail that the contract is only weakly connected with the performer's "domicile" if the other factors connect the contract with two or more different countries.

We are dealing with a presumption. It is, then, obvious that the burden of proof and procedural activity lie with the party demanding the application of another law to the contract than that of the characteristic performer's country of residence. This is of utmost importance for the smooth administration of justice. The party finding support in the presumption does not have to present any facts or search for evidence, until the "rebutter" has come so far in such activities that there is cause for alarm. Only then must he try to strengthen his position by either showing that the characteristic performer's residence is a strong connecting factor and/or adding to his case other connecting factors in the same geographical direction. Here lies the most important difference between Article 4 and the "individualizing method". According to that method, both parties to a law suit must from the very start exhaust themselves equally in arguing the weight of numerous connecting factors.

5. Conclusions

We have critically analysed the Swedish "individualizing method" on mainly two grounds: It had from the start very narrow support in case-law and is now exchanged for another method. Its long-standing support in the legal literature has been shown to have an equally narrow foundation.

Under the influence of the counsel for one party who had found a suitable source in a German academic slightly to the side of the mainstream of German conflict law, the "individualizing method" was introduced by the Supreme Court in 1937 in order to solve a very particular case on the application in Sweden of foreign currency regulations. In its then-presented form, the "individualizing method" was never again used by the Supreme Court. On the contrary, a modern case from 1992 adopted a totally different procedure. The contractual choice of law in the absence of a party agreement was decided by the support of a strong presumption in favour of the characteristic performer's law. The Court's opinion follows the same line of reasoning as if Article 4 of the Rome Convention had been applied.[75]

The first and, after 50 years, still singular effort in the Swedish literature to give a full, argumentative description of the "individualizing method" was shown to be a direct loan from the very same source, Nussbaum, who had inspired the Supreme Court in 1937. Later Swedish writers in favour of the method have only simplified it and, finally, uncritically presented it as the only existing general Swedish rule on choice of law in contract.

When Sweden ratifies the Rome Convention it is crucial that the courts realise the great difference between presumptions and the free weighing of an unspecified set of connecting factors. The subject matter of this article touches upon some very basic principles of substantive and procedural law and the intercourse between them. Where is the ideal point of intersection between a total discretion of the courts in the adjudication of individual cases and fixed rules equitable in typical cases but unfair under particular circumstances? How may demands on predictability be combined with efforts to award individual justice? How far may the strive for procedural economy and practicability be driven? What are the limits for courts and legislators in trying to reduce the need and wish of parties to litigate?[76]

The present author finds the use of strong presumptions to be the best solution so far invented to solve the problems mentioned. Even under strong presumptions there is an opening for contrary solutions in atypical situations. Article 4 of the Rome Convention is built on this foundation. The danger that courts in Sweden will resort to old doctrines by giving support to easy ways of rebutting the presumptions may, hopefully, be reduced if they are aware that the Swedish "individualizing method" – if it ever existed – had its single founda-

---

[75] However, the outcome of the gold bond case *NJA 1937 p. 1* could have been the same even under the Rome Convention. The underlying contract had such a close connection with the United States that the presumption in Article 4(2) may have been rebutted.

[76] A line not followed up here, and not much favoured by the present author, is the function substantive and procedural legal rules have or should have to direct the behaviour of the citizens. If the best behaviour to avoid litigation would be that the parties agree explicitly on the choice of law, the "individualizing method" has at least a deterrent merit.

tion in one now-mostly-forgotten German legal writer's extreme way of construing century-old German case-law.

References

Bar, Christian v.: *Internationales Privatrecht*, vol. II, München 1991: Beck.

Bar, L. v.: *Theorie und Praxis des internationalen Privatrechts*, vol. II, 2. Aufl., Hannover 1889: Hahn'sche Buchhandlung.

Bogdan, Michael: *Svensk internationell privat- och processrätt*, 1 uppl., Lund 1980: LiberLäromedel; 4 uppl., Stockholm 1992: Norstedts.

Bogdan, Michael: '"Tillämplig lag på handelsagentur", *Juridisk Tidskrift vid Stockholms Universitet* 4 (1992–93), pp. 912–916.

Bogdan, Michael: "Fastighetsmäklare och svensk internationell konsumenträtt", *Svensk Juristtidning* 80 (1995), pp. 1–6.

Dennemark, Sigurd: "Om avtalsstatutet", *Svensk Juristtidning* 28 (1943), pp. 675–697.

Dennemark, Sigurd: "Svensk rättspraxis. Internationell privaträtt 1941–1948", *Svensk Juristtidning* 35 (1950), pp. 35–50.

Dicey & Morris on *The Conflict of Laws*, vol. II, 12th ed. by L. Collins et al., London 1993: Sweet & Maxwell.

Eek, Hilding: *The Swedish Conflict of Laws*, The Hague 1965: Martinus Nijhoff.

Eek, Hilding: "Svensk eller utländsk lag?", in: *Exporträtt 4*, Stockholm 1970: Exportföreningens Serviceaktiebolag, pp. 15–96.

Eek, Hilding: *Lagkonflikter i tvistemål*, vol. II, Stockholm 1978: Norstedts.

Gihl, Torsten: "Till frågan om skuldstatutet", in: *Festskrift till Håkan Nial*, Stockholm 1966: Norstedts, pp. 170–203.

Giuliano, Mario & Lagarde, Paul: "Report on the Convention on the law applicable to contractual obligations", *Official Journal of the European Communities* 31 October 1980, C 282, pp. 1–50.

Guldklausulmålet, vols. I–III, with various subtitles, all including *Försäkringsaktiebolaget Skandia v. Riksgäldskontoret*, Stockholm 1935, 1935 and 1937: Norstedts.

Göranson, Ulf: "Förmögenhetsrättsligt lagval i komparativ belysning", in: U. Göranson & M. Jänterä-Jareborg, *Internationell privaträtt. Studiematerial och rättsfall för Terminskurs 6*, 2 utg., Uppsala 1995, Uppsatser pp. 125–147 (stencils).

Hjerner, Lars A.E.: *Främmande valutalag och internationell privaträtt. Studier i de främmande offentligrättsliga lagarnas tillämplighet*, diss. Stockholm 1956: Appelbergs Boktryckeri.

Hobér, Kaj: "In Search for the Centre of Gravity – Applicable Law in International Arbitrations in Sweden", in: *Swedish and International Arbitration 1994*, pp. 7–43.

Hult, Phillips: *Föräldrar och barn enligt svensk internationell privaträtt*, Stockholm 1943: Norstedts.

Hult, Phillips: "Regel, standard och skön", in: *Festskrift tillägnad Nils Stjernberg*, Stockholm 1940: Norstedts, pp. 128–146.

Jänterä-Jareborg, Maarit: "Internationellt tvingande civilrättsregler, fastighetsförmedling och konsumenter – några reflexioner", *Svensk Juristtidning* 80 (1995), pp. 374–384.

Kahn, Franz: "Gesetzeskollisionen. Ein Beitrag zur Lehre des internationalen Privatrechts", first published in *Jherings Jahrbücher* 30 (1891), pp. 1–143, and reprinted posthumously in Kahn, Franz: *Abhandlungen zum internationalen Privatrecht*, vol. I, München und Leipzig 1928: Duncker & Humblot, pp. 1–123.

Karlgren, Hjalmar: *Kortfattad lärobok i internationell privaträtt*, 1 uppl., Lund 1945: Carl Bloms Boktryckeri; 5 uppl., Lund 1974: Gebers.

Karlgren, Hjalmar: [Review of] Nial, Internationell förmögenhetsrätt, *Tidsskrift for Rettsvitenskap* 59 (1946) pp. 336–340.

Kegel, Gerhard: *Internationales Privatrecht*, 6. Aufl., München 1987: Beck.

Knoph, Ragnar: "Omkring guldklausuldommen", *Tidsskrift for Rettsvidenskap* 51 (1938), pp. 46–58.

Lando, Ole: *Kontraktstatuttet. Hovedpunkter af den internationale kontraktsrets almindelige del*, diss. København 1962: Juristforbundets forlag.

Malmar, Folke: "Svensk rättspraxis. Internationell privaträtt 1936–1940", *Svensk Juristtidning* 27 (1942), pp. 399–404.

Michaeli, Wilhelm: *Internationales Privatrecht gemäss schwedischem Recht und schwedischer Rechtssprechung*, Stockholm 1948: Nordiska Bokhandeln.

Nial, Håkan: *Internationell förmögenhetsrätt*, 1 uppl., Stockholm 1944: Norstedts; 2 uppl., Stockholm 1953: Norstedts.

Nial, Håkan: [Review of] Karlgren, Kortfattad lärobok..., *Tidsskrift for Rettsvitenskap* 59 (1946), p. 232.

Nussabaum, Arthur: *Deutsches internationales Privatrecht. Unter besonderer Berücksichtigung des österreichischen und schweizerischen Rechts*, Tübingen 1932: Mohr.

Phillip, Allan: *EU–IP. Europæisk International Privat- og Procesret*, 2. udg., København 1994: Jurist- og Økonomforbundet.

Pålsson, Lennart: "Svensk rättspraxis. Internationell privat- och processrätt 1976–1980", *Svensk Juristtidning* 67 (1982), pp. 214–251.

Pålsson, Lennart: "Svensk rättspraxis. Internationell privat- och processrätt 1986–1990", *Svensk Juristtidning* 77 (1992), pp. 475–503.

Regeringens proposition 1990/91:63 [Government Bill on Commercial Agents Act].

Schnitzer, Adolf F.: *Handbuch des internationalen Privatrechts*, vols. I–II, 2. & 4. Aufl., Basel 1944 & 1957: Recht und Gesellschaft.

Schnitzer, Adolf F.: "Les contrats internationaux en droit international privé suisse", in: *Receuil des Cours de l'Academie de Droit international de La Haye* 123 (1968–I), pp. 541–653.

Zweigert, Konrad: "Die dritte Schule im internationalen Privatrecht. Zur neueren Wissenschaftsgeschichte des Kollisionsrechts" in: *Festschrift für Leo Raape*, Hamburg 1948: Rechts- und Staatswissenschaftlicher Verlag, pp. 35–52.

APPLICATION OF FOREIGN LAW IN SWEDISH COURTS – RECENT DEVELOPMENTS

Maarit Jänterä-Jareborg

Few countries in the world have been blessed with such an outstanding conflict of laws scholar and drafter of private international law legislation as has Sweden through Lennart Pålsson. Lennart Pålsson has often found reason to criticize the decisions of the Swedish Supreme Court in conflicts cases and the Court's lack of courage to create new solutions adjusted to the parties' needs in an international world. Such criticism can also, to some extent, be directed at the Court's contributions to the subject matter of this article. Although the Court may now be considered to have sanctioned the application of the *lex fori* when a party has not requested the application of a foreign law, many related questions still remain open. A question is also whether the Court's reasoning can be reconciled with the objectives behind the unified choice of law rules in the European Union.

1. Introduction

Complications and temptations

The complications invôlved in the application of foreign law are well documented. First of all, the judge has to overcome a psychological barrier, i.e. his dislike for having to apply foreign rules previously unknown to him. In addition, there are all of the practical problems. It is often a difficult and time-consuming procedure to get hold of accurate information on foreign law. The court proceedings may need to be postponed for months for this reason, which increases the costs.

When necessary information has been gained, difficulties of interpretation may arise. Critics have claimed that justice vanishes when foreign law takes the floor. Instead of being applied by a judge who is an expert in that law, the law (or what is claimed to be the contents of that law) is being used by a hesitant beginner.[1] It has therefore been proposed that foreign law should be applied only at the request of a party.

One can suspect that a majority of judges throughout the world would find this proposal appealing. Several studies show that the *lex fori* has been applied by the courts in the majority of conflict cases irrespective of the law identified by the applicable choice of law rules.[2] Still, the doctrine of the *ex officio* application of foreign law is firmly established on the European Continent. It is widely held that choice of law rules are, by nature, of mandatory character. The judge must, therefore, pay tribute to these rules and apply foreign law if they refer to a foreign *lex causae*. Alternative approaches, such as letting the application of foreign law depend on a party's plea (and proof), as in English and US courts, or the closely related "jurisprudence Bisbal" developed by the French *Cour de Cassation*,[3] have been repudiated by the majority of conflict scholars in Europe. These approaches have only had a limited effect on the private international law codifications carried out in Europe during the last two decades.

---

[1] See A. Flessner, "Fakultatives Kollisionsrecht", *Rabels Zeitschrift für ausländisches und internationales Privatrecht* 34 (1970), p. 552.

[2] See, *e.g.*, O. Lando, "Skandinavien", in: *Die Anwendung ausländischen Rechts im internationalen Privatrecht. Festveranstaltung und Kolloquium anläßlich des 40. jährigen Bestehens des Max-Planck-Instituts für ausländisches und internationales Privatrecht vom 6.–8. Juli 1966 in Hamburg*, 1968, p. 129.

[3] In its famous judgment from 1959 in the *Bisbal* case, the *Cour de Cassation* rejected the courts' duty to apply choice of law rules and foreign law *ex officio*. The case concerned the transformation of a legal separation into divorce between spouses who were Spanish citizens. According to the Court, French law is applicable to all private law relationships tried by a French court, provided that a party does not demand the application of foreign law. This standpoint came to prevail in French case-law for almost 30 years (= jurisprudence Bisbal). The content given to it could be described as somewhat arbitrary: Not only had the court the right to apply *French law* when neither party had requested the application of foreign law, but the court could also in such a case refer the issue to *foreign law*! At least since 1988, several of the judgments by the Supreme Court have indicated that the "jurisprudence Bisbal" has now been reconsidered. The new case-law, is, however, not coherent so it has also been claimed that some of the decisions in fact reconfirm the "jurisprudence Bisbal". See F. Vischer, "General Course on Private International Law",

On the contrary, one could claim that these codifications have strengthened the classical position of continental conflict of laws: choice of law rules and the foreign law they refer to are to be applied *ex officio* by the judge.[4] Also, the French Supreme Court has recently returned, more or less, to the classical notions on the application of foreign law.[5]

Scandinavia as the blacksheep of classical private international law?

When conditions for the application of foreign law have been discussed from a comparative perspective, it has not been unusual to regard the Scandinavian countries as constituting a special category in this respect. It has, e.g., been claimed that foreign law is applied in Scandinavia only at the demand of a party.[6] It has also been claimed

---

Recueil des Cours 232 (1992 I), pp. 75–77, and D. Koerner, *Fakultatives Kollisionsrecht in Frankreich und Deutschland*, 1995, pp. 4–29.

[4] This is the prevailing opinion irrespective of whether or not the court's duty to apply at its own initiative the choice of law rules and the foreign law they refer to has been explicitly stated in the new legislation. The first-mentioned model is found, e.g., in the Austrian Act of June 15, 1978 (article 2) and the Turkish Act of May 22, 1982 (article 2). The latter model is used, e.g., in the German Act of July 25, 1986, the Swiss Act of December 18, 1987, and the Italian Act of May 31, 1995. According to von Overbeck, it is so self-evident that a Swiss court is to apply the choice of law rules embodied in 1987 Act *ex officio* that there was no need to include an explicit provision establishing such a duty. A.E. von Overbeck, "Die Ermittlung, Anwendung und Überprüfung der richtigen Anwendung des anwendbaren Rechts", in: Y. Hangartner (ed.), *Die allgemeinen Bestimmungen des Bundesgesetzes über das internationale Privatrecht*, 1988, p. 95. In respect of German law, see: *Gesetzentwurf der Bundesregierung. Entwurf eines Gesetzes zur Neuregelung des Internationalen Privatrechts.* Deutscher Bundestag 10. Wahlperiode. Drucksache 10/504, 20.10.1983, p. 26. See, also, the decision of the German Supreme Court, *BGH, 7.4.1993, Neue Juristische Wochenschrift* 1993, p, 2305. – On the other hand, one can claim that the new rules, compared to the former ones, are so formulated that they more often lead to the application of the *lex fori*, mainly because domicile has been given greater weight as a choice of law criterion and because party autonomy has been extended to new areas.

[5] See F. Vischer, *supra* note 3, pp. 76–77 and F. Herzfelder, "Die Prüfungspflicht der französischen staatlichen Gerichte hinsichtlich kollisionsrechtlichen Fragen, Zur neuen Rechtsprechung des französischen Kassationshofs", *Recht der Internationalen Wirtschaft/ Außenwirtschaftsdienst des Betriebsberaters* 1990, pp. 354–358. Because the new case-law is not coherent, opinions are divided on whether the Supreme Court has at all reconsidered its original standpoint or has, in fact, reintroduced it. See D. Koerner, *supra* note 3, pp. 26–29 with references.

[6] See, *e.g.*, A. Flessner, *supra* note 1, p. 548 ("jedenfalls für den Prozeß mit Verhandlungs-grundsatz").

that foreign law, in the Scandinavian legal systems, is regarded as a matter of fact, including all the consequences such a classification carries with it.[7] Hence, the interested party not only has to plead the application of foreign law but must also prove its content. The application of the foreign *lex causae* may not be revised by the Supreme Court.

Sweden, no doubt, forms a geographic part of Scandinavia. Still, for a Swedish specialist on the subject, such descriptions have made for a more or less confusing reading. They have, in an essential way, contradicted what the legal doctrine has claimed for a century and what has found support in case-law and the *travaux préparatoires* to Swedish conflicts legislation.[8] The principle of *ex officio* application of choice of law rules and the foreign law they refer to has, since the early 1900s, been the cornerstone of Swedish private international law. True, divergent opinions have also been expressed in the Swedish legal literature, but these have until very recently been limited to cautious suggestions questioning the scope of the courts' obligations in respect of claims at the parties' disposal.[9]

A change of course in Swedish case-law

Recent decisions by the Swedish Supreme Court indicate, however, that this traditional standpoint has now been reconsidered by the Court. First, there was a question of affirming that an explicit or implicit procedural agreement concerning the application of the *lex*

---

[7] See F. Schwind, *Internationales Privatrecht, Lehr- und Handbuch für Theorie und Praxis*, 1990, pp. 35–36.

[8] It is tempting to explain these descriptions as generalizations of standpoints taken in Danish private international law, *e.g.*, in the above-mentioned (note 2) article of O. Lando. It must be emphasized that similarities in the procedural treatment of facts and foreign law do not transform also the latter into a question of fact. Such a conclusion is completely foreign to modern Scandinavian law. It is unanimously held that foreign law is law also when applied by the court of the forum. In the late 1800s, it was still normal to consider foreign law as a question of fact which had to be pleaded and proved by a party. See O. Lando, *supra*, note 2, pp. 128–129.

[9] For this reason, one can claim that the Scandinavian position, as described by I. Zajtay, "The Application of Foreign Law", in: *International Encyclopedia of Comparative Law*, Volume III, (1972), Private International Law, Chapter 14, p. 11, gave a too generalized picture in respect of the standpoint in Swedish private international law.

fori is to be respected in cases where the parties in Swedish domestic law may dispose of their rights. This liberty is not restricted to areas where party autonomy in respect of choice of law is well-established, as in contractual law, but also covers permissively regulated ("dispositive") family law matters such as the right to maintenance, marital property rights and inheritance rights. As an example, one can mention the Court's decisions in *NJA 1977 p. 92, NJA 1978 p. 590* and *NJA 1987 p. 815.*

Second, a foreign law may also be chosen by the parties during the court proceedings, provided that there is a natural connection to the chosen jurisdiction. This was confirmed in *NJA 1992 p. 278.*

Third, the Supreme Court's decision in *NJA 1993 p. 341* may be interpreted as sanctioning the application of the *lex fori* when the parties have abstained from pleading foreign law (or such facts in support of their claims which bring about the application of choice of law rules and foreign law) without necessarily having – explicitly or implicitly – agreed upon the application of the *lex fori*. It is tempting to see this decision as the final death-blow to the doctrine of the *ex officio* application of foreign law in matters where Swedish domestic law permits a settlement between the parties.[10] As a consequence, when a settlement is permitted, i.e. when the case, according to Swedish domestic law, concerns rights of which the parties may dispose, foreign law is to be applied only at the request of a party. *Ex officio* application of choice of law rules and foreign law is thus limited to the fairly few matters where the parties in Swedish private law may not dispose of their rights. In modern Swedish conflict legislation, the applicable choice of law rules normally refer in these cases to Swedish law.[11] An inevitable conclusion is that the scope of application of foreign law in Sweden has been drastically reduced.

---

[10] In his commentaries on conflicts cases, Lennart Pålsson has for quite a while been expecting such a desertion of this doctrine. See, e.g., L. Pålsson, "Svensk rättspraxis. Internationell privat- och processrätt 1976–1980", *Svensk Juristtidning* 1982, p. 230.

[11] The explanation is that in modern Swedish family conflicts law, domicile (habitual residence) is considered to be the most important choice of law criterion. Further, in respect of divorce and adoption, the legislation stipulates the application of the *lex fori*. See Act (1904:26 p. 1) on Certain International Legal Relations Concerning Marriage and Guardianship, Chapter 3, section 4, and Act (1971:796) on International Legal Relations Concerning Adoption, section 2.

Consistency with the objectives of uniform choice of law rules within the European Union?

The question is now whether this development runs counter to the development on the European Continent. If so, is it possible to reconcile it with the new duties that, *e.g.* the planned ratification of the 1980 E.E.C. Convention on the Law Applicable to Contractual Obligations will create? Choice of law conventions aim at nothing less than creating uniformity in the choice of the governing law and, as a result, decisional harmony. Of importance in this respect is that according to the prevailing view on the European Continent, choice of law rules found in an international convention are considered to be of a more binding character than autonomous "national" conflict rules.[12] Such a difference is, however, not made in modern Swedish law.[13]

---

[12] In the German conflicts doctrine, advocates of the so-called *Fakultatives Kollisionsrecht*, according to which a prerequisite for the application of choice of law rules and foreign law should be that they are invoked by or relied upon by at least one of the parties, make an exception in respect of conventional choice of law rules. See, *e.g.*, F. Sturm, "Fakultatives Kollisionsrecht: Notwendigkeit und Grenzen", in: *Festschrift für Konrad Zweigert zum 70. Geburtstag*, 1981, p. 342: "Wer kollisionsrechtlichen Abkommen beitritt, übernimmt auch die Verpflichtung, diese Normen in Fällen mit Auslandsberührung anzuwenden, und zwar ohne Rücksicht darauf, ob die Parteien dies wollen oder nicht. Der kleine Schritt, den solche Abkommen in Richtung Rechtsvereinheitlichung und Entscheidungsharmonie tun, rechtfertigt es, Parteiinteressen hintanzusetzen."

[13] In writings originating from the first decades of the 20th century, one finds statements claiming that choice of law rules contained in international conventions ratified by Sweden create an international obligation on Sweden to make use of these rules in relation to the other Contracting States. See, *e.g.*, Ö. Undén, *Internationell äktenskapsrätt enligt gällande svensk lag*, 1922, pp. 5–6. On the other hand, it was not considered justified to make a difference between cases covered by an international convention and other cases. Instead, the judge in both cases was considered obligated to apply the choice of law rules *ex officio*. Å. Hassler & H. Nial, *Internationell privaträtt*, 1948, p. 38. See also, *Nytt Juridiskt Arkiv II*, 1905:5, p. 9. In later Swedish private international law, the question of the existence of an

2. Theoretical foundations for the application of foreign law

Choice of law rules and foreign law must be applied ex officio

In Sweden, private international law started to develop as an area of law in the late 19th century.[14] The Hague Conference on Private International Law played an important role in this development. Sweden ratified, *e.g.*, all the family law conventions adopted at the Conference before the Second World War. The legislation implementing the conventional rules was given universal application, either directly or through analogy in case-law.[15] In the legal doctrine, it was taken for granted that the courts were under the obligation to apply choice of law rules and the foreign law they refer to *ex officio*.[16] No difference was made in this respect between cases where the applicable choice of law rule was contained in an international convention ratified by Sweden and other cases, *i.e.* where it was a question of applying a conventional rule to a situation not covered by the convention (*e.g.* because the other concerned state was not a contracting state) or national autonomous Swedish conflict rules.[17] These doctrinal standpoints also won support in case-law.[18]

---

international obligation to make use of conflict of law rules contained in an international convention has, more or less, fallen into oblivion. This is clearly demonstrated by the Supreme Court's reasoning in *NJA 1993 p. 341*, a case where the applicable choice of law rules were founded on the 1961 Hague Convention on the Conflict of Laws Relating to the Form of Testamentary Dispositions, to which Sweden is a party. See *infra*, section 4.

14 See M. Jänterä-Jareborg, "The Influence of the Hague Conventions on the Development of Swedish Family Conflicts Law", *Netherlands International Law Review* XL (1993), pp. 49–51.

15 See M. Jänterä-Jareborg, *supra* note 14, pp. 50–51.

16 See C.A. Reuterskiöld, *Föreläsningar öfver privat internationell rätt*, II, Handbok i svensk internationell rätt (process-, utlämnings-, straff- och privaträtt), 1912, pp. 33–34; E. Kallenberg, *Svensk civilprocessrätt*, Andra bandet I, 1927, pp. 93–94; Å. Hassler & H. Nial, *Internationell privaträtt*, 1948, p. 38; N. Beckman, *Svensk domstolspraxis i internationell rätt*, 1959, p. 44; H. Eek, *Lagkonflikter i tvistemål, Metod och material i svensk internationell privaträtt*, 1972, p. 137; Hj. Karlgren, *Kortfattad lärobok i internationell privat- och processrätt*, 1979, p. 73. – Contractual obligations would, however, seem to have been an exception.

17 See, *supra*, note 13.

18 At least until the late 1970s, there are decisions where a Swedish court seems to have applied choice of law rules and foreign law at its own initiative, although the case concerned such a subject matter where Swedish domestic law permits a settlement between the parties. See, *e.g.*, *NJA 1937 p. 438, NJA 1978 p. 590* (*infra* section 4), *SvJT 1950 p. 958* and

Assumption of equivalence
between foreign law and Swedish law

The theoretical foundation of *ex officio* application of foreign law was, originally, the assumption of equivalence between foreign law and Swedish law. The following statement, found in a textbook from the 1940s, is illustrative of the underlying reasoning:[19]

> "When due regard is paid to the principle of equivalence it must be considered unacceptable to make such a difference between domestic law and foreign law that the former is to be applied *ex officio*, the latter only at party request. Such a distinction would mean a considerable restriction to the applicability of foreign law. When a party considers himself to have nothing to gain by the application of foreign law he, naturally, refrains from referring to it, not the least because its application may cause him both inconvenience and costs. On the other hand, it could be inconsistent with the requirements of predictability and equal treatment if the choice of the applicable law was dependent on party request. The aim of private international law is that a legal dispute is tried in accordance with the same law irrespective of the forum. For this reason, choice of law rules must be mandatory and applied *ex officio* by the court."[20]

Contrary to original expectations, private international law developed into a national area of law with divergent choice of law rules being applied in different jurisdictions.[21] Much of the justification for *uniformity of result* (decisional harmony, *Entscheidungseinklang*) as the

---

SvJT 1971 rf. s. 18. Case-law has, however, been incoherent in this respect. Hence, there are also cases which have been tried in accordance with Swedish domestic law although there was such connection to another country that application of foreign law should have been considered. See, e.g., *NJA 1967 p. 158, NJA 1974 p. 7* and *NJA 1986 p. 712.* One could well claim that Swedish case-law, in fact, closely resembled the "jurisprudence Bisbal" of the French courts. See above, note 3. – In the great majority of the published conflict cases, the initiative to the application of a foreign law has been taken by a party. This law has then been applied by the courts, provided that its application was in conformity with the Swedish choice of law rules.

[19] Å. Hassler & H. Nial, *supra* note 13, pp. 36–37.

[20] Translation from Swedish by the present author.

[21] The choice of law conventions adopted at the Hague Conference on Private International Law have, as a rule, been ratified by so few states that their unifying effect has been described as negligible. Th. M. de Boer, "The Hague Conference and Dutch Choice of Law: Some Criticism and a Suggestion", *Netherlands International Law Review* XL (1993), pp. 5–6.

ultimate goal of private international law to be observed both in the drafting and in the application of choice of law rules was lost. Hence, decisional harmony is rarely mentioned today as an objective of Swedish private international law.[22] If this objective has, generally, turned out to be unrealistic, one would expect that the principle of *ex officio* application of choice of law rules and foreign law had also been re-examined. A reconsideration in Swedish law could have seemed natural, especially as it has never contained any written provisions explicitly stipulating a duty for the courts to apply foreign law at their own initiative. Also, the decisions of the Swedish Supreme Court have, generally speaking, been vague on this point. It has not been possible to deduce any clear rule from the Court's decisions that would cover all types of private international law cases. Hence, as stated by Pålsson, the guidance given by case-law is limited and has left a wide scope for various possibilities in respect of permissively regulated matters.[23]

The lack of legislative support for ex officio application of foreign law

In the legal literature, such a duty has instead been deduced from the provisions concerning how foreign law is to be substantiated. If foreign law is to be applied and the court does not know its content, the court may, according to these provisions, request a party to prove it. The last such enactment is provided for in Chapter 35, section 2 para. 2 of the 1942 Code of Procedure.[24] Although comparable provisions in foreign legal systems, *e.g.* section 293 of the German Code of Civil Procedure (ZPO), have been interpreted in a similar manner,

---

[22] It has not, however, been completely abandoned. Although Sweden is at present (1995) party to only two choice of law conventions, *i.e.*, the 1955 Hague Convention on the Law Applicable to the International Sale of Goods and the 1961 Hague Convention on the Conflict of Laws Relating to the Form of Testamentary Dispositions, occasionally, when autonomous choice of law rules are being drafted in Sweden it is emphasized that these rules should, as far as possible, be in harmony with rules followed elsewhere. See, *e.g.*, *SOU 1983:25, Internationella faderskapsfrågor*, p. 103.

[23] See L. Pålsson, *Svensk rättspraxis i internationell familje- och arvsrätt*, 1986, p. 37–38.

[24] Because this provision is applicable when the legal proceedings take place in Sweden, there has, since its enactment, not been a need to include similar provisions in the later Acts concerning various areas of private international law.

one can claim that this interpretation in Swedish law exceeds the scope of the provisions from which it is deduced. Literally, these provisions only concern a later issue in a conflict case, when it has already been established (by the initiative of the court or at party request) that foreign law is to be applied. They give the court the mandate to request the parties' assistance when the court does not know the content of the applicable foreign law. Considering this, it can be contested that these provisions implicitly confirm the court's duty to apply the choice of law rules and foreign law of its own motion.[25]

In Swedish legal doctrine, the scope of the *ex officio* application has been debated since the late 1960s. Still, it has taken a long time to gain any clarity in this respect. Not even in the normally extensive *travaux préparatoires* to Swedish enactments does one find any definite standpoint on the issue. Visible is, instead, a general reluctance to take a firm standing on the different questions relating to the application of foreign law.[26] According to the Family Law Reform Commission in its extensive and ambitious report from 1987 aiming at a comprehensive reform of Swedish international family law, such questions may arise in many different cases and in various circumstances. Therefore, it was not considered possible to draft rules which would suit all

---

[25] In foreign conflicts doctrine, such a duty is often explained by referring to the fact that conflicts rules are part of the law of the forum and must, therefore, be applied under the same conditions as the other rules of the *lex fori*. A problem with such an explanation in Swedish and Scandinavian law is that the law of procedure in the Scandinavian countries establishes different conditions for the application of the domestic rules depending on whether or not the subject matter is such that a settlement is permitted. Thus, when choice of law rules in the *lex fori* are equalized with other rules of the forum, the result is the opposite from the one often drawn abroad: The parties may opt out the choice of law rules in all those cases where a settlement is permitted according to the domestic law of the *lex fori*. This can be done in various ways, *e.g.*, by the parties refraining from invoking in support of their claims of the extraneous elements of the case, especially those connecting factors which are of relevance according to the choice of law rules of the forum. The court may take notice of the extraneous elements only if a party has referred to them; it is not enough that they are, *e.g.*, contained in the file. See M. Jänterä-Jareborg, *Partsautonomi och efterlevande makes rättsställning. En internationellt-privaträttslig studie*, 1989, pp. 336–344. This distinction will be dealt with in the following section.

[26] Besides the question *who* – the court or a party – is to take the initiative to the application of foreign law, these include questions such as burden of proof of foreign law and what solution is to be chosen when the content of the foreign law is not known. Etc.

situations.[27] The development of the law in these issues has been left to the courts.

3. Differentiation between cases depending on whether or not a settlement is permitted

At first sight, even the latest Swedish private international law doctrine seems to be bound by tradition. *Ex officio* application of choice of law rules and the foreign law these rules refer to is pointed out to be the traditionally prevailing view in Sweden and the opinion of the majority.[28] Interestingly enough, the equivalence between foreign law and domestic law, on the one hand, and decisional harmony, on the other, is given little emphasis.[29] Application of foreign law is explained as taking place in the interests of the forum state. "Foreign law is not applied because it as such is 'better' than Swedish law, but because its application from a practical point of view is considered by the Swedish legislator to lead to a more appropriate result than the use of Swedish domestic law adjusted to the circumstances prevailing in Sweden", writes Michael Bogdan in the leading Swedish textbook on private international law.[30] Decisive to the choice of the applicable law is to what country the legislator has considered the case to have its most relevant connection.

A closer look, however, reveals that the traditional standpoint is today far less categoric than it was a few decades ago. A clear difference is now made between cases concerning rights of which the parties may not dispose (= a settlement is not permitted) and cases where the issue at stake is at the parties' disposal and, thus, a

---

[27] *SOU 1987:18, Internationella familjerättsfrågor*, pp. 323–324.

[28] See M. Bogdan, *Svensk internationell privat- och processrätt*, 1992, p. 41. Lennart Pålsson points, however, that such a description is inadequate and misses the many variations in the system, not the least the various techniques used in the drafting of choice of law rules. The system contains, *e.g.*, a number of so-called elective choice of law rules which give the parties the right to set aside the applicable law and, instead, request the application of another law, likewise identified by the actual choice of law rule. The parties may also, to a large extent, agree on the applicable law. See, L. Pålsson, *supra*, note 23, p. 36–38.

[29] See, *e.g.*, M. Bogdan, *supra* note 28, pp. 26–30 and p. 22.

[30] M. Bogdan, *supra* note 28, p. 27. Translation from Swedish by the present author.

settlement is permitted. The nature of the case as falling into the first or second category is decided in accordance with Swedish domestic law.[31]

It is unanimously held that in matters where a settlement is not permitted (= a so-called indispositive case) the court must, at its own initiative, take account of the choice of law rules and apply foreign law, if referred to by these rules. A public interest is involved in these cases which is why the parties' wishes or agreement concerning the applicable law has been considered to be without relevance. This position is in conformity with case-law.[32] Where the case is instead such that a settlement is permitted in Swedish law (= a so-called dispositive case), the *ex officio* application is contested. Diverging opinions have been expressed concerning the conditions under which the court may apply the *lex fori*.[33] In this respect, there is a series of interesting decisions by the Supreme Court which, in my opinion, clarify the position of present Swedish private international law.

4. Development in case-law

Since the 1970s, the Supreme Court has made a number of interesting statements concerning the conditions for the application of foreign law. In the following, I will shortly comment upon the most important of these statements. In my opinion, they are to be seen as a whole where each new decision has cast further light on the question. The

---

[31] The justification of such a classification can, naturally, be contested in a conflicts case. It has been considered as an almost inextricable question whether the free disposition of the claim should be asserted on the strength of the *lex fori* or be decided in accordance with the *lex causae*. F. Vischer, *supra* note 3, p. 78. See also M. Bogdan, *supra* note 28, p. 40.

[32] In *NJA 1962 p. 123* concerning the annulment of the presumption of paternity, the parties had explicitly, during the court proceedings, wished to be subjected to Swedish law. This request was ignored by the Supreme Court which, in accordance with the applicable choice of law rule, found that Italian law was to be applied. See also *NJA 1973 p. 57* concerning the choice of the applicable law to the establishment of paternity, *infra*, section 4.

[33] See L. Pålsson, "Schweden", in: Bülow & Böckstiegel & Geimer & Schütze (Hrsg.), *Der Internationale Rechtsverkehr in Zivil- und Handelssachen*, 1992, p. 8.

Supreme Court could, however, have been more explicit and striven at creating clear, generally applicable rules. The quotations are my translations from Swedish.

NJA 1973 p. 57

This case concerned paternity and maintenance of a child born out of wedlock. The child and its mother were German citizens habitually resident in Germany whereas the respondent, *i.e.* the alleged father, was a Swedish citizen habitually resident in Sweden. In the District Court and in the Appellate Court, the case was tried in accordance with Swedish law, probably because the parties had explained in court that they had agreed that Swedish law should be applied. However, when the Supreme Court brought the question of the applicable law to the parties' attention, the respondent claimed that German law was to be applied. The petitioners, in turn, denied his right to unilaterally withdraw from the agreement on the governing law.

The Supreme Court found that German law was to be applied to the establishment of paternity, without dwelling on the effect of the earlier agreement on the application of Swedish law.[34] The child's right to maintenance was, according to the Court, "to be decided in accordance with the objective circumstances of the case since the parties are no longer in agreement on the applicable law". As a result, this question was also tried in accordance with German law.

What makes this case interesting is that the Supreme Court in fact deduced the parties' right to decide on the applicable law during the proceedings from whether the issue considered rights of which the parties may dispose in Swedish domestic law. Since questions of paternity are mandatorily regulated there, the agreement was disregarded in this respect.[35] Maintenance issues, on the other hand, are permissively regulated in Swedish law. The Court's reasoning in-

---

[34] At this time, there was support in case-law for application of the law of the state where the child became a national at the time of its birth, especially if the child was also habitually resident in that state. See L. Pålsson, *supra* note 23, p. 87. New choice of law rules were introduced through the Act (1985:367) on International Questions of Paternity.

[35] See also *NJA 1962 p. 123.*

dicates that the parties' agreement could have been recognized in this respect if they had still been of one opinion concerning the application of Swedish law.[36] This is interesting because at that time there was no support for party autonomy in maintenance matters.

NJA 1977 p. 92

A citizen of both Syria and Lebanon had initiated proceedings against a Swedish company claiming commission from the company on the grounds that he had acted as an agent for the company.

The extraneous elements of this case were obvious. Still, it was tried in accordance with Swedish law in all of the three court instances. One finds an explanation to this only in the judgment of the Supreme Court:

> "This case has extraneous elements, in particular the fact that the agency was to be carried out in Syria. The question could, therefore, arise whether foreign law is to be applied. The parties have, however, presented their claims as if Swedish law was applicable to the dispute. The subject matter of the dispute is such that a settlement is permitted and there is connection to Sweden. For this reason, the case is to be tried in accordance with Swedish law."

It is worth noticing that the Supreme Court explicitly judged the nature of the dispute in accordance with Swedish domestic law. Since, in Swedish law, the case concerned rights of which the parties may dispose, it followed that the parties also had the right to dispose of the choice of the applicable law. The dispute's connection to Sweden seems, in the Court's reasoning, to have justified the choice of Swedish law.[37]

---

[36] The decision has given rise to speculations concerning whether a party may at a later stage of the proceedings unilaterally freely withdraw from an earlier agreement on the applicable law. The Supreme Court's decision in *NJA 1987 p. 815* has clarified this issue. According to this decision, there must be exceptional reasons for a party to be given the right to such a unilateral revocation. See M. Jänterä-Jareborg, *supra*, note 25, pp. 335–336.

[37] Two interpretations have been found possible concerning the Court's statement. The first one is that the Court found that the parties had implicitly agreed upon the application of Swedish law. According to the second one, the Court was not willing to apply foreign law without the demand by a party in a case where Swedish domestic law permits a settlement between the parties. See, *e.g.*, M. Bogdan, *supra* note 28, pp. 43–44.

NJA 1978 p. 590

The case concerned a spouse's duty to pay alimony to the other spouse, both before and after the divorce. The claimant was a citizen of Yugoslavia whereas the respondent was a Romanian citizen. Only the respondent was found to be habitually resident in Sweden.

In the District Court, the dispute was tried in accordance with Swedish law without any explanation in the judgment. The Appellate Court, on the other hand, applied Romanian law as the husband's *lex patriae*, apparently *ex officio*.[38] After the judgment had been appealed to the Supreme Court, the parties agreed that Swedish law was to be applied. The Supreme Court approved of this agreement "since the dispute concerns an issue in respect of which Swedish law permits a settlement". As in respect of *NJA 1973 p. 57*, this explanation is interesting because at that time party autonomy could not be regarded as well-established in maintenance matters.

NJA 1987 p. 815

A marital property contract had been concluded between a Danish citizen and a Norwegian citizen before marriage. After marriage, the spouses took their habitual residence in Switzerland, but they later moved to Sweden. According to the contract, all the property belonging to the spouses was to be regarded as each owner's separate property. After the marriage had been dissolved by divorce, a dispute arose between the parties concerning whether proceeds of separate property were also to be considered as separate property. During the proceedings, the parties agreed that the question was to be solved in accordance with Swedish law.

This agreement was recognized by all three court instances. The Supreme Court stated: "In Swedish domestic law, the parties may make a settlement on the subject matter of this dispute. Both parties

---

[38] The choice of the applicable law was complicated by the fact that this case was not covered by the choice of law rules in the Act (1912:69) on Certain International Legal Relations Concerning the Legal Effects of Marriage which at that time was still in force. In this respect, a prerequisite according to that Act was that the spouses were nationals of the same state.

have clear connection to Sweden. Under such circumstances, the agreement between the parties concerning the application of Swedish law is to be respected."[39] It should be pointed out that party autonomy in respect of matrimonial property relations was recognized by the legislator some years later in Act (1990:272) on Certain International Questions Concerning Matrimonial Property Relations.

NJA 1992 p. 278

In this maintenance case, the respondent had since 1985 been habitually resident in Sweden whereas the claimants, *i.e.* his wife and two children, were habitually resident in Chile. All the parties were Chilean citizens.

After the proceedings had been initiated, the parties declared that they wished their dispute to be tried in accordance with Chilean law and provided information on that law. This agreement was recognized by the courts, but without any explanations.

Since the party choice of the applicable law in all of the previous cases referred to Swedish law, this case casts additional light on the scope of the parties' freedom to choose the governing law during the proceedings. It must be taken for granted that a prerequisite for a valid choice of a foreign law must be the existence of some reasonable connection to the chosen jurisdiction.[40] (In the present case, application of Chilean law would have been well justified and in conformity with case-law even without the parties' agreement.[41]) For reasons of legal certainty, there should be an explicit party choice of law, contrary to what has been required in respect of the *lex fori*.[42]

---

[39] When expert opinions, acquired later on, indicated that the outcome according to Swedish (domestic) law might differ from that according to Norwegian law, the ex-husband wanted to withdraw from the choice of law agreement and claimed that Norwegian law was to be applied. This withdrawl, which took place as late as in the Supreme Court, was not accepted by the Court. According to the Court, the husband had not invoked sufficient grounds to be able to unilaterally withdraw from the agreement at this stage of the proceedings. See *supra, NJA 1973 p. 57*.

[40] See also L. Pålsson, "Underhållsfrågor och internationell privaträtt", *Svensk Juristtidning*, 1993, p. 621.

[41] See L. Pålsson, *supra* note 40, pp. 621–623.

[42] In the Swedish system, the required certainty can be easily gained by the court's inquiry addressed to the parties.

NJA 1993 p. 341

This case concerned whether a document drawn up in England, just before the death of a Swedish citizen habitually resident there, could be considered valid as a testamentary disposition, *i.e.* whether the form requirements of the so-called emergency will were fulfilled. The case came to focus on the proper interpretation in this respect of the Swedish Code of Inheritance. The petitioner's claim was directly founded on this Code. At least in the first two court instances, the parties seem to have been in agreement on the application of Swedish domestic law.[43] As is normal in a legal dispute, their opinions on the content of the law were, however, different.

In the District Court and in the Appellate Court, the case was tried in accordance with Swedish law without the courts making any reference to the choice of law rules in the Act (1937:81) on International Legal Relations Concerning Estates, Chapter 1, section 4, which implement the 1961 Hague Convention on the Conflict of Laws Relating to the Form of Testamentary Dispositions. The Supreme Court, in turn, drew attention to these rules and their content but then pointed out that neither party had claimed that the document would be considered a valid will under English law. "The question whether there exists an emergency will must therefore, as the courts have done, be judged in accordance with Swedish law", the Court stated.[44] The Court paid no attention to the fact that the applicable choice of law rules were conventional. Therefore, it also failed to consider the special purpose and nature of the rules embodied in the 1961 Hague Convention. The decision is in conflict with the opinion that alternative choice of law rules contained in an international

---

[43] It is stated in the protocol of the District Court that the parties were in agreement on the application of Swedish law. The present author thanks Professor Michael Bogdan for a copy of this unpublished document.

[44] This statement closely resembles the justification given by the Danish Supreme Court in *UfR 1918. 212 (H)* in support of the application of Danish law. The case concerned the right of a child born in Chile to the estate of the mother's husband in the capacity of a child born in wedlock to the deceased. In the opinion of the Court, there was no reason to apply foreign law, already for the reason that no party had requested it. The voting protocol of the Court shows that the Court wanted to take an explicit standpoint on the question. A. Philip, *Dansk International Privat- og Procesret*, 1976, p. 54.

convention must be regarded as mandatory and hence are to be applied *ex officio* by the courts.[45]

The published judgment of the Supreme Court gives no explanation as to why the Court, contrary to the lower courts, paid attention to the choice of law rules embodied in the (revised) Act of 1937. Against the background of the statements made by the Court in the previous decisions and the still remaining uncertainty in respect of the conditions for the application of choice of law rules and foreign law, a natural conclusion seems to be that the Court found this necessary. The foreign connecting factors were obvious although neither party, in light of the report, had referred to them in support of the party's claim. As the Supreme Court's statement is formulated, it can only be interpreted as meaning that it is a duty of the interested party to refer to foreign law in support of his claim. If no such reference is made, then Swedish law is to be applied.[46]

In my opinion, the Supreme Court in this decision in fact repudiated the doctrine of *ex officio* application of choice of law rules and foreign law in cases where Swedish domestic law permits a settlement.[47] Whether intentional or not, the straightforwardness of the

---

[45] See F. Vischer, *supra* note 3, p. 83. Vischer is, however, in favour of exceptions in respect of rights of which the parties may freely dispose.

[46] The unpublished documents of the case indicate, however, that in the Supreme Court the respondent suddenly found reason to refer to the 1961 Hague Convention, ratified by all the concerned states. Since, according to this convention, several laws may be alternatively applicable, the respondent now referred to expert opinions on the content of both Danish law and English law. The petitioner objected to this on the ground that the applicability of Swedish law had been uncontested from the beginning. (That Danish law was also considered important by the respondent is explained by the fact that an expert opinion indicated that the deceased, who at her death was married to a Danish citizen and had previously been living in Denmark, was under English law considered to be domiciled in Denmark.) This reference by a party to the 1961 Convention may, naturally, have been the real reason for the Court's attention to the choice of law rules. A Supreme Court decision must, however, be interpreted as it stands and in light of the published report. Unpublished information available only on demand at the courts can not be given any decisive importance.

[47] An earlier decision by the Labour Court, *AD 1988 nr. 177*, had strongly indicated that foreign law is applied only at party request. The subject matter of this case had solely to do with the Finnish labour market. The dispute (alleged breach by the employee of the terms of the contract) came to be tried by a Swedish court only because the respondent, *i.e.* the former employee, had moved to Sweden after the termination of the employment contract in Finland. The plaintiff was a Finnish municipality. It is difficult to find any other explanation to the application of the *lex fori* than that neither party had insisted on the

Court's reasoning is striking. Unlike in its earlier decisions, the Court abstained from referring to the existence of an (earlier) agreement between the parties on the application of Swedish law. Instead, the Supreme Court made it clear that since no party had pleaded the application of foreign law, *i.e.* claimed that the document would be considered as a formally valid will in English law, Swedish law was to be applied. As the decision is reported, it can be claimed to clean Swedish private international law of unnecessary fictive elements. It is at least tempting to claim that from now on such complicated questions as where the borderline is between a tacit agreement on the application of Swedish law and a presumed such agreement are without relevance.

5. Conclusions

In Swedish private international law the parties may, during the court proceedings, opt for the *lex fori* if the case concerns rights which in Swedish domestic law are at the disposal of the parties. Equally, the parties may opt for a foreign law, provided that there is a natural connection to the chosen law.

The parties' agreement on the applicable law has, in fact, for quite a long time been acknowledged in the field of contractual obligations where party autonomy was already well-established in Swedish case-law in the 1930s. It has, gradually, been extended to all such issues in respect of which Swedish domestic law permits a settlement. In this way, the parties have also been given the right to dispose of the applicable law in areas where party autonomy is otherwise not yet recognized.

Recent case-law confirms that, today, a prerequisite for the application of foreign law is that at least one of the parties has requested it, when claims are at issue of which the parties may dispose. This development has reduced the scope of the *ex officio* application of choice of law rules and the foreign law they refer to those relatively

---

application of Finnish law to the dispute. See, also, L. Pålsson, "Svensk rättspraxis, Internationell privat- och processrätt 1986–1990", *Svensk Juristtidning* 1992, p. 477 and p. 491.

few areas where Swedish domestic law does not permit a settlement between the parties.

From a practical point of view, this development can be justified. The notion of choice of law rules as mandatory is, today, generally not convincing due to the failure of these rules to guarantee decisional harmony. It is much more appealing to both the courts and concerned parties in the Swedish legal system if these rules are applied under the same conditions as rules of domestic law. The justification is that they are a part of the law of the forum and subject to the law-finding process generally prevalent there. In Swedish law, the predominance of issues in respect of which a settlement is permitted also gives the parties a far-reaching right to opt out the choice of law rules. The parties' settlement is respected to the extent that it is in conformity with mandatory rules.

Is it, then, possible to reconcile this point of view with the objectives of international conventions aiming at the unification of choice of law rules?

Generally speaking, I believe so, *e.g.* with respect to the Hague conventions open for ratification or accession by a great number of states from all parts of the world, at least when mainly pecuniary interests of the parties are at stake. The parties are not deprived of the protection afforded by the unified choice of law rules because they may always request their application.[48]

The question is more complicated when dealing with regional conventions, *e.g.* the 1980 E.E.C. Convention on the Law Applicable to Contractual Obligations. The aim of this Convention is to facilitate the economic integration within the Community through unified choice of law rules concerning contractual obligations. The Convention can also be seen as a complement to the E.E.C. Convention on the Recognition and Enforcement of Judgments in Civil and Commercial Matters (= Brussels Convention, 1968). It has been argued that if recognition of a judgment given in one member state is mandatory

---

[48] A complicated issue is, however, how and to what extent should the court look after the interests of the parties, *e.g.*, their possible lack of knowledge of the applicable choice of law rules and bring these rules to their attention. This important question must, unfortunately, be ignored in this article. For further reference concerning the Scandinavian discussion on the subject, see M. Jänterä-Jareborg, *supra* note 25, pp. 344–349.

throughout the Community, then the courts throughout the Community should apply the same law.[49] According to article 18 of the Contractual Obligations Convention, in the interpretation and application of the uniform rules regard shall be had to their international character and to the desirability of achieving uniformity in their interpretation and application. If *forum shopping* is to be avoided, then it can be argued that the same conditions should prevail in all the member states for the application of rules embodied in the Convention.

Evidently, this is not the case at present. Lacking access to comprehensive studies concerning the application of the Convention in the various contracting states, I shall confine myself to opinions expressed in the legal literature.

The most straightforward of these – and probably the one best in line with the Swedish standpoint – is the statement made by the Danish expert Allan Philip. According to Philip, the questions that are not dealt with in the Convention, *e.g.* the conditions for the application of foreign law, are, in Danish law, subject to the general principles of private international law.[50] A consequence of this is that the Convention does not create a more far-reaching duty to apply foreign law than that which prevails in respect of non-conventional choice of law rules. According to the Danish position, if party autonomy is recognized in a certain area, then foreign law is applied only at the demand of a party.[51] An effectually similar view based on the prevailing national traditions in English private international law is expressed by Peter North. According to him, complete harmony cannot be achieved through the Convention because the differing rules of evidence may often be just as significant to the outcome of a case as differing choice of law rules.[52]

---

[49] See P. North, *Private International Law Problems in Common Law Jurisdictions*, 1993, p. 123. According to North, this was strongly felt by the original six member states to the Community but less so in some of the newer ones.

[50] A. Philip, *EU-IP. Europeisk International Privat- og Procesret*, 1994, p. 135.

[51] A. Philip, *supra* note 44, p. 57. – It could be claimed that a drawback of such an attitude is that it stimulates "lex forism" at the expense of predictability.

[52] P. North, *supra* note 49, p. 123. Of interest in this connection would seem to be that in English law, a party interested in the application of foreign law must plead and prove it.

The conclusion to be drawn from these statements is that Sweden should be able to ratify the Convention without necessarily needing to re-examine the prevailing conditions for the application of foreign law. Seen, on the other hand, from a Community perspective, the different traditions in the member states constitute a serious threat to the Convention. If, *e.g.*, foreign law in Sweden is applied only at the request of a party, is not article 4 of the Convention in such case more or less meaningless? This article identifies the applicable law in the absence of a party choice of law.

In my opinion, this risk for disregard of the in fact most important choice of law rule of the Convention[53] speaks strongly in favour of a reconsideration of when to apply the rules embodied in the Contractual Obligations Convention. Mere silence in respect of the question of choice of law should not be enough for the application of Swedish law. A prerequisite should, instead, be that the court be able to establish a common accord between the parties on the application of the *lex fori*.[54] In such a case, the situation can probably be considered to be covered by article 3 of the Convention sanctioning a party choice of law.

The divergent national practices concerning the application of foreign law within the member states of the European Union is a question of growing importance. It seems to me that this question has so far been given too little attention. In Sweden, the country's recent entry into the European Union gives an excellent reason to consider the need for clear rules in this respect, legislative or judge-made.

"The onus of proving that it", *i.e.*, the foreign law, "is different, and of proving what it is, lies upon the party who pleads the difference. If there is no such plea, or if the difference is not satisfactorily proved, the court must give a decision according to English law, even though the case may be connected solely with some foreign country." *Cheshire and North's Private International Law*, 1992, p. 106. – Also Kohler draws attention to similar problems. Ch. Kohler, "Einheit, Vielheit und Relativität im Kollisionsrecht der EG-Mitgliedstaaten", *Praxis des internationalen Privat- und Verfahrensrechts* 12 (1992), p. 281.

[53] Experience shows that even within international trade, the parties seldom make use of party choice of law in advance. See M. Bogdan, *supra* note 28, p. 234.

[54] See F. Vischer, *supra* note 3, p. 79.

Bibliography

Beckman, Nils: Svensk domstolspraxis i internationell rätt, Stockholm 1959: P.A. Norstedt & Söners Förlag.

Bogdan, Michael: Svensk internationell privat- och processrätt, Fjärde upplagan, Stockholm 1992: Norstedts Juridik.

Cheshire and North's Private International Law, 12th edition by P.M. North and J.J. Fawcett, London 1992: Butterworths.

de Boer, Th. M.: "The Hague Conference and Dutch Choice of Law: Some Criticism and a Suggestion", Netherlands International Law Review XL (1993), pp. 1–13.

Eek, Hilding: Lagkonflikter i tvistemål, Metod och material i svensk internationell privaträtt, Stockholm 1972: P.A. Norstedt & Söners Förlag.

Flessner, Axel: "Fakultatives Kollisionsrecht", Rabels Zeitschrift für ausländisches und internationales Privatrecht 34 (1970), pp. 547–584.

Gesetzentwurf der Bundesregierung: Entwurf eines Gesetzes zur Neuregelung des Internationalen Privatrechts, Deutscher Bundestag 10. Wahlperiode, Drucksache 10/504, 20.10.1983.

Hassler, Åke & Nial, Håkan: Internationell privaträtt, Efter föreläsningar av professor Åke Hassler, Tredje upplagan, Reviderad efter föreläsningar av professor Håkan Nial, Stockholm 1948: Stockholms Högskolas Juridiska Förenings Förlag.

Herzfelder, François: "Die Prüfungspflicht der französischen staatlichen Gerichte hinsichtlich kollisionsrechtlichen Fragen: Zur neuen Rechtsprechung des französischen Kassationshofs", Recht der Internationalen Wirtschaft/Außenwirtschaftsdienst des Betriebsberaters 1990, pp. 354–358.

Jänterä-Jareborg, Maarit: Partsautonomi och efterlevande makes rättsställning, En internationellt-privaträttslig studie, Uppsala 1989: Iustus Förlag.

Jänterä-Jareborg, Maarit: "The Influence of the Hague Conventions on the Development of Swedish Family Conflicts Law", Netherlands International Law Review XL (1993), pp. 49–65.

Kallenberg, Ernst: Svensk civilprocessrätt, Andra bandet I, Lund 1927.

Karlgren, Hjalmar: Kortfattad lärobok i internationell privat- och processrätt, Femte upplagan, Lund 1979: Liber Läromedel Lund.

Koerner, Dörthe: Fakultatives Kollisionsrecht in Frankreich und Deutschland, Tübingen 1995: J.C.B. Mohr (Paul Siebeck) Tübingen.

Kohler, Christian: "Einheit, Vielheit und Relativität im Kollisionsrecht der EG-Mitgliedstaaten", Praxis des Internationalen Privat- und Verfahrensrechts 12 (1992), pp. 277–284.

Lando, Ole: "Skandinavien", in: Die Anwendung ausländischen Rechts im internationalen Privatrecht. Festveranstaltung und Kolloquium anläßlich des 40. jährigen Bestehens des Max-Planck-Instituts für ausländisches und internationales Privatrecht vom 6.–8. Juli 1966 in Hamburg, pp. 128–140. Im Institut bearbeitet von Dierk Müller, Berlin & Tübingen 1968.

North, Peter: Private International Law Problems in Common Law Jurisdictions, Dordrecht-Boston-London 1993: Martinus Nijhoff Publishers.

Philip, Allan: Dansk international privat- og procesret, 3. udgave, København 1976: Juristforbundets Forlag.

Philip, Allan: EU-IP, Europæisk International Privat- og Procesret, 2. udgave, København 1994: Jurist- og Økonomforbundets Forlag.

Pålsson, Lennart: "Schweden", in: Bülow & Böckstiegel & Geimer & Schütze (Hrsg.), Der internationale Rechtsverkehr in Zivil- und Handelssachen, 1992, pp. 1–12.

Pålsson, Lennart: Svensk rättspraxis i internationell familje- och arvsrätt, Stockholm 1986: Norstedts.

Pålsson, Lennart: "Svensk rättspraxis, Internationell privat- och processrätt 1976–1980", Svensk Juristtidning 1982, pp. 214–251.

Pålsson, Lennart: "Svensk rättspraxis, Internationell privat- och processrätt 1986–1990", Svensk Juristtidning 1992, pp. 475–503.

Pålsson, Lennart: "Underhållsfrågor och internationell privaträtt", Svensk Juristtidning 1993, pp. 613–633.

Reuterskiöld, C.A.: Föreläsningar öfver privat internationell rätt, II, Handbok i svensk internationell rätt (process-, utlämnings-, straff- och privaträtt), Stockholm 1912.

Schwind, Fritz: Internationales Privatrecht, Lehr- und Handbuch für Theorie und Praxis, Wien 1990: Manz Verlag.

SOU 1983:25: Internationella faderskapsfrågor, Betänkande av utredningen om internationella faderskapsfrågor, Stockholm 1983: Allmänna Förlaget.

SOU 1987:18: Internationella familjerättsfrågor, Slutbetänkande av familjelagssakkunniga, Stockholm 1987: Allmänna Förlaget.

Sturm, Fritz: "Fakultatives Kollisionsrecht: Notwendigkeit und Grenzen", in: Festschrift für Konrad Zweigert zum 70. Geburtstag, pp. 329–347, Herausgegeben von Herbert Bernstein, Ulrich Drobnig, Hein Kötz, Tübingen 1981.

Undén, Östen: Internationell äktenskapsrätt enligt gällande svensk lag, Lund 1922: C.W.K. Gleerups Förlag.

Vischer, Frank: "General Course on Private International Law", Recueil des Cours 232 (1992 I), pp. 9–255.

von Overbeck, Alfred E.: "Die Ermittlung, Anwendung und Überprüfung der richtigen Anwendung des anwendbaren Rechts", in: Yvo Hangartner (Hrsg.), Die allgemeinen Bestimmungen des Bundesgesetzes über das internationale Privatrecht, St. Gallen 1988, pp. 91–113: Veröffentlichungen des Schweizerischen Instituts für Verwaltungskurse an der Hochschule St. Gallen.

Zajtay, Imre: "The Application of Foreign Law", International Encyclopedia of Comparative Law, Private International Law, Volume III, Chapter 14, Tübingen 1972.

BEING FIRST.
ON USES AND ABUSES OF THE LIS PENDENS
UNDER THE BRUSSELS CONVENTION

Ole Lando

1. Why be first?

The Brussels Convention on Jurisdiction and Enforcement of Judgments in Civil And Commercial Matters is in force in 12 of the EU Member States and membership will eventually comprise all 15 Member States.[1] The Lugano Convention on the same subject matter, between the EFTA Countries and between them and the Union States[2] which now comprises 6 additional Contracting States, brings the entire network up to 18 European States.[3] As the provisions of the two conventions are almost identical, both will hereinafter be called the Convention.

The Convention has been a success. Debt collection has become easier and foreign debtors domiciled in a Contracting State have become more ready to pay their debts.[4]

The Convention has two set of rules: one on jurisdiction and the other on enforcement of judgments. The first part provides uniform rules on the international jurisdiction of the courts of the Contracting States. The main rule is the *actor sequitor forum rei* in art 2: Persons domiciled in a Contracting State shall be sued in the courts of that State. To this rule must be added the rules on special jurisdiction in

---

[1] Made in Brussels on September 27, 1968 and amended three times (1978, 1982 and 1989). Latest consolidated version is published in O.J.E.C. 1990 No 6 189/1.

[2] See O.J.E.C. 1988 No L. 319/9.

[3] Of the present Members of the Lugano Convention Austria, Finland and Sweden are expected to join the Brussels Convention.

[4] This proposition is based on interviews with Dutch, French and German lawyers.

arts 5 and 6 and other rules which confer jurisdiction on courts other than those of the defendant's domicile. Thus, under art 5 no 1 in matters relating to a contract, a person domiciled in a Contracting State may be sued in the courts of the place of performance of the obligation in question; under art 5 no 3, in matters relating to torts, such person may be sued in the courts of the place where the harmful event occurred. These and other rules will often leave a plaintiff with a choice as to where, i.e. in which country, he can bring his action. He can then choose the court which he expects will give him the best chance of winning his case, hereinafter called a friendly court.

Important are also the rules on lis pendens[5] in art 21–23.[6] These

---

[5] There is an abundance of literature on the subject. References can be found in Pålsson, *Luganokonventionen*, Stockholm, 1992, pp 182–191, Dicey and Morris on the Conflict of Laws, 12 ed, general editor Lawrence Collins, London, 1993 with 1995 Supplement, chapters 11 and 12 (specialist editor Lawrence Collins). H. Gaudemet-Tallon, *Les Conventions de Bruxelles et de Lugano*, Paris, 1993, Chapter 8 (pp 191–209), J. Kropholler, *Europäisches Zivilprozessrecht*, 4 ed. Heidelberg, 1993, pp 241–253 and A. Philip, *EU-IP*, 2 ed. Copenhagen, 1994, pp 98–102. See also Göransson in "Vänbok till Robert Bomann", Uppsala 1990 p 107. The lis pendens as a legal institution has been treated by Pålsson in Tidsskrift for Rettsvitenskap 1967, 537.

[6] The texts of articles 21–23 now read:

Section 8
Lis Pendens – Related Actions

Article 21

Where proceedings involving the same cause of action and between the same parties are brought in the courts of different Contracting States, any court other than the court first seised shall of its own motion stay its proceedings until such time as the jurisdiction of the court first seised is established.

Where the jurisdiction of the court first seised is established, any court other than the court first seised shall decline jurisdiction in favour of that court.

Article 22

Where related actions are brought in the courts of different Contracting States, any court other than the court first seised may, while the actions are pending at first instance, stay its proceedings.

A court other than the court first seised may also, on the application of one of the parties, decline jurisdiction if the law of that court permits the consolidation of related actions and the court first seised has jurisdiction over both actions.

For the purposes of this Article, actions are deemed to be related where they are so closely connected that it is expedient to hear and determine them together to avoid the risk of irreconsilable judgments resulting from separate proceedings.

Article 23

Where actions come within the exclusive jurisdiction of several courts, any court other than the court first seised shall decline jurisdiction in favour of that court.

rules, and notably art 21, give the party who seizes a court first an advantage. He can bar the defendant from suing elsewhere within the network in the same cause of action. This opportunity has, as we shall see, been used in a number of cases and has also been abused. As the Convention does not provide a general clause to the effect that actions brought before an inconvenient forum may be dismissed,[7] such an action must be tried by the court first seized, if it has jurisdiction, even if this is unfair.

The lis pendens rules have often been applied. A frequent situation has been the following: A believes he has a claim against B, a belief which B does not share or at least claims that he does not share. B therefore brings an action against A in a friendly court to get a declaratory judgment to the effect that A does not have a claim against B. Being first, B will prevent A from suing in another court within the network of the Convention.

There have been a number of such cases where a plaintiff has seized a "friendly" court in order to get a declaratory judgment.

2. The Italian Case

In a case which was finally decided by the English Court of Appeal on December 19, 1991,[8] the plaintiff, a Swiss company named Marc Rich & Co A/G, had bought crude oil from the Italian defendant, Societa Italiana Impianti. The facts relating to the conclusion of the contract were as follows: On January 23, 1987 Marc Rich made a telex offer to buy a quantity of Iranian crude oil on f.o.b. terms from Impianti. On January 25 Impianti accepted the offer subject to certain further conditions. On January 26 Marc Rich sent an additional telex message setting out the terms of the contract under which it was to be governed by English law and included a clause referring all disputes to arbitration in London.

---

[7] The forum non conveniens principle which has been established by the British courts, see Dicey and Morris op cit note 5, 398 ff, was rejected by the working party which prepared the first amendment to the Brussels Convention, see the Schlosser Report in OJEC 1979 C/69 at p. 125 (no 181).

[8] Marc Rich & Co. A.G. v. Società Italiana Impianti P.A. (No 2) [1992] Lloyd's Rep. 624 (CA).

When the oil was delivered Marc Rich claimed that it was contaminated with water. Samples of the oil were taken and analysed.

On February 18, 1988 Impianti summoned Marc Rich to appear before the Italian Tribunale in Genoa seeking a declaration of non-liability. As Marc Rich was – at that time – a "non-convention" defendant, the Genoa court could assume jurisdiction on the ground that the contract had been concluded in Italy where Impianti had received Marc Rich's acceptance.

Marc Rich tried to avoid the Genoa court. It contested the jurisdiction of the court invoking the arbitration clause; on February 29 it commenced arbitration proceedings in London in which Impianti refused to take part. In May 1988 Marc Rich commenced proceedings before the High Court in London in order to have an arbitrator appointed. There, Impianti contended that the real dispute between the parties was linked to the question of whether or not the contract contained an arbitration clause; this dispute fell within the scope of the Convention and should therefore be adjudicated in Italy. Marc Rich took the view that the dispute fell outside the scope of the Convention by virtue of art 1 (4), a view which the High Court supported. It held that arbitration should be continued in England. This meant that the High Court was of the opinion that Impianti had validly agreed to arbitration in London.

On appeal, the English Court of Appeal asked the European Court whether the exception in art 1 (4) of the Convention should extend to a litigation where the initial existence of an arbitration agreement was at issue. It got the answer that art 1 (4) must be interpreted to mean that the exclusion provided therein extends to litigation pending before a national court concerning the appointment of arbitrators, even if the existence or validity of an arbitration agreement is a preliminary issue in that litigation.[9]

This answer was given by the European Court on July 25, 1991.

Meanwhile, the Genoa Court had ruled that it had jurisdiction in the matter. On November 22, 1988 Marc Rich lodged a petition in the Italian Supreme Court seeking a declaration to the effect that, by

---

[9] See [1991] ECR I 3855.

reason of the arbitration agreement, the courts in Italy lacked jurisdiction to try the dispute. The judgment of the court was delivered on January 25, 1991. The court held that there was no binding arbitration agreement between the parties because there was no agreement in writing as required by art 2 of the New York Convention on the Recognition and Enforcement of Foreign Arbitral Awards, and because there was no basis for assuming that there had been a tacit acceptance by Impianti of the proposal to submit the dispute to arbitration.

The case then continued in Genoa, and in May 1991, before the European Court had spoken, Marc Rich defended its case on the merits.

The answer given by the European Court would not have prevented the British Courts from nominating an arbitrator as requested by Marc Rich. However, in October 1991 Marc Rich sought to obtain an order from the English High Court restraining Impianti from pursuing the action in Italy pending the appointment of an arbitrator under article 10 (3) of the English Arbitration Act of 1950. This application was dismissed by the High Court and, on appeal, by the Court of Appeal, mainly on the ground that in his defence of May 1991 Marc Rich had submitted to the jurisdiction of the Italian Court and could therefore no longer contend it.[10]

By being first Impianti succeeded. For the British courts the dispute came to turn on whether they had to pay heed to the Italian proceedings which had been instituted before the proceedings in Britain. It is not to tell how the dispute would have been decided in England and Italy if Marc Rich had been first, but by being second Marc Rich was at a disadvantage right from the beginning.

The Italian interpretation of art 2 of the New York Convention requiring arbitration agreement to be in writing was stricter than the English but, it is submitted, not unfair. It must also be borne in mind that during the written negotiations Marc Rich originally accepted the counter proposals of Impianti and then, two days later, sent a telex containing the additional terms comprising the arbitration

---

[10] See note 8 supra.

clause. It may be argued that these additional terms never became part of the contract and that Impianti did not accept them by performing the contract.

However, the case shows the importance of being first. It may be better to seek a declaration of non-liability in a friendly court than to wait until the other party brings an action in damages in another court or before an arbitral tribunal. One can see from subsequent cases that this idea has spread. As will be mentioned below, it may have adverse consequences.

3. The Dutch Case

A subsequent case before the European Court involved the owners of a cargo of soya bean oil laden on board the ship Tatry and the owners of the ship Maciej Rataj, C 406/92.[11] Part of the cargo had been carried on the ship Tatry which belonged to Polish shipowners, from Brazil to Rotterdam and the rest to Hamburg. The cargo owners complained to the shipowners that in the course of the voyage the cargo had been contaminated with, among other things, diesel oil.

In November 1988 the shipowners brought an action before the District Court of Rotterdam against some of the owners of the cargo seeking a declaration that they were not liable or not fully liable for the alleged contamination. In September 1989 some of those cargo owners who had been sued in Rotterdam, in addition to some who had not, had the ship Maciej Rataj, which belonged to the same owners as the Tatry, arrested in Liverpool. The former cargo owners then brought an action in the English High Court against the Tatry and the Maciej Rataj. It was unclear whether this action was in personam only or both in rem and in personam. The latter owners brought an action in rem. Both actions were brought under the Arrest Convention and continued in England after the ship had been released from arrest against guarantee.

---

[11] See [1994] E.C.R. I 5439 and [1995] Lloyds Rep. 302, [1992] 2 Lloyd's Rep. 552 (C.A.).

The English Court of Appeal asked the European Court a number of questions relating to the lis pendens and related actions rules in art 21 and 22. One was whether art 21 barred those cargo owners who had not been sued in Holland from suing in England. The European Court answered that following a proper construction of article 21, where two actions involve the same cause of action and some but not all of the parties to the second action were the same as the parties to the action commenced earlier in another contracting state, the second court seized is required to decline jurisdiction only to the extent to which the parties to the proceedings before it are also the parties to the action previously commenced; it does not prevent proceedings from continuing between the other parties. This, the European Court admitted, could involve a fragmentation of the proceedings. However, article 22 mitigated that unhappy consequence by allowing the second Court seized to stay proceedings or to decline jurisdiction on the ground that the actions were related, assuming the conditions of art 22 were satisfied. The Court also ruled that for the application of art 22 it is sufficient for the two parts of the same cargo belonging to different owners to be shipped under the same conditions and under contracts which are identical, and that separate trial and judgment would involve the risk of conflicting decisions. The parties to the actions need then not be the same.

The Court finally held that, under a proper construction of art 21, action to have the defendant held liable in damages has the same cause of action as earlier proceedings brought by the defendant seeking a declaration that he is not liable and that a subsequent action has the same cause of action even if it is called an action in rem. In this case the shipowners had their case tried in the court they preferred.

Like the Italian case, this suit confirms that a party which brings an action seeking a declaration of non-liability against the other party before the latter brings his action seeking damages can prevent the other party from bringing his action in another court. Even if a party was not sued in the first action, but his cause of action was the same as that of the party who was previously sued, he may see his action stayed or dismissed if it is related to the first action and there is a risk of conflicting judgments as laid down in art 22 of the Convention.

This is perhaps a circumstance which speaks against the too generous admission of actions seeking a declaratory judgment.

4. The Greek Case

A year before the ruling of the European Court in the Dutch case, the English Court of Appeal delivered a judgment in the case of Continental Bank N.A. v. Aeakos Compania Naviera S.A. and others.[12] The plaintiff, American Bank, had granted a loan of US 56 million to the defendant companies and had obtained a guarantee from three Greek individuals who were also defendants in the case. The loan agreements contained the following clauses:

> "21.01. This agreement shall be governed by and construed in accordance with English law.
>
> 21.02. Each of the borrowers...hereby irrevocably submits to the jurisdiction of the English courts and hereby irrevocably nominates Messrs. Aegis (London) Ltd....England, to receive service of proceedings in such courts on its behalf, but the bank reserves the right to proceed under this agreement in the courts of any other country claiming or having jurisdiction in respect thereof."

The borrowers defaulted in their payment of installments and interest and, after a rescheduling agreement had been made, also in the rescheduled payments.

Before the plaintiff bank brought an action against the borrowers and guarantors in an English court, the defendants sued the bank in the Court of First Instance of Athens, Greece where the defendant companies were managed. The borrowers claimed damages from the bank totalling approximately US 63 million and a declaration that the guarantors were released. The cause of action was based on art 919 of the Greek Civil Code which provides that "whoever intentionally in a manner which violates the commands of morality causes damages to

---

[12] [1994] 1.W.L.R. 588 (C.A.).

another is bound to make reparation of any damage thus caused". The defendants alleged that the bank had exercised its rights under the loan agreements contrary to business morality. The action brought appears to have been an action in tort or delict.

After the complaint in the Greek proceedings had been served upon the bank in Chicago, the bank issued a writ in an English action seeking an injunction to restrain the defendants from continuing the Greek proceedings in breach of the jurisdiction agreement. The defendants sought an order that the bank's writ be struck out or the action be stayed under art 21 and 22 of the Convention. In the High Court the judge held that the defendants were in breach of contract by suing in Greece in spite of the jurisdiction agreement, and that art 21 and 22 did not require the English court to stay proceedings in England. He granted a final injunction restraining the defendants from taking any further steps in the Greek proceedings.

The Court of Appeal dismissed the defendants' appeal. The English court had jurisdiction to enjoin the defendants from continuing with the Greek proceedings, even though the Greek courts had been first seized. English law which governed the contract and the jurisdiction agreement applied to the subject matter of the Greek proceedings. The claim in Greece was alleged to be mainly in tort but to have contractual aspects as well. In proceedings in England by the bank to recover the loan or to obtain an injunction to restrain the Greek proceedings, the jurisdiction clause also applied to claims in tort. The common sense view was that the purpose of the clause was to submit disputes in connection with the loan facilities to the jurisdiction of the English courts.

The Court of Appeal also held that the jurisdiction agreement granted the English courts exclusive jurisdiction under art 17 of the Convention and that it deprived the Greek court of jurisdiction. Art 17 took precedence over art 21 and 22; if it were otherwise, a party would be allowed to override a jurisdiction agreement governed by art 17 with a pre-emptive suit in the courts of another Contracting State. The court of the latter state would then be the court first seized and the court chosen by the parties would have to decline jurisdiction or, if the jurisdiction of the other court was contested, to stay proceedings. In this way, a party in breach of contract would be able to set at naught an exclusive jurisdiction clause which was a product of the free will of the parties. If the injunction was not granted, the defendants would persist in their breach of contract and the plaintiff's legal rights, as enshrined in the jurisdiction agreement, would prove to be worthless. The continuance of the Greek proceedings would amount to vexatious and opperessive conduct on the part of the defendant and an injunction was therefore appropriate.

In the proceedings before the Court of Appeal, the defendants argued that the Court should grant a stay of the proceedings until the Greek court had decided whether it had jurisdiction (see art 21 (1) of the Convention). The English court should have left it to the court first seized to decide whether it had jurisdiction; the Court of Appeal ought to have trusted the Greek court.

It is respectfully submitted that the Brussels Convention must lead to this result. Nothing in the Convention or its travaux préparatoires suggests that the enforcement of a jurisdiction clause takes priority over the effect of lis pendens. If, as in the present case, the issue is whether the dispute is covered by the jurisdiction clause, this question must be left to the court first seized to decide. The court second seized must await the decision of the court first seized. Under this system, the British rules, under which a British court can enjoin a foreign party from continuing proceedings in another Contracting State, appear to be incompatible with the Convention rules on lis pendens.[13]

Furthermore, the court second seized must obey the decision of the court first seized; if that court assumes jurisdiction, the court second seized must decline its jurisdiction even if the court first seized would not have jurisdiction under the rules of the Convention. This the European Court told the English Court of Appeal on June 26, 1991 in the Case of Overseas Union Insurance Co v. New Hampshire Insurance Co.[14]

It is not unlikely that, if asked by the Court of Appeal, the Euro-

---

[13] See on the judgment, Dicey and Morris, op cit note 5, 1995 Supplement at pp 401, 422 and 437, and the literature and other British cases referred to there.

[14] [1991] E.C.R.I. 3317. See also Gaudemet-Tallon op.cit. note 5, no 290, Kropholler op.cit. note 5, p 248.

pean Court would have given an answer along these lines. However, the Court of Appeal entertained no doubts about the answer to the question and rejected an application by the defendants for an order to refer it to the European Court.

In support of the decision taken by the Court of Appeal it may be argued that the case is a clear example of the abuse of the lis pendens rules of the Convention. The two experts on Greek law who were heard in the proceedings before the Court of Appeal both confirmed that the Greek court would assume jurisdiction over the dispute in spite of the jurisdiction clause. The reason for this was not stated, but it was probably that the action in the Greek court was considered to be in tort and not in contract. However, in British eyes the case was, as the Court said, a paradigm case for the granting of an injunction.

In our view the case is a paradigm example of a clash between the rules of the Convention and justice, a clash caused by the piecemeal harmonisation of the rules of procedure of the Contracting States. The rules of the Convention have not been accompanied by sufficient guarantees against abuse by unscrupulous parties (see No. 6 below).

5. The Retrocession Case

This case was never decided by the court seized. It was instead settled before the jurisdiction issue was even tried. The facts were as follows:

The defendant, an English insurance company which had rein-sured a portfolio of insurance contracts, had "retroceded" these con-tracts to the plaintiff, a Nordic insurance company. The signing of the contracts had been preceeded by oral negotiations in London with a reinsurance broker. The contracts led to considerable claims by the English company against the Nordic company. Some of the claims were paid, but very substantial sums were still outstanding. The total losses which the defendant had recovered and still claimed from the plaintiff exceeded twenty times the premiums which the defendant had paid the plaintiff for the retrocessions.

The Nordic company refused to cover further claims made by the

English company and brought an action in a court of its own country claiming that the English company had misled it as to the character of the insured risks. It sought a declaration that the retrocession contracts were null and void due to misrepresentation, and claimed repayment of the amounts already paid.

This case also reflects the eagerness to be first and to choose a friendly court. Knowing that the defendant might try to recover the amounts outstanding and for this purpose bringing an action in an English court which, as we shall see, would have jurisdiction under art 5 no 1 of the Convention, the Nordic company brought an action in its own country thereby preventing the English company from bringing an action in England. The Nordic company claimed that the court had jurisdiction under art 5 no 1, the relevant part of which provides that a person domiciled in a Contracting State may in matters relating to contract be sued in the country for the place of performance of the obligation in question. The plaintiff maintained that *matters related to contract* included a claim that the contract be declared null and void; that *the obligation in question* was the duty of the defendant to give the plaintiff correct information concerning the risks involved – a duty which the defendant had breached – and that *the place of performance* of this duty was the plaintiff's domicile in the forum country.

All three of these points gave rise to dispute.

On the first issue, was a claim that the contract be declared null and void, a matter related to contract, the plaintiff invoked Effer S.p.A. v. Kanter,[15] where the European Court had ruled that under art 5 no 1 of the Convention a national court had jurisdiction to try an objection by the defendant that the contract on which the plaintiff relied was invalid.

However, in the Effer-case the European Court had also said that "the national court has power to consider the existence of the...contract itself since that is indispensable in order to enable the national court...to examine whether it has jurisdiction under the Convention".

---

[15] [1982] E.C.R. 825. See on this issue Gaudemet-Tallon op.cit. note 5 no 159, and in *Revue critique de droit international privé*, 1983, 510, Kropholler op.cit. note 5 at p 86 (note 6), Pålsson op.cit. no 5 p 75.

The common sense interpretation of this dictum seems to be that if the Court finds the contract nonexistent, it must decline jurisdiction. So, if in the retrocession case the Nordic court were to find for the plaintiff and hold the contracts to be null and void, it would also have to decline jurisdiction. The Nordic court would have jurisdiction to try the case only if it were to find for the defendant and consider the contracts to be valid and enforceable, a decision which the plaintiff did not seek.

The plaintiff claimed that the obligation in question was the defendant's duty to supply correct and adequate information when the contracts were negotiated. Bilateral contracts, like retrocession contracts, give rise to obligations on both sides. One party, the insurer, assumes risks and undertakes to pay the claims to the insured party when the risks materialize. The other, the insured party, must pay the insurance premiums and thereby pay for the risks which the insurer assumes. These are the primary principal obligations of the parties. Besides these obligations, the parties have a number of other duties to each other. When the contract is being negotiated, the insured party must give correct and adequate information on the relevant facts about the risks; when a loss is suffered, he must provide the insurer with adequate information about it. The performance of these and other obligations may be conditions for the other party's duty to cover the risks, but they are not the principal obligations.

In several of its decisions the Court of Justice of the European Community has stated that it is the policy of the Brussels Convention to avoid a multitude of fora. In de Bloos v. Bouyer[16] the Court said that it is the purpose of the Convention to avoid, as far as possible, a situation in which a number of courts have jurisdiction in respect of the same contract. Therefore, the term 'obligation in question' cannot be interpreted as referring to any obligation whatsoever arising under the contract in question. It must refer to the contractual obligation forming the basis of the legal proceedings, i.e. that which corresponds to the contractual right on which the plaintiff's action is based. In a case where the plaintiff asserts the right to be paid damages or seeks a

---

16 [1976] E.C.R. 1497.

dissolution of the contract on the ground of the wrongful conduct of the other party, the obligation referred to in art 5 no 1 is still that which arises under the contract, the non-performance of which is relied upon to support such claim.

In Shevenai v. Kreischer[17] the European Court repeated the dictum on the need to avoid the many fora in the de Bloos case. After having refused to rely solely on the performance of the obligation which characterizes the contract, as the Court had done in Invenel v. Schwab[18] in respect of an employment contract and which in certain cases may create uncertainty, the Court said:

> "On the other hand no such uncertainty exists for most contracts if regard is had solely to the contractual obligation whose performance is sought in the judicial proceedings. The place in which that obligation is to be performed usually constitutes the closest connecting factor between the dispute and the court having jurisdiction over it; it is the connecting factor which explains why, in contractual matters it is the court of the place of performance of the obligation which has jurisdiction. Admittedly, the above rule does not afford a solution in the particular case of a dispute concerned with a number of obligations arising under the same contract and forming the basis of the proceedings commenced by the plaintiff. However, in such a case the court before which the matter is brought will, when determing whether it has jurisdiction be guided by the maxim *accessorium sequitur principale*, in other words, where various obligations are at issue, it will be the principal obligation which will determine its jurisdiction"...

The message seems to be clear: In order to avoid the plaintiff's being able to rely on a multiplicity of fora under art 5 no 1 of the Convention, the Court will base jurisdiction only on the principal obligation of each party as the obligation in question and will disregard accessory duties.[19]

The rule that the principal obligation is the obligation in question should apply generally. It should govern not only when the plaintiff charges the defendant with having violated both a principal and an accessory obligation, but also when the plaintiff accuses the defendant of having violated one or more accessory duties which are in-

---

[17] [1987] E.C.R. 239.

[18] [1982] E.C.R. 1891, 1900.

[19] See also Kropholler op cit note 5 p 89 (note 9).

cidental to his own duty to perform his principal obligation. If such accessory obligations were to be considered the obligation in question, art 5 no 1 could create a multitude of fora which has, as we have seen, not been the policy of the Court of Justice.

It must also follow from the structure of art 5 no 1 that the obligation in question is the principal obligation. Art 5 no 1 second sentence provides that any obligation arising out of an employment contract is to be performed where the employee habitually carries out his work in any one country. This also applies when the defendant has violated an accessory duty. If, for instance, an employee who carries out his work in England was employed after negotiations in a Nordic country where he told lies about his qualifications and if, for that reason, the employer wants to sue him for damages, the employer can not do so in the Nordic country on the ground that the duty of the employee to tell the truth was to be performed there. The place of performance will remain the place where the employee performs his principal obligation to work. Art 5 no 1 second sentence on employment contracts is different from the first sentence dealing with all other contracts only in that instead of two principal obligations, the employee's duty to work and the employer's duty to pay him for his work, the obligation in question is reduced to one – the employee's performance of work. From this it must follow that each party's obligation under the first sentence must refer to his principal obligation and not to an accessory duty to give correct information. As repeatedly stated by the European Court, the obligation in question can only be the principal obligation of each party. In the Retrocession Case the obligation in question was for the plaintiff to cover the risks under the reinsurance contracts, a duty from which he sought to be relieved.

It is therefore submitted that it was the plaintiff's obligation to provide coverage for the risks assumed, which was the obligation in question, and that it was the place of performance of this obligation which was the foundation of jurisdiction under art 5 no 1 of the Lugano Convention. It was this obligation from which the plaintiff sought relief so that he would not have to pay further sums to the defendant and so that he could recover the sums already paid. The obligation in question remained the same whether it was the reinsured party who would claim the sums insured or the re-insurer who sought a declaration to the effect that he did not owe further amounts under the contracts and who claimed back the sums already paid.

Finally, the plaintiff contended that the place of performance of the obligation in question was in his home country.

As was laid down by the Court of Justice in several cases, the place of performance of the obligation in question is to be determined by the national court seized with the matter. It is for this court to determine, in accordance with its own choice of law rules, which law is applicable to the contract and to have that law define the place of performance. If, in the present case, the Court had found that it was the law of the forum which was applicable to the contracts, that law would determine the place of performance; if it came to the conclusion that English law governed the contract, English law would determine the place of performance. However, in this case, both English and Nordic law came to the same conclusion.

If, as the defendant alleged, the obligation in question was the plaintiff's duty to cover the risks, the place of performance of this money obligation would be the same regardless of whether the law of England or the law of a Nordic country governed the contract.

Under English law, unless otherwise agreed by the parties, money debts in contract are to be paid at the creditor's place of business, which in this case was London.[20]

Nothing in the case indicated that the parties agreed that the payment of the sums insured was to be made at the plaintiff's domicile. Therefore, if English law was applicable to the obligation in question, the Nordic Court would not have jurisdiction under art 5 no 1 of the Lugano Convention.

If the Court had found that its own law was applicable to the contract, it was for that law to determine the place of performance. Under the Uniform Nordic Instrument of Debts Act, the performance of a money debt is to be made at the creditor's place of business. Under this provision, the result would have been the same as if

---

[20] See Treitel, *The Law of Contract*, 9th ed. London 1995, p. 669 and Chitty on Contracts 27th ed. vol 1, London, 1994, p. 21.043.

English law was applied and the Court would not have jurisdiction under art 5 no 1 of the Lugano Convention.

The plaintiff finally realized that the action was hopeless and gave it up. The case, however, shows that in order to be first a party is willing to bring an action even with small chances of success.

6. Conclusions

We have seen four examples of the rush to the courts which the lis pendens rules of the Convention have brought about. This, it is submitted, may have unhappy consequences. It encourages both parties to try to be first in court instead of trying to reach a settlement before proceedings are started. The rush increases costs for the parties and the number of actions in the courts of Europe.

To restrict the use of actions seeking negative declarations or similar actions to avert claims, rules may be considered which limit their application. We know that actions for negative declarations are viewed with suspicion by the English courts.[21] The Community is already considering taking action to harmonize national rules of civil procedure.[22] To limit the right to obtain declaratory judgments should perhaps be considered.

The Greek Case and the Retrocession Case show that actions for declaratory judgments may be abused and that the law in its present state does not provide sufficient guarantees against such abuse. Here, the Community system could be set to prevent such situations from arising. The court second seized should be allowed to disregard proceedings before the court first seized if the action brought there is an abuse of the Convention.[23] The concept of an abuse of a right is known in French law[24] and in some other EU laws.

---

[21] See Dicey & Morris 406 f and cases there cited. On Danish law see Gomard's *Civilprocessen*, 3 ed., 1990, 264 ff.

[22] See "Rapprochement du droit judiciaire de l'Union éuropénne, Approximation of judiciary law in the European Union", Storme, M. (ed) Dordrecht, 1994.

[23] The ruling of the European Court in Overseas Union Insurance Co. v. New Hampshire Insurance, 1991, ECR I-3317 will prevent national courts from doing that.

[24] See Ghestin & Goubeaux, *Traité de droit civil* vol 1, Paris, 1983, 612 ff.

However, to permit a national court to enjoin a party from continuing proceedings before another national court in the network, as the English Court of Appeal did in the Greek case, is, it is submitted, not compatible with the Convention.

SWEDISH SNUS CONFRONTS BASIC EU PRINCIPLES

Hans Henrik Lidgard*

1. Federation or . . .

In his first book about the European Community – which became the standard in Swedish legal education on European law – "Celebrator" speculated whether the collaboration in Europe should be characterized as a "federation" or something else. I have always recalled that Lennart Pålsson preferred to use at most the words "a pre-federative organization".[1]

In spite of all the learned opinions in the book, it is still these initial remarks that have followed me throughout the years. One must still ask: What is the proper characterization of the European collaboration, has it changed over time and where is it heading in the future.

As is well known, the member states have approached this discussion with the utmost concern to avoid using the "F-word" in official texts. Countries in favour of integration and a deepening of the collaboration would indeed not oppose it.

---

* The author presented his academic dissertation on "Sweden, EEC and Competition" in 1977 under the supervision of professor Lennart Pålsson. Special gratitude is conveyed to Kanslirådet Ninna Rösiö, another research fellow tutored by Lennart Pålsson, for support with material and advice to this paper. The paper was completed in July 1995.

[1] My memory has served me right. See L. Pålsson, *EEC-Rätt*, 1970, p. 22. "I de fall där de supranationella momenten är tillräckligt starkt utvecklade, talar man inte längre om en internationell organisation utan om en *federal statsbildning* (exempel Canada, Schweiz, USA). Det finns de som velat karakterisera EEC som en sådan federation. Detta är dock åtminstone på nuvarande utvecklingsstadium en betydande överdrift. På sin höjd skulle man – beroende på den framtida utvecklingen – kunna tala om en 'prefederal' organisation."

Others suggest, with a typical "de Gaulle ring" to it, that Community collaboration is a collaboration between free and independent states. They prefer to characterise the collaboration as an economic community or a union. The problem is that such notions do not give a definite and clear picture of the content of the collaboration or what can be expected in the future. Each interpreter adds his personal note to the definition and only the future will tell where it all ends.

The Treaty on European Union signed in Maastricht on February 7, 1992 ("TEU" or the "Maastricht Treaty")[2] did not eliminate the uncertainties, but rather added on new ones. "We have ... a union without real unity, a building half-built with an institutional 'géométrie variable' and a 'rendez-vous' in 1996 to try to improve on what was achieved in Maastricht."[3]

The loopholes in the Maastricht Treaty necessitate further discussions, as predicted at the time of the signing of the Maastricht Treaty. A new conference was called for within five years to undertake the requisite supplementation to the legislation.[4] Today the member states are at a preparatory stage for this Intergovernmental Conference 1996 ("IGC 1996"), where the first task is to define which of the many open issues shall be the subject of priority. Many are called for, but only few can be chosen if the conference shall have any chance of success. The "F-question" will – perhaps without being discussed as such – underlie those issues which are to be debated.

It is not going to be easy to find detailed solutions to many open items without a basic agreement on the characterization of the European collaboration. One escape route that worked at Maastricht in 1992 and which many function again is the "subsidiarity principle".

---

[2] The use of abbreviations is a constant problem. EEC, EC and now EU have been used at different times to describe the Community collaboration. This paper uses the notions and abbreviations established in 1993: European Union (EU), Treaty on European Union (TEU), Treaty establishing the European Community (ECT), European Council, Council (of the European Union), (European) Commission, European Parliament (EP), European Court of Justice (EJC) etc., unless the text would be misleading by such use.

[3] E.P. Wellenstein, "Unity, Community, Union – what's in a name?", Guest-editorial, *Common Market Law Review*, (1992), p. 209.

[4] Article N(2) TEU referes to those provisions of the Treaty for which revision is provided. Article 3b ECT on subsidiary is not included – which will not prevent that this provision will be part of the IGC 1996 discussion.

It becomes easier to transfer competence to the central level if the member states believe that it is not an exclusive, but rather a shared competence and that they retain ultimate control.[5]

Subsidiarity was one important issue in the snuff discussion within the Community during the first years of the 90s. The purpose was to allow Swedes to continue their age-old habit of putting moist tobacco under the upper lip.[6] The snuff debate touched upon Community concepts which will again be of relevance in the IGC 1996. The legality, subsidiarity and proportionality principles were all referred to. When the matter resurfaced during the accession negotiations, a compromise solution was found which led to a new form of restrictions on the free movement of goods. The snuff case was also of interest as an experience in approaching community authorities – a lobbying practice[7] that Swedes must be familiar with.

The purpose of this paper is to present the snuff discussion as it took place and especially as it relates to the subsidiarity concept and then to attempt conclusions relevant for IGC 1996.

2. Moist snuff

2.1 A barbarian Swedish habit

Swedes know "snus" as a "fine-cut", non-fermented tobacco with a 50 % water content. The product, whether in loose form or portion packed in small paper bags, is put under the upper lip – thereby

---

[5] See for an overall Swedish analyses SOU 1994:12, "Suveränitet och demokrati", *Betänkande av EG-konsekvensutredningarna: Subsidiaritet* which is an official Swedish Royal Commission for investigating and reporting on how sovereignity and democracy in Sweden are affected by a membership in the European Union. Lennart Pålsson was one member of the Royal Commission. See also P. Cramér, "Noteringar rörande subsidiaritetsprincipens tillämpning i framtidens EG/EU", *Svensk Juristtidning* (1973) pp. 533–547.

[6] Responsible for the lobbying efforts were Stefan Gelkner, president of Gotia Tobacco and Roland Perlström, vice president Swedish Match.

[7] The word "lobbying/lobbyist" has been regarded as a new and unknown feature in Sweden – involving networking and greasing the palms of contacts. More correct is probably to define the lobbyist as a representative or an "ombudsman" as the word is commonly used in the Swedish language. His/her knowledge about Community procedures is vital; the net work is important but paramount is the interest he is representing and the strength of the opinion advocated. The authorities are presently preparing rules of conduct which shall govern the relationship between community officials and lobbyists.

allowing the active nicotine substance to penetrate the mucus membrane.

In Europe Swedes are almost unique in their snuffing habit. Our Nordic neighbours have adopted the custom to a limited extent and a minuscule amount of snuffers exist in Germany. The Germans rather use "Kau-Tabak" which has the curious instruction on the package: "Nicht zum kauen". Kau-Tabak is also granulated tobacco compressed into small pieces which when placed on the tongue release the nicotine buccaly. In addition, North Africans living in France snuff – a habit that they have brought from their home region. Their product, which is produced in Belgium, differs from the Swedish. Otherwise Europeans more elegantly "sniff" a dry powder form of tobacco through the nose.

Snuffing also occurs outside Europe in certain disparate countries and it is interesting that no logic can easily explain how the habit has developed and spread. Some US states have adopted the snuff habit with products like Red Man, Skoal Bandits and Copenhagen (as if this most Swedish habit emanated in Denmark). The products are all similar to Swedish "snus", but differ in that the tobacco has been fermented. To underscore the difference, the snuffing American will put his snuff under the lower lip. A special form of snuffing – "snuff-dipping" – has spread among women in the Southern states. A moistened stick is dipped in the snuff and thereafter massaged between the teeth and the gum and the nicotine is thereby introduced into the bloodstream.

Oral snuffing is also widespread in countries like India, Pakistan and in certain African countries. Oddly, Sudan has a per capita snuff consumption that is as high as Sweden's.

The snuffing habit is approximately 150 years old in Sweden. Initially it started among the working population – fishermen and foresters – but gradually it has spread to society at large. One reason is that snuffing has been regarded as a less harmful alternative to smoking. Almost 20 % of the grown male population in Sweden occasionally snuff. Surprisingly 2 % of the female population also more or less regularly use portion packed snuff.

It has been discussed whether snuffing is an introduction to the habit of smoking for young people. If the answer is "yes", statistics show that Swedish youth smoke proportionally less than youth in other countries. The assumption is therefore that if the young Swedes had not started snuffing they would have smoked instead.

2.2 Snuff becomes a European matter

Europeans consume approximately 6,000 tons of snuff each year. The small eight million Swedish population uses 5,300 of the 6,000 tons and 370 million other Europeans the remaining 10%. The figures verify that the consumption of oral moist snuff is primarily a Swedish habit.

As stated, snuffing is also widespread in certain US states and the total American consumption is larger than the European. One leading US producer decided in the mid 80s to increase its efforts to export American fermented snuff to the unexploited European continent. The company obtained permission and UK government support to establish a snuff factory in Scotland. In parallell it initiated marketing of its products in a number of European countries with efficient American marketing concepts primarily directed towards young people. It intended to build a long-term market by creating a habit among the young.

United Kingdom, Ireland and Belgium responded to the American marketing methods by prohibiting the product in their respective markets. The legal enactments were all appealed by the producing industry. An Irish court upheld the prohibition arguing that the prohibited product had side effects detrimental to health.[8] The UK court – based on equitable grounds – set the administrative decision aside. The product was considered harmful, but authorities could not allow the establishment of a production unit while prohibiting the

---

[8] The Irish legislation banning oral smokeless tobacco products was contained in the Tobacco (Health Promotion and Protection) Act 1988 S.I. No. 39 of 1990. Section 6 stipulates that: "(1) Any person who imports, manufactures, sells or otherwise disposes of, or offers for sale or other disposal, or advertises, an oral smokeless tobacco product shall be guilty of an offence..." The High Court in case 1990 No. 871p between United States Tobacco (Ireland) Limited and United States Tobacco International Inc (plaintiffs) and Ireland, Minister for Health and Attorney General (defendants) upheld the legislation. Judgment of Mr. Justice Blayney delivered the 19th day of February 1991.

sale of the resulting product.[9] In Belgium the matter was appealed through the ordinary system, but due to a dragged-out procedure no judgment was issued before the matter was raised on the European level and therefore withdrawn by the applicant.[10]

3. The initial European process

3.1 The Commission initiates activities

In 1989, during the national appeal procedures, the European Commission initiated a separate investigation. Intervention became necessary because the same product was now allowed in certain member states and prohibited in others. The overriding principle of free movement of goods in Europe required a consistent treatment of the product throughout the Community.

Within the Commission, the task force "Europe against Cancer" was appointed to handle the snuff issue. In combating cancer, the task force had made the struggle against tobacco one of its main priorities. Having assigned the task force the matter meant that health issues were an important factor in the future discussion, whether this was a Community competence or not. Concern for free trade became a secondary issue.[11]

During an initial 10 month period the Commission invited interested parties to submit their observations, among them representatives from the Swedish tobacco industry. Unfortunately, the Swedes were not fully aware of how important their first contact with the Commission was. They made their observation and left Brussels

---

[9] The English legislation is contained in Oral Snuff (Safety) Regulations 1989 (SI 1989 No. 2347). The legislation was set aside by Decision of 21.12.1990: Secretary of State for Health – ex parte United States Tobacco International Inc. – Lord Justice Taylor – Queens Bench division [1991] 3 WLR 529.

[10] The appealed Belgian legislation – l'Arrêté Royal du 13/8/90 – stipulated in Article 2, § 2b): "Il est interdit de mettre dans le commerce le tabac à sucer en sachets destiné à être mis dans la bouche tel quels." The matter was referred to the Conseil d'Etat, matter G/A 43927/III/12037, but withdrawn in view of the up-coming European process which would impact on the Belgian legislation as well.

[11] The secondary interest for the rules on free movement is demonstrated by the ultimate solution, described in Section 5.2 below. Therefore, the European oral tobacco market is today as fragmented as before the Commission initiated its initiative – if not more.

with the impression that their arguments had some impact. In retrospect the Swedish case would have been better served if complete scientific argumentation had been presented at this stage. Once the institutional bodies have made their assessment it becomes difficult – on the verge of impossible – to introduce additional evidence which could tip the balance in favour of a different decision.

In November 1990 the Commission had completed its investigations and prepared a draft Directive prohibiting the release on the market of oral moist snuff tobaccos.[12] The Directive was based on Article 100a ECT and not Article 235 ECT. A reason was that the Commission expected opposition from at least one member state to its different tobacco initiatives.[13] The use of Article 100a ECT was questioned by EP Legal Committee as not satistfying the legality principle but never really challenged. Following Community procedures, the draft was next submitted to the Council.

The definition of the prohibited product under thist first proposal was crucial.[14] It covered the marketing and sale of tobacco in powder

---

[12] Proposal for a Council Directive amending directive 89/622 on the approximation on the laws, regulations and administrative provisions of the Member States concerning the labelling of tobacco products. COM (90), Brussels, 12 November 1990.

[13] See H. Rasmussen, *EU-ret og EU-institutioner i kontekst*, 1994 pp. 48. Rasmussen suggests that the Commission is deliberately manipulating the legal basis in order to achieve political results (p. 50). EJC has always supported the Commission if there has been a reference to a legal objective even if the true underlying reason came outside the competence of the Community. Note, however, case C 155/91, *E.C. Commission v. E.C. Council*, [1993] 1ECR, 939 at para. 10 and 14–15 where the Court helt that an environment measure fell under the specific environmental rules and did not come under the rules of free movement of goods. This judgment was followed in case C 187/93, *European Parliament v. E.U. Council*, [1995] CMLR volume 73(7) p. 309 where ECJ held at para. 25 that "the mere fact that the establishment or functioning of the internal market is involved is not enough to render Article 100A of the Treaty applicable and recourse to that article is not justified where the act to be adopted has only the ancillary effect of harmonising market conditions within the Community."

[14] The original Council Directive 89/622/EEC, OJ No. L 359, 8.12.1989 on the approximation of the laws, regulations and administrative provisions of the Member States concerning the labelling of tobacco products – defines "tobacco products" as "products for the purpose of smoking, sniffing, sucking or chewing in as much as they are, even partlyl, made of tobacco."

The Commission Proposal op.cit. (*note 11*) added the following definition: "(4) "oral moist snuff tobaccos" means all products made wholly or partly of moistened tobaccos in fine cut, ground or particular form or in any combination of these two forms which are for oral use other than smoking.

or particular form for oral consumption to which water had been added and it had been carefully designed not to affect any form of non-smoking tobacco already existing in the Community. Dry snuff for nasal consumption as well as German "Kau-Tabak" and chewing tobacco escaped the prohibition. The difference was not the tobacco form, but rather its water content – even if water as such has never been alleged to have a detrimental effect on human health!

The proposal was one of the few instances where a prohibition has not covered the harmful substance, but one special form of it – the moist powder form. Throughout the process it has therefore been argued that the Commission's approach was an unlawful discrimination between one product and another essentially similar one in breach of the principle of non-discrimination. Such discrimination could only be accepted if the authorities had proven that the prohibited form was more harmful.[15]

As a factual basis for its proposal, the Commission relied on certain scientific studies made in USA and India which suggested that oral, moist snuff indeed caused mouth cancer. The preamble of Directive 92/41 states ". . . in accordance with the conclusions of the studies conducted by the International Agency for Research on Cancer, tobacco for oral use contains particularly large quantities of carcinogenic substances; whereas these new products cause cancer of the mouth in particular."

The Swedish snuff industry argued that these studies were of limited relevance as they related to different products having different mode of actions. No conclusive long term study had been made on Swedish products. On the contrary, scientific work performed in Sweden rather suggested that the eventual harm caused by Swedish "snus" could be reversed once the habit was abandoned. A persuasive argument by the industry was that, considering the large proportion of Swedish snuffers, it could be expected that Sweden would have a far higher incidence of oral cancer than any other country. In

---

[15] The principle of equality or non-discrimination requires that similar situations should not be treated differently unless the differentiation is objectively justified. In case 13/63, *Italy v. Commission*, (1963) ECR 177 ECJ observed in para. 4 that "Material discrimination would consist in treating either similar situations differently or different situations identically."

reality, however, Sweden has the lowest rate of oral cancer per capita in Europe. 150 years of widespread consumption had not had any impact on the health of the Swedish population. Not only had the Commission not carried its burden of proof, evidence even lay against the Commission.

3.2 Lobbying the European Parliament

During an almost two-year period the snuff matter went back and forth between the institutions in the Community according to the then existing decision-making process. Although oral snuff had no great significance in the Community, the debate was considerable.

In the European Parliament ("EP"), The Environmental Committee under its rapporteur Vernier and the Legal Committee advised by its rapporteur Lord Inglewood produced two different opinions. The Environmental Committee agreed without reservations with the Commission and argued in favour of a prohibition. The Legal Committee was not convinced that the Community had the legal competence (see below) to deal with snuff matters and stalled its decision.

During the parliamentary process lobbyists approached parliamentarians and, though the Swedish representatives came from a non-member country and advocated in favour of a tobacco product, they were well received. Evidence and arguments were presented in "big brown envelopes" as the Swedes were out solidly to prove their case. The question is, however, whether this massive scientific information was not counterproductive. Members of the European Parliament (MEPs) have a hectic agenda and are unlikely to study large dossiers regarding such a remote issue as oral snuff.

The personal and oral approach also applied was far more successful. It is the experience of most lobbyists that MEPs are quite receptive to short, condensed oral presentations of facts and arguments that show other aspects than those in favour of a proposal. Lacking this additional view, the MEPs would have to rely on information produced by the Commission, which is perhaps not always complete and free from bias.

3.3 The legal arguments

As indicated, the snuff lobbyists argued that the Directive was a discrimination against snuff over other tobacco products and also advocated against the Commission's evaluation of the impact on health. No suggestion was made that the Swedish product was healthy, but rather that the Commission had failed to prove that snuff was harmful and especially more harmful than any other tobacco product. The more forceful arguments pleaded were that several fundamental Community concepts were infringed by the proposed Directive:

1. The "Legality Principle"[16] was – as indicted by the hesitation of the EP Legal Committe – not satisfied. The snuff prohibition was in reality based on health concerns that were then not a part of its competence.[17]

2. The "Subsidiarity Principle"[18] was also infringed as the matter was not an exclusive EC competence and it was not established

---

[16] The legality principle has been recognized as a fundamental principle of Community law and Article 3b ECT now confirms this principle by providing that "The Community shall act within the limits of the powers conferred upon it by this Treaty and of the objectives assigned to it therein."

[17] Article 129 ECT as amended by the Maastricht Treaty now stipulates that "The Community shall contribute towards ensuring a high level of human health protection by encouraging cooperation between the Member States and, if necessary, lending support to their action. . . . Health protection requirements shall form a constituent part of the Community's other policies." It is questionable if even this stipulation could give EU competence to enact a snuff prohibition. In fact, Article 129 ECT is a good expression of the subsidiary principle in the sense that legislation shall primarily be undertaken at state level and the Community shall support such actions.

[18] The subsidiarity principle can be referred back to Thomas Aquinas. It has especially been adopted and discussed by the Catholic church. See L.F. Eklund, "Subsidiaritets-principen dess bakgrund och innebörd", *Expertrapport till SOU 1954:12, Suveränitet och demokrati*. It has its equivalence in different federal constitutions. In the Constitution of the United States of America, Amendment X it is stipulated that: "The powers not delegated to the United States by the Constitution, nor prohibited by it to the States, are reserved to the States respectively; or to the people." This is a stipulation seldom referred to in court proceedings. Of greater interest is the definition of congressional powers in Article I, Section 8, which when read together with Section 10 actually contains a division of powers between federal and state level in the form of detailed listing. A detailed listings has been inserted in the German constitution. See below (*note 56*). In spite of all the years of federal experience the underlying idea of a balance of power between central and local authority remains un-precise.

that it coulg not be handled on a national level just as efficiently as on the Community level (see below).[19]

3. Finally, the "Proportionality Principle"[20] was disregarded. It would have been more adequate and less burdensome for the interested parties if snuff was allowed but made subject to the relevant restrictions on marketing and sale used for general tobacco products: i.e. restrictions on sale to younger persons, on advertising and perhaps coupled with gradual reduction of alleged harmful substances like nitrosamines.

The remarks made were indeed timely as they just preceded the Maastricht treaty. In fact, Article 3b ECT now contains direct references to the three principles referred to.

The legality and proportionality principles are well known in Community law whereas the reference to the subsidiarity principle was a more novel approach.

The underlying idea was simpel: The habit of snuffing is primarily practised in Sweden. Therefore, let the Swedes handle the matter as Swedish authorities are fully competent to take the required precautions and so is any other member country affected by the habit. Nothing would prevent these countries from taking adequate measures required to protect the health and well-being of their citi-

---

[19] Compare Rasmussen, op. cit. (*note 12*) P. 48, who argues that the proposed parallel prohibition on Tobacco Advertising – proposed directive (Com (92) 196 Final). Brussels 30/4 1992 – infringed the subsidiarity principle – especially in view of the prohibition on harmonization in Article 129:4.

[20] Case C-331/88 *The Queens v. Minister of Agriculture, Fisheries and Food and the Secretary of State for Health, ex parte FEDESA and others ("Hormones")* CMLR 1991 p. 407 at para. 13: "The Court has consistently held that the principle of proportionality is one of the general principles of Community law. By virtue of that principle, the lawfulness of the prohibition of an economic activity is subject to the condition that the prohibitory measures are appropriate and necessary in order to achieve the objectives legitimately pursued by the legislation in question; when there is a choice between several appropriate measures recourse must be had to the least onerous, and the disadvantages caused must not be disproportionate to the aims pursued." The proportionality principle is now recognized by Article 3b: "Any action by the Community shall not go beyond what is necessary to achieve the objectives of this Treaty."

zens.[21] There was no need for an intervention by the Community which should rather confine itself to supporting the member states in their efforts.

The arguments were made in spite of the fact that Sweden was still not a member of the Union, but relying on the 1972 Free Trade Agreement between Sweden and the EEC and subsequently the European Economic Area agreement (EEA). This latter agreement should have the same legal consequences as Community law. A prohibition of the product in the Union would promptly have to be extended to the EEA in the form of an EEA directive and subsequent national implementation. Therefore the same principles should apply in the interpretation of the EEA agreement as would apply in Community law.

The subsidiarity argument was not evident and several commentators deny that such a concept existed at so early a stage in the Community development.[22] Arguments in favour of a prior existence underline that the preamble of the treaty of Rome refers to an ever closer union. Through Article 235 ECT the possibility of adding new areas of competence is included in order to achieve objectives foreseen by the Treaty. Likewise, the use of directives foreseen in Article 189 ECT could also be seen as an expression of the subsidiarity idea.

On each point it could, however, be argued that they rather speak in the opposite direction and that the basic concept of the ECT is that of transfer of defined areas of competence from the member states to the Community institutions. In recent times it has been necessary to adopt a more flexible approach in order to achieve political consensus on adding new competencies to the Community. With the Single European Act ("SEA") in 1987 the subsidiarity concept was intro-

---

[21] Case 120/78 *Rewe-Zentral AG v. Bundesmonopolverwaltung für Branntwein (Casis de Dijon)* CMLR 1979 p. 494. See the recently published dissertation by C.M. Quitzow, *Fria varurörelser i den Europeiska gemenskapen. En studie av gränsdragningen mellan gemenskapsangelägenheter och nationella angelägenheter*, 1995, pp. 295–330.

[22] D.Z. Cass, "The word that saves Maastricth? The principle of subsidiarity and the division of powers within the European Community", *Common Market Law Review* 29 (1992), pp. 1107–1136 explains the gradual development of the subsidiarity concept in Community law. A.G. Toth, "The Principle of Subsidiarity in the Maastricht Treaty", *Common Market Law Review* 29 (1992), pp. 1079–1105, especially at p. 1081 opposes the prior existence.

duced in relation to the environment with an express reference. Such a clause would not have been necessary if subsidiarity already was a fundamental principle in Community law.[23]

4. The decision making process

4.1 Parliament votes in the first reading

Lobbyists referring to both health arguments and underlying Community concepts and the Legal Committee hesitation had some impact on the decision-making in Parliament, but it was not enough. In the end the proposed directive carried in July 1991 with a small 19 vote majority in the first reading.[24]

In parallel the Economic and Social Committee ("ECOSOC") dealt with the Commission proposal. As the opinion of this institution carries less weight in the community decision making process, the Swedes did not actively lobby it. At about the same time as the decision in Parliament the committee eventually arrived at a recommendation following the proposal of the Commission. ECOSOC added that portion packed snuff especially should be prohibited.[25]

4.2 Council adopts a Common Position

As the next step in the Community decision making process the Council, based on the advice from Parliament and ECOSOC had to adopt its "common position" – which should be subject of a second reading in the Parliament before finally adopted by the Council. Lobbying activities towards the Council and the member states were, of course, crucial.

At this time the Swedish Parliament had instructed its government

---

[23] Article 130r(4) ECT provided that: "The Community shall take action relating to the environment to the extent to which the objectives referred to in paragraph 1 can be attained better at Community level than at the level of the individual Member States."

[24] The Parliament gave its opinion on 8 July 1991, OJ No C 240, 16.9.1991 p. 24.

[25] The Economic and Social Committee gave its opinion on 29 May 1991, OJ No C 191, 22.7.1991 p. 37. The proposed prohibition of portion-packed snuff has been inserted in directive 92/41/EEC in spite of the fact that it is not clear why a product which is already prohibited by the directive shall be "especially prohibited".

to support any snuff-defending activities.[26] Snuff thereby became a national Swedish concern and the lobbyists received official Swedish support in accessing important decision-makers. Even if it is not easy for diplomats to argue in favour of a tobacco product, the minister responsible for European matters – Mr. Dinkelspiel – and the diplomatic corps did so in line with their instructions.

COREPER was approached, but also member states siding against the proposal. For reasons of constitutionality Germany opposed the snuff-prohibition. Similarly Italy would vote against a prohibition – but for different and perhaps not so obvious reasons. All that was required was a no-vote from one additional country – large or small – to create a blocking minority and thereby prevent the Council from adopting its common position.

United Kingdom, which under ordinary circumstances would be a safe opponent to Community tobacco legislation and a supporter of subsidiarity, had an active anti-snuff position. It was therefore not prepared to vote against the Directive. Denmark – where moist snuff is both produced and used – also seemed a likely no-voter. Denmark was, however, defending its cigarette producing industry and not prepared to dilute its efforts in favour of snuff. Holland, finally, had been ambivalent towards a prohibition, but now held the presidency of the Council which led it to a more Community-oriented approach.

The "common position"[27] – which was adopted in November 1991 – contained several amendments: The original definition had been altered, but still achieved the same purpose as in the initial Commission proposal. The particular prohibition for portion packed snuff suggested by the Economic and Social Committee was included in the definition in spite of its lack of logic and in the preamble of the Directive it was now clarified that "traditional products" were ex-

---

[26] Parliamentary Standing Committee on Industry and Commerce 1990/91: NU 47 suggested that the EU proposal amounted to a restriction of trade. In addition a prohibition would infringe the liberty of the tenth of the Swedish population which comprises the country's snuff consumers. See Svenska Dagbladet 10/4 1994 "Näringsutskottet vill rädda snuset".

[27] Position Commune arretée par le Conseil le 11.11.1991 en vue de l'adoption de la directive modifiant la direcitve 89/622/CEE. Doc 8657/91.

empted.[28] For a brief period this latter passage was interpreted to mean that also Swedish snuff would come under the exemption. Commission officials clarified – in keeping with accepted Community law principles[29] – that this exemption would only apply to traditions EU products. Such products would have come outside the operative definition of the Directive anyway as it had been carefully designed not to cover any product within the Community.

4.3 The second reading in Parliament

With the new procedural rules under the Maastricht agreement, Parliament could either oppose the common position or amend it by a qualified majority of all MEPs. It was regarded as highly unlikely that 260 members would come out against proposed legislation taking a negative approach to a tobacco product which was neither produced nor consumed in the Union. This certainly "was not a hill to die for".

Undiscouraged by the impossible mission and more experienced this time, the Swedish lobbyists changed their tactics compared to the first reading. No "thick brown envelopes" or complicated arguments regarding discrimination, health and Community concepts. Lobbying activities were concentrated on group leaders and key parliamentarians. Support from political forces in Sweden was also strong. The distributed information was clear and above all simple – contained in

---

[28] The preamble of the Commission amended proposal, COM (91) final – SYN 314, Brussels, 188 September 1991 stipulates for the first time in the end: "Whereas, the sales bans on such tobacco already adopted by three Member States have a direct impact on the establishment and operation of the internal market; whereas it is therefore necessary to approximate Member States' laws in this area taking as a base a high level of health protection; whereas the only appropriate measure is a total ban; whereas however, *such a ban should not affect traditional tobacco products for oral use* (emphasis added) which will remain subject to the provisions of Directive 89/622/EEC as amended by this directive applicable to smokeless tobacco products;" This statement in the preamble was adopted by the Council common position (see below).

[29] The fact that the exemption for traditional products appears only in the preamble is significant. The ECJ made clear in case 215/88 *Casa Fleischhandel v. BALM*, (1989) ECR 2808 at para. 31 that: "whilst a recital in the preamble to a regulation may cast light on the interpretation to be given to a legal rule, it cannot in itself constitute such a rule." Accordingly the reference to traditional products is only valid as to those products which do not come under the operative provisions of the directive. It is no more than an explanation. It cannot be used to create derogations from what is otherwise prohibited.

1-page "flyers". Personal contacts with as many MEPs as possible were added on top of the strategic contacts.

At this stage of the debate it had become obvious that Swedish public opinion was much affected by the EU approach to a product which quickly became identified with the Swedish national character. Was the prohibition of that products what the Union was all about?

It would be difficult to secure a Swedish "yes" to EU membership if no sensible solution to the snuff issue was found. For those MEPs who favoured an enlargement of the Union this was indeed an important argument. In addition several parliamentarians now saw the snuff-legislation as a good example of when the new subsidiarity principle should be applied.

Based on the discussion, the Swedish industry representatives drafted an amendment to the proposed Directive which would exempt traditional "European" (in a wider sense) products from the prohibition.[30] In the end only products produced in other parts of the world would come under the prohibition – which was not a concern of the Swedish producers. The draft amendment was endorsed and signed by more than 60 MEPs.

In the parliamentary debate which followed, Mr. Tom Spencer, leading British conservative and a strong advocate of Swedish membership in the Union, urged the Commission to accept the amendment.[31] Commissioner Ripa Di Meana riposted that it would not be necessary as Swedish "snus" came under the exception for tradition-

---

[30] The proposed amendment contained the following text: "Tobacco for oral use, for the purpose of Article 8a, means all products for oral use *which are not of a traditional European type*, made wholly or partly of tobacco, in powder or particulate form or in a form resembling a *confectionary* products."

[31] See European Parliament minutes from debate 10.3.92 p. 71. Mr. Spencer said that "At the moment there is a reference in the revised Common Position [to traditional products] which might make things easier. But at the moment it is only in the recitals. It is not in the operational parts of the Directive. It is my concern and that of many friends in Sweden that this matter should made absolutely clear. . . . The Swedes have the lowest rate of oral cancer in Europe. In fact the highest rates of oral cancer, as far as we can tell, appear to be connected with Calvados drinking. That is a figure given us by the Belgian cancer authorities."

al products.[32] Mr. Spencer then suggested that the reference to traditional products should be included in the operative text of the directive which the Commissioner did not think necessary as the explicit recital should be sufficient to achieve an exception for Swedish "snus".

Again, lobbying seemed to work – but by a small margin the final vote in March 1992 turned out against the proposed amendment. Out of the required 260 votes, 240 voted in favour of the amendment, 46 voted no and yet another 8 abstained.[33] However, considering the views expressed by the Commissioner it appeared as if Swedish "snus" would according to the view of the Commission come under the exception for traditional products.

4.4 The Directive enacted

The voting result in the Parliament indicated that the MEPs were strongly in favour of exempting Swedish snuff, but an overwhelming majority of those voting was not enought at this stage of the Community decision making process. The qualified majority rule required 260 if favour – no less. Shortly after the vote in Parliament, the Council therefore enacted the final directive.[34]

Directive 992/41 defines in Article 1:2 the prohibited tobacco for oral use as:

> ". . . all products for oral use, except those intended to be smoked or chewed, made wholly or partly of tobacco, in powder or particulate form or in any combination of these forms – particularly those presented in sachet portions or porous sachets – or in a form resembling a food product."

---

[32] See above (*note 31*). The Commissioner said: "Taking the Swedish case as an example, I would like to say that the Directive will be applied as regards *ex novo* presentation of such products but that it will not apply to consumption of traditional products. In the opinion of the Commission, this point is already sufficiently clear in Clause 17 of the text of the proposed Directive."

[33] Parliament debate see OJ No. C 94, 13.4.1992.

[34] Council Directive 92/41/EEC OJ L 158/30 11.6.92, amending Directive 89/622/EEC on the approximation of the laws, regulations and administrative provisions of the Member States concerning the labelling of tobacco products, adopted by the Health Minister Council on May 15, 1992.

In spite of all the years of discussion and all the ink spilled on carving out a precise definition, the final wording leaves room for substantial discussion. Should the sentence be read as a prohibition on all products for oral use except the excluded ones that follow? That is clearly not the intention – but is it not what the defintion actually says? Furthermore, snuff is neither in "powder or particulate form" but "fine-cut". This word was contained in the original Commission proposal, but eventually deleted. Will this fact make the fine-cut Swedish "snus" escape the prohibition? The prohibition itself is related to the placing on the market of oral tobacco products as defined. What happens to the producer who markets the same product for "nasal consumption", but the consumer is using it orally? What is the real meaning of the exception for traditional products? How many years of how wide-spread use does it take for a product to be traditional?

This unclear provision should have been implemented in the different member states before 1 July 1992 – i.e. one and a half months after the decision was finally made by the Council and some two weeks after it was published in Official Journal. This, of course, did not happen. Step by step the individual countries have introduced legislation at their convenience and often with their own little twist to make up for the deficiencies in the Directive. The implementation phase is still in 1995 not completed to the entire satisfaction of the Commission.[35]

5. Subsidiarity and compromises – a part of a new EU flexibility

5.1 The Subsidiarity Concept develops

References to the subsidiarity principle during the second reading in Parliament were still somewhat hesitant due partly to the emphasis

---

[35] Denmark has made clear that it regards loose snuff as a traditional product which does accordingly not come under the ban. Germany has still not finalized its implementing legislation. Finland has prohibited snuff in accordance with the directive, but interestingly Åland is making use of its autonomous position and does not intend to prohibit snuff in any form.

put on Swedish membership in the Union, but also to the preliminary stage of the development of the principle – even if it had now been reduced to writing in the Maastricht Treaty. A clear interpretation could only be given by the ECJ and the Swedish tobacco industry prepared for legal proceedings promptly after the debate in Parliament had ended.

The first problem was to find a legal basis for bringing the matter to the Court, as member states were not likely to challenge the Directive. Any legal action would have to await not only the final adaptation of the Directive but also national implementation. Referral to the ECJ had to be arranged under an article 177–184 procedure.[36]

The Maastricht treaty which had been signed in February 1992 affected several of the areas which had been subject of the snuff debate. For one thing the Union had obtained a limited competence in health matters through the inclusion of Article 129 ECT. Furthermore, the discussion regarding the widening of Community competencies was balanced by a stipulation in Article 3b ECT dealing with subsidiarity:[37]

> "In areas which do not fall within its exclusive competence, the Community shall take action, in accordance with the principle of subsidiarity, only if and in so far as the objectives of the proposed action cannot be sufficiently achieved by the Member States and can therefore, by reason of the scale or effects of the proposed action, be better achieved by the Community."

It has been argued that subsidiarity in Community law is a poor concept. It hampers integration rather than promoting it.[38] No doubt, the rule adds to the confusion by being imprecise in referring to notions such as "sufficiently achieved", "reasons of scale and effect"

---

[36] The possibility of injunctive remedies in Great Britain to prevent a Council decision or UK implementation of the Directive post adoption was considered, but abandoned.

[37] There are at least three references to the subsidiarity principle in TEU: The preamble states that the Member States are resolved "to continue the process of creating an ever closer union among the peoples of Europe, in which decisions are taken as closely as possible to the citizen in accordance with the principle of subsidiarity." Likewise Article A, second paragraph in Title I provides that decisions should be taken "as closely as possible to the citizen" and Article B, last paragraph in Title I requires that the conditions and the timetable shall be adhered to "while respecting the principle of subsidiarity as defined in Article 3b . . ."

[38] See Toth, op. cit. (*note 22*) at p. 1103.

and "better achieved". All leave room for differing interpretations. On the other hand it was the solution without which it is unlikely that the member states would have proceeded with other parts of the Maastricht Treaty.[39]

The Commission now underlines that subsidiarity allows both centralization and decentralization in the decision-making process.[40] Clearly, exclusive Community competencies fall outside the principle.[41] Likewise, in areas where the Community has no competence, the subsidiarity principle is of no relevance.[42] It is only applicable in areas of shared competence where a division of power becomes necessary. Initially there were few areas of shared competence in the Treaty of Rome. Over time this situation has changed and today shared competencies exist in areas like energy, environment, social, consumer and regional policies. These areas are generally speaking extended new competencies and the use of the subsidiarity principle has been a condition for the extensions.

It is difficult to understand the provision as anything but a presumption that legislation shall be enacted at national level. It is only where the member states cannot in a sufficient way achieve the objectives, but the Community can, that legislation shall be performed at Community level.

The EU authorities must from now on in accordance with Article 190 ECT consider subsidiarity aspects in their new legislative enactments with an indication in the preamble of new proposals why Community legislation is required.

---

[39] See SOU 1994:12, op. cit. (*note 5*), at p. 124.

[40] Rapport sur le fonctionnement du Traité de l'Union Européenne. Préparer l'Europe du XXIème Siècle. Bruxelles 10/5 1995.

[41] Included in the exclusive competence are e.g. foreign trade policy, agriculture and fishery, transport and antitrust – at least to the extent the latter affects trade between member states. See Cramér, op. cit. (*note 5*) p. 539–540. Competition law is a good example for collaboration between EU and national authorities and application of subsidiarity in the best sense. Editorial Comment, "Subsidiarity in EC competition law enforcement", *Common Market Law Review*, (1995). The Commission has also suggested that the four freedoms are covered by the exclusivity. According to EF-Karnov 1993, p. 41, this would be to go too far. The principle should apply to any area where the member states may effectively legislate until Community law has been enacted.

[42] Examples of areas not covered by Community law are family law, criminal law, general torts and damages. See L. Pålsson, *EG-Rätt*, (1978), p. 75.

In spite of the restriction referring to the acquis communautaire in Article C TEU,[43] the European Council in Lisbon of June 1992 instructed the Commission to make a report on subsidiarity. Herein the Commission identified legislation or proposed legislation which should be withdrawn because it came under the principle.[44] This affected the proposed Directive on Tobacco advertising[45] – but not the Snuff directive, which remains valid.

5.2 The Swedish exception

The result of the EU procedure intended to introduce a prohibition of the marketing of oral tobacco products was the banning of an ill defined product for questionable reasons – with a wide general exception providing that the ban "should not affect traditional tobacco products for oral use".

Swedish "snus" in loose form undoubtedly satisfies any possible definition of a traditional product as the product has been widely used in Sweden for more than 150 years. Even the portion packed product – which is loose snuff surrounded by a bag made of approved paper – satisfies normal traditional requirements having been marketed in Sweden for some 20 years. The portion packed product has throughout its years of existence gained market share because it has been regarded as a more hygienic and milder product.

If Swedish "snus" were regarded as a traditional product in the Community it would escape the prohibition of the Directive and could be sold both in Sweden and other parts of the Community without any restrictions. This was probably the legal position after the enactment of Directive 92/41. Commissioner Ripa Di Meana already during the parliamentary debate indicated that this would be the case.

Unfortunately for the Swedish tobacco industry, the relative un-

---

[43] Article C TEU stipulates: "The Union shall be served by a single institutional framework which shall ensure the consistency and the continuity of the activities carried out in order to attain its objectives while respecting and building upon the *acquis communautaire*."

[44] "Commission Report to the European Council on the adaptation of Community legislation to the subsidiarity princple." Brussels 24/11 1993.

[45] Proposed Directive, Com (992) Final, Brussels 30/4 1992.

certainty surrounding the fate of the Swedish "snus" led the Swedish authorities to bring the matter up for clarification both in the Swedish negotiations for accession to the European Union and in the context of the EEA-agreement. In the membership negotiations Sweden requested that the Directive should not be applicable to "snus" in Sweden. The EU side granted a derogation for "snus" both in loose and portion packed form – but not for "snus in forms resembling food products" – on condition that Sweden would introduce an export ban in respect of all member states except Norway.[46]

In March 1994 the matter was the subject of a decision in the EEA Joint Committe as Directive 92/41 was part of the "pipeline acquis communautaire" which had been adopted in the EU after 31 July 1991 (which was the stop date for EU legislation included in the EEA agreement). In this decision[47] the Joint Committee amended Protocol 47 and certain annexes to the EEA agreement. Chapter XXV dealt with tobacco and stipulated that the Community prohibition on oral tobacco should not apply to marketing in Iceland, Norway and Sweden. Again the exception did not apply to "snus" in forms resembling food products. Furthermore it required the three countries to ban export of the products to all other contracting parties.

Sweden complied in a timely manner with its obligation under both the Accession Agreement and the EEA agreement through a

---

[46] The concession is contained in a one page document titled Sweden-Norway, Conference on accession to the European Union, Brussels, 21 December 1993, CONF 8/93 (General). Subject: Chapter 29: Other – Union common position on Swedish and Norwegian requests concerning "snus". It is a Community declaration rather than an agreement, but the document is exhibited to the Accession Agreement.

[47] Decision of the EEA Joint Committee No. 7/94 of 21 March 1994 amending protocol 47 and certain Annexes to the EEA Agreement. "1. The following shall be added in point 1 (Council Directive 89/622/EEC): "as amended by: – 392 L 0041: Council Directive 92/41/EEC of May 15 1992 (OJ No. L 158, 11.6.1992, p. 30), The provisions of the Directive shall, for the purposes of the present Agreement, be read with the following adaptions: a) The prohibition in Article 8 . . . shall not apply to the placing on the market in Iceland, Norway and Sweden of the products defined in Article 2.4 . . . However, this derogation shall not apply to the prohibition of sales of "snus" in forms resembling food products. Furthermore, Iceland, Norway and Sweden shall apply an export ban on the product defined in Article 2.4 . . . to all other Contracting Parties to the present Agreement."

governmental regulation[48] which prohibits export of defined oral tobaccos to Finland, Austria and the member states of the Union. The Swedish law does, however, make an exception for export for personal use, which is important for all Swedes sojourning in the Community.

The above process satisfies several overriding political concerns both in Sweden and the Community. Swedish snuffers would no longer oppose Swedish membership in the Union as they could continue their age-long and peculiar habit. The Commission had found a solution which allowed it to successfully close the dossier without interfering with the Swedish tradition and yet securing that the product would not be traded in the Community at large. At one stage it was suggested that the Commission would on application from the member states approve and list the "traditional products" in Europe. This was no longer necessary and no precise list has been made. With the Swedish snus issue cleared away, remaining oral tobacco products – if any – coming under the prohibition probably did not matter as national peculiarities are hard to export anyway. On an overall political note it could be said that a flexible solution in line with the requirements of the subsidiarity principle had been found.

From a legal perspective, however, the procedure leaves room for considerable doubts. Already during the Community internal process it had been questioned whether fundamental Community concepts like the legality-, equity-, subsidiarity- and proportionality principles had been adhered to in a correct way. The exemption for "traditional products" introduced during the final stage of the decision making had removed these concerns as the reach of the prohibition would in any event be limited.

With the measures adopted during the accession negotiations and

---

[48] Förordning om förbud mot export av snus; utfärdad den 16 juni 1994. "1 § Varor som anges i bilaga får inte exporteras till Finland, Österrike eller medlemsstat i Europeiska unionen. Förbudet i första stycket gäller inte varor som medförs av en resande och som är avsedd för dennes eller dennes familjs personliga bruk eller som gåva till närstående för personligt bruk." The exhibit identifies the product using the customs classification system and defining it in the same terms as the Directive: "Tobak för användning i munnen utom sådana produkter som är avsedda att rökas eller tuggas, och som helt eller delvis är framställda av tobak i pulver- eller partikelform eller i någon kombination av dessa former – i portionspåsar eller porösa påsar – eller i en form som påminner om ett livsmedel."

in the context of the EEA agreement the matter again became important for Swedish tobacco industry. The end result was that the Union in an unprecedented way had barred access for Swedish traditional products to the Community in conflict with the prohibitions contained in ECT Articles 30 and 34 and EEA Article 12 on quantitative restrictions.

The notion of "traditional product" is not available for Swedish oral tobacco on similar terms as for traditional products from other member states. The use of the word "snus" in the Community declaration of December 1993 appears to clarify that the Swedish oral tobacco is subject to a special treatment for which there is no explanation and no reason given. The consequence is that "snus" produced in Denmark – which in fact exists – is a traditional product which can be sold freely in the Community – even to Sweden, but when the same product is produced in Sweden it cannot be sold back. In fact, the Commission could argue that evan the imported Danish product cannot be reexported to the country it came from.

Considering general Community concepts the result of the legislation is absurd and recourse to legal remedies may be a solution. The Swedish "snus" producers could initiate export of their products to a well situated continental member state – like e.g. Denmark och Germany. This export will contravene the Swedish export ban and may also be regarded as prohibited in the country of importation. The Swedish legislation should then be challenged as infringing fundamental Community concepts whereas the importing country should be requested to respect a traditional product from another member state. Both steps may very well require the intervention of the EJC.[49]

After several years of political wrestling it appears as if time has come for a judicial determination of whether the authorities in their

---

[49] The main problems today appears to be that the Community position on Swedish "snus" has been exhibited to the Accession Agreement in the form of a document under the heading MISCELLANEOUS (AA–AFNS page 608). In the case C 191/90 Genevizs UK Ltd and Another v. Smith Kline and French Laboratories Ltd, [1993] I C.M.L.R. 89 at paras 32 and 41, the ECJ established that Articles 47 and 209 of the Spanish and Portuguese Accession Agreement contained valid derogations from the free movement of goods within the Community. The question therefore is if the document annexed to the Swedish Accession Agreement has the same legal status as the very precise and clear exception established in the Spanish and Portuguese agreements.

lawmaking have adhered to fundamental Community concepts – among them the non-discrimination and the subsidiarity principles – when constructing the complicated legal web now discriminating against Swedish "snus".

5.3 The 1996 Intergovernmental Conferecne

The application of the subsidiarity principle remains in a state of flux and must be subject to development in the future. Such precision will affect relations between the Community and the member states – but it also has a bearing on private interests as is demonstrated by the snuff case.

At the moment of writing, Europe is preparing the agenda for the forthcoming IGC 1996. The Community institutions have submitted their reports on the functioning of the Union and the member states are gradually presenting their views in preliminary position papers.

Is there going to be a "widening" or a "depending" of the Community in 1996? The answer is that it must be both. Several Eastern European states are far advanced in the European integration process and politically there is hardly a way back. Enlargement can not, however, happen without substantial reforms covering such fields as institutions, decision making, and agriculture to name a few.[50]

A study of the national and institutional comments submitted so far indicates the risk of an overwhelming agenda. The problems of Maastricht may rapidly become a reality also in 1996. There could even be a possibilty that those forces in the Community which remain reluctant to further enlargement of the Union could jeopardize IGC 1996 by taking an overambitious approach. Preparation, a carefully selected agenda and skilful compromising may lead to results.

The fundamental question is still what characterization of the European collaboration can unite the diverse opinions. One option is to build on the free market concept and to combine general in-

---

[50] A. Olander, "1996 års regeringskonferens – avstamp för ett annorlunda EU?" *Briefing från UD* 3/95 pp. 3–8.

tergovernmental collaboration with national autonomy. The alternative is support for a strengthened central authority. In order to be successful the member states may have to confine themselves to what is absolutely necessary to allow for the planned enlargement towards the east rather than to solve all outstanding issues.

It appears that subsidiarity will be a high priority for IGC 1996. The concept has been dealt with in almost all the preliminary position papers submitted before the summer vacation 1995:

The European Commission[51] underlines in its report to the Council that several major problems in Europe today have a Community dimension and must be handled accordingly. The conclusion is not that everything must be done centrally. In accordance with the subsidiarity principle the right solution shall be found in the individual case. The Commission points out that the principle is too often invoked to weaken the Union. This is wrong, subsidiarity also has a positive dimension in explaining that certain matters are better handled at the EU level.

The European Parliament also comments upon subsidiarity in its Resolution to the Council.[52] Under the heading "Clarifying competencies" Parliament suggests that the present Article 3b TEU should be maintained. There is no need to establish a fixed list identifying competencies as it would be too rigid and too hard to achieve.

The ECJ[53] only briefly refers to the subsidiarity concept by noting that several cases relating to the interpretation of Article 3b have now been referred to the Court.

The member states have dealt with subsidiarity in their different position papers and other statements. The dividing line appears to follow their general attitude to Community collaboration. UK, France, Germany and the Nordic countries favour collaboration be-

---

[51] Commission report op. cit. (*note 40*).

[52] Resolution on the functioning of the Treaty on the European Union with a view to the 1996 Intergovernmental Conference – Implementation and development of the Union, 17/5 1995 PE 190.441.

[53] Report of the Court of Justice on certain aspects of the application of the Treaty on European Union. Luxembourg May 1995. The Court refers to the following pending cases relating to subsidiarity: Case C-84/94 *United Kingdom v. Council* and Case C-233/94 *Germany v. Parliament and Council*.

tween independent countries while Spain, Italy and the Benelux have developed a more integrationistic approach.[54]

The Federal German Government wants to extend the scrutiny of documents tested for compatibility under Article 3b. The subsidiarity principle needs to be strengthened through precise definitions of the respective areas of competence. Furthermore, the second element in Article 3b: "and can therefore, by reasons of scale or effects of the proposed action, be better achieved by the Community" should be deleted. The German Länder are going further by requesting a clear separation of powers through a precise list per subject area.

Due to the Presidential election France did not take any position during spring of 1995. During his electoral campaign Mr. Chirac made clear references to the subsidiarity principle as a way to shift powers back to the member states.

The UK – which already during the Maastricht discussion favoured a subsidiarity clause – had not developed its ideas in this context during spring 1995. Spain, which took the opposite view to the UK in Maastricht, has again come out aggressively against the subsidiarity concept. Spain will firmly oppose any listing of Community powers. Subsidiarity must not be used as an instrument to limit or increase competencies for either the Community or the member states. It should only be used in cases of shared competence to determine "who should do what". The official Spanish view is that subsidiarity is nothing but an aid to establish if a matter can be more effectively carried out at Union or at member state level.

Considering that the subsidiarity issue is but one – albeit important – of many critical issues for the IGC 1996 and that the different positions are already at this early stage fairly locked it is easy to understand the challenge facing the negotiators. Tabling problems

---

[54] The national positions have been summarized and are constantly updated by the European Parliament, Political and Institutional Affairs Division in its "Note on the positioning of the Member States of the European Union with respect to the 1996 Intergovernmental Conference". Luxembourg 12 April 1995. First updated version. Germany p. 8–16, France p. 22 and Spain p. 45.

will not help as there are too many important concerns which must be addressed.[55]

6. Concluding reflections

It has been suggested that a federal structure is by definition one in which powers or competencies are shared between constituent bodies, usually on a regional basis. The European Union could qualify as a federation under this definition.[56] Yet, few suggest that the Union has a federative character today.

When does a pre-federation become a federation? The above quoted definition is far from complete.[57] Is the essential feature related to where the decision making power lies? In a federation it is centralized – whereas in other forms of international collaboration the states maintain the control over development. Other elements are also significant.

The European Union remains under the control of the member states. It is only in areas where competence has been transferred (explicity or implicity) that a Union competence exists. Further development is subject to additional transfer of power at the discretion of the states. In the European Economic Community of six it was still possible to find political consensus whereas with the enlarged European Union it becomes increasingly difficult. The risk is that integration could halt at its present stage due to the impossibility of finding political agreements acceptable to all member states.

---

[55] How should the two criteria of Article 3b which determine who shall take action in a specific matter be interpreted; who will decide which level has competence; is the Court competent to interpret the principle; does it have a direct effect etc.

[56] See Cass, op. cit. (*note 22*), with further references. The Union contains several federative elements: the directly elected parliament, majority decisions in the Council, direct effect, priority for Community law, plans for a common currency, Union citizenship etc. See SOU 1994:12, op. cit. (*note 5*) p. 99.

[57] SOU 1994:12, op. cit. (*note 5*), p. 94 defines a federation as an organization where both the federal level and the state level have democratically elected decision making bodies. In case of conflict, the law of the higher (federal) level will have priority over the lower (state) level – a situation which will arise without any decision being required at the lower. The common order has the character of a constitution.

The concept of subsidiarity adds a new dimension to the development. Subsidiarity is often interpreted as decentralization with decision-making as close to the people as possible. In Denmark and Sweden the concept has frequently been translated to "närhetsprincipen" or the "nearness principle". President Chirac referred during his electoral campaign to the subsidiarity principle as a way of shifting power back to the member states. This is, however, not a complete interpretation of the principle. Subsidiarity is also a way for the members in a collaboration to agree to perform certain tasks jointly because it affects them all and/or because it is more efficient. Accordingly, the concept contains a centralizing aspect as well.

As applied in the Union subsidiarity contains a good number of uncertainties and is a concept still under development. A part of the IGC 1996 discussion will be devoted to whether these uncertainties shall be settled or left hanging in the air. Some of the member states favour precise definitions and wordings whereas others would rather leave matters to a case by case development.

To take a too Lutheran and formalistic approach to the subsidiarity notion requiring prompt and exact determination of its real meaning would deprive the concept of its inherent dynamic possibilities. Finding very precise words and exhaustive lists identifying which entity has competence to act in every situation would also be a cumbersome exercise as suggested by the European Parliament. In fact it would require the same kind of political decisions as would an amendment to the Treaty. The varied views on the European collaboration would make such a mission, if not impossible, at least very difficult.[58] The strength of the subsidiary concept as presently encapsulated in Article 3b TEU is that it will allow a gradual development in par with the underlying political will, but avoiding too rigid formalism and possibilities to abuse veto rights.

In areas of shared competence the subsidiarity principle in its present form allows the dynamic development to continue. In certain

---

[58] Germany has in its constitution been able to make catalogues for exclusive legislation (Article 73) and concurrent legislation (Article 74) which defines the distribution of competencies within the Federal Republic. P. Hallström, "Några tankar om subsidiaritetsprincipens tillämpning i EG-rätten", Svensk Juristtidning, (1972), pp. 177–187 favours a similar solution for the Unione.

fields Sweden favours such dynamics[59] whereas in others it takes a more hesitant approach. This is precisely the challenge. Member states are forced to look for politically acceptable compromises before the collaboration and the Community competencies can be extended to new areas.

The ECJ will ultimately decide if the institutions have used their powers under the subsidiarity principle in a correct way.[60] Yet the Court must move cautiously if it intends to alter political decisions reached by representatives of the member states. When legislation is made by way of application of an essential political discretion, the Court will only intervene in cases of flagrant abuse of the principle.[61]

Will the Union at some stage become a federation? Due to lack of precise definitions it may depend on where the real decision-making power will lie in the future. If it is the member states who retain the control, the answer is no. The collaboration is rather intergovern-mental. The more unanimity is abandoned in favour of qualified majority in the decision making and the more the European Parliament is influencing the distribution of competence the more suprana-tional the organization becomes.

The conclusion therefore is that the Union remains at its pre-federative stage. At some future date a situation may appear where European nations and people have gained so much confidence in their Union that they are prepared to write a clear and simple consti-tution and allow the central institutions to control the future devel-opment under democratic forms. At that time it may be appropriate to use the "F-word". Meanwhile, the present Union with all its deficiencies subscribing to the concept of subsidiarity may prove to

---

[59] Crime preventions and environmental collaboration are two areas identified by the Swedish government in its preliminary position paper for IGC 1996, "Svenska principiella intressen inför EU:s regeringskonferens 1996", Regeringskansliet, juli 1995.

[60] The principle is a part of the operative text of the ECT and not the preamble as was suggested by some member states during the Maastricht negotiations. One effect of this structure is that the EJC is competent to interpret it.

[61] In the Hormones case op. cit. (*note 20*) the Court at para. 14 stipulated with respect to the Common Agricultural Policy that "the Community legislature has a discretionary power . . . the legality of a measure adopted in that sphere can be affected only if the measure is manifestly inappropriate having regard to the objective which the competent institution is seeking to pursue."

be just the right solution, allowing a dynamic collaboration to develop at the same time as diversity in Europe is protected.

Bibliography

Cass, Deborah Z., "The word that saves Maastricht? The principle of subsidiarity and the division of powers within the European Community", *Common Market Law Review* 29 (1992), pp. 1107–1136.

Cramér, Per, "Noteringar rörande subsidiaritetsprincipens tillämpning i framtidens EG/EU", *Svensk Juristtidning* (1973) pp. 533–547.

Eklund, Lars F., "Subsidiaritetsprincipen: dess bakgrund och innebörd", *Expertrapport till SOU 1954:12. Suveränitet och demokrati: Subsidiaritet.*

Hallström, Pär, "Några taknar om subsidiaritetsprincipens tillämpning i EG-rätten", Svensk Juristtidning, (1972), pp. 177–187.

Olander, Anders, "1996 års regeringskonferens – avstamp för ett annorlunda EU?" *Briefing från UD 3/95 pp. 3–8.*

Pålsson, Lennart, EEC-Rätt, Lund 1970, Studentlitteratur.

Pålsson, Lennart, *EG-Rätt,* Lund 1978, Studentlitteratur.

Quitzow, Carl Michael, *Fria varurörelser i den Europeiska gemenskapen. En studie av gränsdragningen mellan gemenskapsangelägenheter och nationella angelägenheter,* Göteborg 1995, Fritzes Förlag.

Rasmussen, Hjalte, *EU-ret og EU-institutioner i kontekst,* København 1994, Karnow.

SOU 1994:12, "Suveränitet och demokrati", *Betänkande av EG-konsekvensutredningarna: Subsidiaritet.*

Toth, A.G., "The Principle of Subsidiarity in the Maastricht Treaty", *Common Market Law Review* 29 (1992), pp. 1079–1105.

Wellenstein, E.P., "Unity, Community, Union – what's in a name?", Guest-editorial, *Common Market Law Review,* (1992), p. 209.

European Commission, Rapport sur le fonctionnement du Traité de l'Union Européenne. Préparer l'Europe du XXIème Siècle. Bruxelles 10/5 1995.

European Parliament, Resolution on the functioning of the Treaty on the European Union with a view to the 1996 Intergovernmental Conference – Implementation and development of the Union. 17/5 1995 PE 190.441.

European Court of Justice, Report of the Court of Justice on certain aspects of the application of the Treaty on European Union. Luxembourg May 1995.

Political and Institutional Affairs Division, European Parliament, "Note on the positioning of the Member States of the European Union with respect to the 1996 Intergovernmental Conference". Luxembourg 12 April 1995. First updated version.

Regeringskansliet, *"Svenska principiella intressen inför EU:s regeringskonferens 1996"*, Stockholm 1995.

HUMAN RIGHTS AND UNIVERSITY POLICY

Göran Melander

Year 1789, when the French Declaration on Human Rights was adopted, will always be a propriety year in the history of human rights. Most likely the same applies with year 1989, when the Berlin walls were pulled down. That event marks the beginning of a new era in Europe, not only because that became the beginning of the definite end of the Cold War and that market economy became the leading star in the former socialist countries. Equally remarkable is the new awakened interest for democracy and human rights, in particular civil and political rights all over the world.

The change in Europe was totally unexpected. The adjustment have taken place without any carefully planned processes. Governments in the East and the West have been forced to improvise. Accordingly, the changes have not taken place without agonies. New problems have emerged and European States have not been prepared to meet the new challenges.

Rascism and xenophobia is growing in Europe. There is no immigration policy in European States and as a consequence migrants who want to come to Europe are treated in an unacceptable way. Deterrent measures have been initiated in order to discourage asylum seekers from arriving; in some countries the hostility against foreigners have taken violent forms and serious riots have taken place. On the other hand such atrocities have also been met with spontaneous measures of solidarity. People have reacted against the persecution of aliens which has been led by a small group of activists. However, the proletariat of aliens is growing in Europe and only few States seem prepared to try to find solutions. The consequences of rascism and xenophobia hit refugees who have well-founded reasons for their presence in Europe and who are granted asylum. Little is undertaken by States to combat such evils.

Minority problems are another threat to peace in Europe. Between the two World Wars various activities were initiated in the Balkan countries to combat discrimination against minorities and to strengthen equality. During the socialist era little was done to combat the underlying causes for antagonism between ethnic groups. As soon as socialism has been abandoned the old minority problems have emerged again. The division of former Yugoslavia and the war between the new states in the region are tragic examples of the incapability of people to cooperate and the failure to solve ethnic conflicts.

The situation in former Yugoslavia is, however, not an isolated example. So far, it represents the case where the conflict has been brought to the open and led to a most cruel and unmerciful war. Other "minor" conflicts have emerged in Azerbadjan, Armenia and Georgia where fighting takes place now and then. The potential areas of conflicts are numerous and that because of discrimination or alleged discrimination against a minority population. Treatment of minorities do not fulfil international standards and such conflicts may be a threat to peace and security.

Discrimination of ethnic minorities and lack of affirmative action is the reason for group conflicts. Members of an ethnic minority may be denied access to the labour market; religious intolerance may lead to clear persecution; minority languages may be suppressed; minorities may be denied to enjoy their own culture.

Minority problems are, however, not impossible to solve. There are numerous cases, not least in Europe, where tolerance has replaced the antagonism between groups. As examples may be mentioned the border area between Denmark and Germany, France and Germany, the situation inside Switzerland just to mention a few cases.

When minorities are being discriminated there is a clear lack of respect for human rights. The most elementary principles are not being applied and little is being done to promote respect for human rights. It should be noted that there exist numerous international agreements, prescibing for the strict observance of the principle of non-discrimination. As examples reference can be made to the UN Covenant on Civil and Political Rights, art 2 para.1, the UN Covenant on Economic Social and Cultural Rights, art 2 para.2, the UN Convention on the Elimination on Racial Discrimination, i.e. treaties which have been ratified by many of the States where discrimination presently takes place.

It may then be argued that various activities for the promotion and development of human rights undertaken after World War II are useless. This is clearly an erroneous presumtion. Generally speaking it is quite notable that there is a growing respect for human rights. Within the UN and regional organisations a system of monitoring human rights agreements has been developed and such systems have been surprisingly effective. Today few states openly admit that human rights violations take place within its borders and if so, they are most anxious to improve its international reputation. States violating human rights risk to be internationally condemned and no state is willing to accept such condemnation. All states have a self-interest to respect human rights. However, the population must be aware of the fact that discrimination constitutes a violation of human rights and those discriminated against must learn how to make use of the international machinery. On top of that minority problems must be solved by affirmative actions, i.e. special measures in favour of minorities in order to create equality.

In order to create an athmosphere of respect for human rights many actors have a role to play. The international community, in particular the UN and other intergovernmental organisations will have to find solutions to various minority problems. It may be that a more active Security Council is needed and that the UN is willing to undertake the task of peace-keeping and prevention of hostilities. Individual States also have a resonsibility in trying to convince parties to a potential conflict to settle disputes by peaceful means. Non-governmental organisations are an important factor. Through concerted actions such organizations may serve as watchdogs and alert the international community when human rights values are being violated.

An essential element for the promotion of human rights is dissemination and education thereof. As repeatedly has been stated, human rights are useless unless you know them. It has also been clearly demonstrated that lack of knowledge of human rights leads to human rights violations and inversely that knowledge of human rights contributes to a better respect for human rights. The existing monitoring system regarding the principle of non–discrimination is clearly underused. It is, for instance, possible for minorities in the former Soviet Union, faced with discrimination, to make communications to the UN Human Rights Committee. That possibility has, however, so far never been used.

Education and dissemination of human rights lies within the mandate and responsibility of UNESCO and it could have been expected that the organization should have taken various initiatives to stimulate human rights education. UNESCO could, for instance, have published textbooks in human rights for various school levels. Such products hardly exist. It could also have been expected that UNESCO should have taken the lead to coordinate human rights education on the universal level. Plans of action have been adopted but not implemented. It could have been expected that UNESCO efter the events in 1989 had given human rights education a higher priority, but in this context nothing has been achieved. To be fair to the organization is must be admitted that the economic constraints of UNESCO have been an effective obstacle for every initiative. However, it is a question of priorities and the organization could have devoted a greater interest to these problems. Already the institutional framework clearly demonstrates the organization's indifference for the subject. Human rights deserves to be a subject for an independent department, directly under the Director–General. Presently, it is downgraded and lies within the Division of Human Rights and Peace, with a most limited budget.

Other UN agencies may also have a role for the dissimination and education of human rights and as a matter of fact the UN Center for Human Rights have taken some initiatives. That organ is presently responsible for so–called technical assistance programmes, i.e. human rights education in various parts of the world. The World Campaign for Human Rights is another initiative which has led to the publishing of a number of human rights instruments and information booklets in the official languages of the United Nations. The existance of such material is, however, fairly unknown. All documents published within the framework of the World Campaign is free of charge and can be ordered from the UN Center.

When the international organizations have limited possibilities to disseminate human rights non-governmental organizations will have to fil the gap. Important activities are carried out by organizations like Amnesty International, International Commission of Jurists and numerous national NGOs.

Another actor which can have an important role is the universities. It is, however, surprising that human rights education is lacking at most universities all over the world. The absence of such education may have a logical explanation with respect to universities in the former socialist countries where at least civil and political rights erroneously were considered as a Western/capitalist invention. And perhaps the respect for human rights were considered as self-evident in the Western societies and that education and dissemination was not needed. In the world of today the absence of human rights within the university system is notable.

According to international instruments education in human rights is an obligation incumbent on States. Article 26 of the Universal Declaration of Human Rights prescibes that education shall be directed to the strengthening of respect for human rights and fundamental freedoms. An identical article can be found in the UN Covenant on Economic, Social and Cultural Rights (art. 13, para.1). A more explicit obligation is laid down in the UN Convention on the Elimination of All Forms of Racial Discrimination: States Parties undertake to adopt immediate and effective measures, particularly in the fields of teaching, education, culture and information, with a view to combating prejudices which lead to racial discrimination. According to the UN Convention against Torture and Other Cruel, Inhuman and Degrading Treatment or Punishment each State Party "shall ensure that education and information regarding the prohibition against torture of law enforcement personnel, civil or military officials and other persons who may be involved in the custody, interrogation or treatment of any individual subjected to any form of arrest, detention or imprisonment" (art. 10). The Convention on the Rights of the Child prescribes that States Parties have to make the principles and the provisions of the Convention widely known, by appropriate and active means, to adults and children alike (art. 42).

UNESCO is the UN organ which is responsible for the coordination of human rights education. A number of resolutions and recommendations has been adopted within the organization to strengthen this goal. In 1974 the UNESCO General Conference adopted a Recommendation concerning education for international understanding, cooperation and peace and education relating to human rights and fundamental freedoms. The recommendation lays down detailed principles for education and dissemination of human rights and humanitarian law. Member States should i.a. consider international cooperation to be a responsibility in developing international education. They should organize, or help appropriate authorities and non-governmental organizations to organize, an increasing number of international meetings and study sessions on international education. Reciprocal visits by various professional groups are encouraged. Exchanges of information should be organized.

An International Congress on the Teaching of Human Rights was arranged in Vienna in 1978. One of the purposes of the Congress was to give fresh input to the development of human rights teaching and education. It was also proposed to study the desirability of preparing a UNESCO Convention on human rights teaching and education.

In the recommendation of the Congress it was stressed that human rights curricula in law and political science programmes should be conceived broadly and incorporate civil and political rights as well as economic, social and cultural rights. It was stressed that since practice in the field of human rights depends on knowledge of the legal means of action which are available, the teaching of human rights must necessarily include courses on law. Research on human rights should be encouraged and developed in a number of themes and research should be facilitated by freedom of access to source materials. The teaching of human rights should be included in the continuing education of professionals, including, among others, doctors and lawyers, as a prerequisite for certification and relicensing where applicable.

The plan of action adopted by the Congress was most ambitious. However, it must be admitted that when it comes to the implementation of the various recommendations of the Vienna Congress not much has been achieved and no Convention on human rights teaching and education has been adopted.

UNESCO organized a second International Congress on Human Rights Teaching in Malta in 1987. A number of similar recommendations were adopted. The Director-General of UNESCO should promote the training in human rights of professionals, particularly those concerned by human rights. Particular importance should be given to the training of teachers and other educators who will be responsible for teaching human rights. Research in the field of human rights should be encouraged. The question of human rights should be included as an area of research at faculty level and UNESCO should assist in the creation of human rights centres. Research should be sponsored on the interaction between individual human rights and the rights of ethnic, religious, political and other minorities, as well as the interaction between individual rights and group or community rights. Research should be encouraged on situations of extreme discrimination and include a component of massive human rights violations, and research should be sponsored on the violations of human rights as a result of armed conflicts and violence, etc. Once again, the programme of action was most detailed and ambitious – and once again the practical result of the recommendation is far from impressive.

A third international Congress on Education for Human Rights and Democracy was arranged by UNESCO in Montreal in 1993. The Congress should be seen as a preparation for the 1993 World Conference on Human Rights in Vienna in June 1993. In a Working Document presented to the Congress (SHS93/CONF.402/3) some obstacles for an effective human rights education was stressed. It is mentioned that teachers seldom have the specific training they need which makes some teachers apprehensive about failing to grasp the content of the subject they are expected to teach. It is stressed that in higher education there are few faculties offering courses on human rights. On the positive side it is stressed that UNESCO has established Chairs in human rights in various universities and has decided (in 1992) in collaboration with the UN Centre for Human Rights to prepare a manual for the teaching of human rights at the university level – to be published in 1998.

International instruments prescribe for the obligation of human rights education and the international community has repeatedly stressed the importance of such education. With respect to higher education the responsibility for establishing human rights education lies within the universities themselves. Within universities there are numerous target groups for human rights education. Some universities in Europe arrange programmes of Core Curriculum. If that is the case it should be a clear possibility to arrange general courses in human right which can lead to a basic knowledge of the subject.

Law students are obvious target groups and a basic knowledge in human rights and the international system for the protection of human rights should be a compulsory element. Besides special courses in the subject ought to be arranged when such courses fit into the curricula.

It is, however, a mistake if human rights should be seen as a subject to which lawyers have the sole right. Other faculties also have a reponsibility. In the education of teachers human rights education should be a self-evident part of the curriculum, in particular teachers in social science. It is of extreme importance to educate the educators. Also for other professions basic knowledge in human rights is important. Medical personnel need to learn medical ethics; natural scientist need to learn about the right to environment as a human right; economists will have to adhere to some ethic principles, just to mention a few examples. It should be added that among students themselves there is growing interest in human rights education.

Research in the field of human rights should be encouraged. Through UNESCO special professorships in human rights can be established – provided UNESCO is able to find funds for chairs and provided universities are willing to accept them. Scholarships for research in human rights should be given priority. States should be encouraged to raise special funds for these activities, funds which can be administered by the universities themselves, by non–governmental organizations or by intergovernmental organizations like the UN Center for Human Rights. In the first place the universities should try to establish a machinery for cooperation in the field of human rights education. It may concern an exchange of curricula but also of researchers and teachers. New textbooks and other material for human rights education can be published in international cooperation.

In the former socialist countries special activities are needed. There is a great interest in human rights education but there is also a lack of competence within the universities. Such competence can be built up by offering possibilities for interested staff members to visit such university institutions where human rights research has a high priority. A conscious and planned exchange of researchers can be initiated and be given a priority.

Research in the field of human rights is difficult if not impossible in the former socialist countries. The main obstacle is lack of resources which i.a. is due to an almost complete lack of modern literature in the field. In the Magna Charta of the European Universities it is stated that "Universities – particularly in Europe – regard the mutual exchange of information and documentation, and frequent joint projects for the advancement of learning, as essential to the steady progress of knowledge". In practice this statement has not been realized, at least not within the field of human rights. An obvious, simple and not too expensive assistance would be that the richer universities in the West equip the poor universities in the East and the South with the basic human rights literature.

An exchange of students is desirable. To this end the Magna Charta of the European Universities declares that "they encourgae mobility among teachers and students". Between universities in Western Europe students may enjoy the advantage of the ERASMUS and similar programmes. They are, however, limited to students within the area, i.e. Western Europe. The possibilities for an exchange programme comprising students from the former socialist countries are developing. Particular programmes should be initiated and priority should be given to students in the field of human rights.

Concerted and coordinated efforts for human rights education are needed. For some universities it is a question of a revised priority and for others a question to raise funds. Generally speaking it seems as if universities fight a losing battle for money. To achieve the best result coordination and cooperation between universities is essential.

SCOPE OF APPLICATION, CHOICE OF LAW AND JURISDICTION IN THE NEW NORDIC LAW OF CARRIAGE OF GOODS BY SEA

Allan Philip

1. Introduction

Maritime legislation in the Nordic Countries is to a large extent based upon international conventions which, by common Nordic efforts, have been incorporated into their largely identical national laws. In this context the Nordic countries are Denmark, Finland, Norway and Sweden. Although the national maritime legislation in the Nordic countries complies with the convention requirements, the tradition is not to transform the convention texts as such into national law, but rather to legislate on the subject in question in a general way and to incorporate the solutions of the conventions into such legislation. This is also what has usually been done in the field of carriage of goods by sea.

The first important modern international effort at unification in the area of carriage of goods by sea and which achieved widespread acceptance was the International Convention for the Unification of Certain Rules Relating to Bills of Lading of August 25, 1924, the so-called Hague Rules. The Convention was incorporated into the Nordic maritime codes in the thirties. It contained no rules on jurisdiction nor rules of choice of law in the traditional sense. It did, however, in its art. 10, provide a rule on its scope of application simply stating that its provisions should apply to all bills of lading issued in a contracting state.

The Hague Rules were amended by a protocol of February 23, 1968, the so-called Visby Rules. They were incorporated into the Nordic maritime codes in the seventies. Art. 5 of the Visby Rules amended art. 10 of the Hague Rules and provided for a more comprehensive rule of scope of application to which we shall later return. The Visby Rules likewise contain no jurisdiction rules nor any choice of law rules in the traditional sense of the word.

The Hague-Visby Rules were later amended to permit the introduction of rules on SDR's (Special Drawing Rights). These rules were incorporated into Nordic law in the eighties.

The conventions and protocols just mentioned were all adopted within the old regime of the Brussels Conferences. In the eighties, however, the subject of carriage of goods by sea was at the initiative of UNCTAD taken up by UNCITRAL. That work resulted in the United Nations Convention on the Carriage of Goods by Sea, adopted in Hamburg on March 31, 1978, the so-called Hamburg Rules. That Convention has not so far been ratified by the Nordic countries. It came into force in 1992 between about 20 nations, most of which were developing countries. The Convention has, however, had considerable influence on Nordic law as it stands since a revision in 1994. However, the Nordic countries have not denounced the Hague-Visby Rules nor ratified the Hamburg Rules. The scope of application rules of the Hague-Visby Rules, therefore, still apply as rules of minimum application of the Hague-Visby Rules.

It is the intention in the following to discuss the scope of application, choice of law and jurisdiction in the successive Conventions as well as in their incorporation into Nordic law as exemplified by Danish law. There are no important differences between Danish law and the law of the other Nordic countries in this respect.

2. Scope of application and choice of law[1]

Choice of law rules determine the scope of application of, respectively, the law of the forum and of foreign law. They do it by indicating, with a substantive reference, the area of law or the type of

---

[1] Cf. generally about these problems Siesby, *Søretlige Lovkonflikter*, 1965, p. 267 and 281, William Tetley, *International Conflicts of Laws*, 1994, p. 291, Uffe Lind Rasmussen, *Jurisdiktionsklausuler og Voldgiftsklausuler i Søtransportkontrakter*, *Marjus* nr. 90, 1984 and Kristina Maria Siig, *Forum og Lovvalg vedrørende Transportansvaret*, *Marjus* nr. 215, 1995.

legal relationship they govern and by indicating with a connecting factor the relevant geographical or other criteria which determine the law of which country must be applied in cases of this nature. In principle, choice of law rules require no investigation of the substantive contents of the chosen law. It must be applied as it is, subject only to ordre public.

Conventions on uniform private law, such as the maritime law conventions, may also contain choice of law rules. They will then replace the choice of law rules otherwise applicable in the member states. However, in most cases the choice of law problems are not regulated by uniform private law conventions but rather left to the law of the forum to be decided. If a case is before the courts of a forum state which has ratified and implemented a convention and the law of that forum state is applied, the convention will be applied to that case. If, on the other hand, according to the choice of law rules of the forum state a foreign law applies, whether the convention is part of the foreign law to be applied or not depends upon whether in the country of origin of the relevant foreign law the convention is ratified and implemented. If the convention is not accepted into that law it will not be applied regardless of the fact that the forum state has ratified and implemented it. This is the general situation.

It happens, however, that a convention contains, not choice of law rules, but rules defining its scope of application. All conventions, of course, contain provisions defining what their subject is; that is not what we are concerned with here. Some conventions contain provisions regulating their geographical scope by requiring the application of the convention when certain facts take place in, or are otherwise connected with, a specific geographical area. A typical example is art. 10 of the Hague Rules. It applies to bills of lading issued in a Contracting State.

It is, of course, a question of interpretation of such provisions in a convention how such a rule must be understood and applied. It may be understood as being subsidiary to the choice of law rules of the forum. That may even follow expressly from the convention, such as e.g. is partly the case with art. 1 of CISG. That means that the convention applies only when it is part of the law of the forum or of the foreign law which is applicable according to the choice of law rules of the forum and not otherwise, and, of course, within that scope of application, only where it is applicable according to its own scope of application rules. Then, no conflict arises between the scope of application rule of the convention and the choice of law rules of the forum.

It may, however, be that the scope of application rule of the convention is meant to apply regardless of any choice of law rules. That undoubtedly is the case with art. 10 of the Hague Rules and art. 13 (old art. 12) of the Maritime Liens and Mortgages Convention. The consequence is that the court must somehow ensure the application of the convention, even if there is a conflict with its choice of law rules which would lead to the application of a law which has not incorporated the convention.

That does not necessarily mean that the court must always apply the lex fori. Application of the lex fori is just one way of ensuring the application of the convention.

It is, however, also possible to ensure the application of the convention when applying foreign law. It may be done by limiting the application of foreign law to cases where the convention has been ratified by the country of origin of that foreign law. That means making the application of the choice of law rule dependent upon information about the ratification of the convention by the country of the chosen foreign law.

Or, it may be done by applying the foreign law only to the extent that it does not conflict with the contents of the convention.

Personally, I prefer the latter solution. Conventions rarely regulate the whole of the area of the law with which they are concerned. They only regulate certain aspects, e.g. the liability of the shipowner for carriage of goods by sea. The remainder of the legal relationship is governed by national law. That a convention has deemed it expedient to require its application in all cases where a certain connection exists is no reason for extending the application of lex fori to all other aspects of such cases which are not covered by the convention. That is particularly so in contractual relationships.

Different methods of complying with the scope of application rules in the international carriage of goods by sea conventions have been followed successively in Nordic law. They shall be mentioned in the following. In this context, it should be remembered that at present Denmark as well as the other Nordic countries are not bound by the Hamburg Rules, but still adhere to the Hague-Visby Rules.

3. The Hague Rules

As mentioned above, art. 10 of the original Hague Rules provides for the application of the provisions of the Convention to all bills of lading issued in a Contracting State. Art. 2 further defines the area of application as the responsibilities and liabilities, rights and immunities of the carrier in relation to the lading, handling, stowage, custody, care and discharge of goods. Remaining rules on carriage of goods by sea fall outside the scope of the Hague Rules.

The Danish Act of 1937 on incorporation of the Hague Rules in fact was, contrary to what was said above about the ordinary method of incorporation used in the Nordic countries, limited to incorporating the provisions of the Hague Rules. In Section 8 provision was made for the application of the Act to carriage between Denmark and other convention-countries, i.e. whether to or from Denmark, and to carriage from Denmark to non-convention countries. Thus, it did not apply to carriage between non-convention countries or to transport from non-convention countries to Denmark. That was in accordance with art. 10 of the Hague Rules, but as formulated, section 8 did not apply either to carriage from one foreign convention country to another or to a non-convention country. In the latter two cases it would be a breach of the convention to not apply it. It may have been thought at the time that such cases would not come before the Danish courts, although that might well happen even if no cases in point are apparently reported.

It is worth noticing that no scope was left in the Act for ordinary choice of law rules. There was no question of choosing between the Danish or foreign convention-based legislation. The cases where the Hague Rules applied were exhaustively enumerated in the Act, exclusively providing for application of the lex fori. It was of no concern to the Act which maritime law would apply to the case in respect of other matters not regulated in the Hague Rules. As mentioned above, the Act only applied to such problems which were covered by the Hague Rules. All other problems that arose in a case would be subject to the ordinary Danish Maritime Code *or* to a foreign maritime law, depending on the ordinary Danish choice of law rules. As an example may be mentioned a case where goods are carried to Denmark in a Swedish ship from a Convention country. It might well be that Swedish law or the law of the port of loading would otherwise apply to the case. Nonetheless, the Danish Hague Rule Act would apply to Hague Rule problems, not the Swedish Act nor the corresponding Act applicable in the port of loading. There might, thus, be cumulative application of the Danish Hague Rule Act to Hague Rule problems with some other law to all other carriage of goods problems.

However, notwithstanding the contents of the Act, there is no doubt that the application of the Act or corresponding foreign legislation might be extended to other cases, first of all by a paramount clause. Further, where according to section 8 the Act did not apply, the courts would undoubtedly be bound to apply either the Act or a foreign convention-based legislation, if required by art. 10 of the Convention to apply it, because it is a principle of Danish law to apply the law, if possible, in such a way as to not get into conflict with conventions to which Denmark is a party.

4. The Hague-Visby Rules

Art. 5 of the Visby protocol amended the provision in art. 10 of the Hague Rules. No changes were made in art. 2, so the area of substantive application remained the same as before.

The amended article provides that it is a rule of minimum application and that the Hague-Visby Rules may be given a wider scope of application by the member states, i.e. to bills of lading which would not be comprised by art. 10 or even to seaway bills or other transport documents.

The cases to which, according to the amended art. 10, the Convention must be applied, are those where carriage takes place between two different states and where:

1) either the bill of lading is issued in a Convention–state or –
2) the carriage takes place from a Convention-state or –
3) the parties have agreed on the application of the Convention or the law of a convention-state (Paramount Clause), regardless of the nationality of any interested person.

The practical difference from the old art. 10 is not very significant. It relates to item 2 and to the express mention of the paramount clause-cases.

A different approach was chosen in 1973 when the Visby protocol was incorporated into Danish law. The Maritime Code and the Hague-Visby Rules legislation were merged and the separate Hague Rules Act repealed. The choice of law rule contained in section 169 of the Maritime Code, like section 8 of the old Hague Rules Act, related only to the application of the Hague-Visby Rules. No statutory regulation was made with respect to the choice of the maritime law generally applicable to carriage of goods by sea other than the Hague-Visby Rules. That was left to general rules of choice of law in contract.

However, contrary to the old provision in section 8 of the Hague Rules Act, section 169 was not merely a rule about application of the Danish version of the Hague-Visby Rules. It provided for the possibility of a choice of law from among the Hague-Visby Rules law of all countries which had adhered to them. The law applicable, failing any paramount clause, would be the legislation incorporating the Hague–Visby Rules of the country where the bill of lading was issued or, if that was a non-Convention State and carriage took place from a Convention State, then the law of that State would apply. This was all in accordance with the Hague-Visby Rules. In case of carriage to a Nordic port from a non-Convention State, the Convention-legislation of the port of discharge would apply. Paramount clauses referring to the Convention-legislation of another Convention State were accepted.

Although section 169 was limited to choosing the national Hague-

Visby Rules version to be applied, it thus permitted, contrary to what was the case in the earlier legislation, the application of foreign law based upon the Hague-Visby Rules. It is likely that, in many cases, the law of the same country would in fact also be applied to other aspects of maritime law than the Hague-Visby aspects, but that did not follow from section 169.

It should be noted that from July 1, 1984 the Rome Convention came into force in Denmark but not in the other Nordic countries. However, a special protocol to that Convention reserved the application of section 169 of the Danish Maritime Code. This applies, of course, only to the choice of law rules in section 169 relating to the Hague-Visby Rules. Maritime law outside the scope of the Hague-Visby Rules was subject to the choice of law rules of the Rome Convention. Art. 4, paragraph 4 of that convention provides for a rebuttable presumption subject to the general rule in paragraph 1 on the closest connection. The presumption is that the contract has its closest connection to the country where the carrier has his principal place of business, provided that that is the country where the cargo is loaded or discharged or where the shipper has his principal place of business.

5. The Hamburg Rules

Before treating the most recent Nordic legislation, it is practical to look at the scope of application rule in art. 2 of the Hamburg Rules.

It should be remembered that while the Hague and Hague-Visby Rules apply only to cases where a bill of lading is issued, the Hamburg Rules apply to any contract of carriage of goods by sea. They also extend the period during which they apply as compared with the Hague and Hague-Visby Rules.

As with the Hague and Hague-Visby Rules, the Hamburg Rules apply if the bill of lading or any other document evidencing the contract is issued in a Contracting State. The Hamburg Rules apply in a number of other cases as well, i.e. where according to the contract the port of loading, the port of discharge or one of the optional ports of discharge which is also the actual port of discharge is in a Contracting State. The Hamburg Rules also apply in case the contract contains a Paramount Clause to that effect, referring either to the Convention itself or to the legislation of a Contracting State. In cases other than those mentioned expressly, the Hamburg Rules leave open which law to apply, even within their substantive scope of application. Thus, even a law based upon another regime than the Hamburg Rules may be applicable.

6. The new Nordic legislation

We shall now look at the most recent Nordic legislation.[2]

As mentioned above, the Nordic Maritime Codes were revised in 1994. The Nordic countries still adhere to the Hague-Visby Rules and, in principle, the liability regime of the Codes is that of the Hague-Visby Rules. However, wherever the Hague-Visby Rules so permit, the provisions in the Codes on carriage of general cargo are strongly influenced by the Hamburg Rules. They apply to carriage under all types of transport documents, not only bills of lading. Plus, they apply to the whole of the period when the cargo is in the charge of the carrier. Even a number of detailed rules are inspired or heavily influenced by the Hamburg Rules. Those include the rules of choice of law and jurisdiction.

The provisions on choice of law are found in section 252 of the Danish Maritime Code. It is a very complicated provision which contains a number of choice of law rules applicable to different situations, but it is not exhaustive. The choice of law rules contained in the provision indicate their own scope of application. Certain situations remain which are not covered by any of these choice of law rules. It must be concluded that in these remaining cases general rules of private international law apply. In Denmark, they are the provisions of the Rome Convention. With some delay the same will be the case in Sweden and Finland due to their entry into the EU.

The first provision relates to intra-Nordic trade. In Denmark, the

---

[2] For a critical appraisal cf. Hugo Tiberg in *Svensk Juristtidning* 1995.323.

provisions of the Danish Maritime Code must be applied to all carriage between the four Nordic countries as well as inside Denmark, while in respect of carriage inside one of the other countries the law of that country must be applied. Corresponding provisions exist in the three other countries. Thus, the law of another Nordic country will be applied to internal carriage in that country, but the importance thereof is small because of the great similarity between the laws of the four countries. Otherwise, lex fori is applied.

With one exception, the second provision is based directly upon art. 2 of the Hamburg Rules. Yet, while that article regulates only the scope of application of the Hamburg Rules, section 252 regulates choice of law but reaches the same result by providing a lex fori solution. Lex fori, i.e. in a Danish court Danish law and in a court of one of the other Nordic countries the law of that country must be applied, if the agreed port of loading is in a Contracting State, or the transport document is issued in such State or the transport document contains a paramount clause referring to the Hague-Visby Rules or a national law based upon them. In the latter case Danish law must thus be applied regardless of which law the transport document refers to.

Article 2 of the Hamburg Rules also provides for their application when the agreed port of discharge, or one of several optional ports of discharge which is also the actual port of discharge, is in a contracting state. Section 252 restricts the application of its lex fori rule to cases where the port of discharge in one of these situations is in a Nordic country.

The third provision seems to make an exception from the second, although it is not absolutely clear in all respects. According to the provision, if neither the agreed port of loading nor the agreed or actual port of discharge is in one of the Nordic countries, the parties may agree to submit the contract of carriage to the law of any state party to the Hague-Visby Rules.

It must be presumed that this provision only applies to cases which would otherwise be subject to the second rule and is an exception to that rule and does not extend to any of what has above been called the remaining cases. The uncertainty arises because the provision speaks without qualification about the actual port of discharge. The second rule speaks only of an agreed optional port of discharge, which is also the actual port of discharge. It must be presumed that the same is meant in the third rule.

In practical terms, it follows that all carriage within, to or from the Nordic countries is subject to the Nordic Codes, usually as lex fori. Lex fori also applies in a Nordic country in most other cases where carriage takes place from a non-Nordic Hague-Visby Rule country or the transport document is issued in such a country or contains a paramount clause referring to the Hague-Visby Rules or national law based upon them. In such cases, however, it may be agreed to apply the law of another Hague-Visby Rule country.

A paramount clause will usually be read as a reference to the law of a foreign Hague-Visby Rule country in all cases where it is permissible under the Code to do so.

What cases are left which are not covered by section 252 and where, therefore, ordinary choice of law rules apply?

It can never be carriage within or from the Nordic Countries. With respect to carriage to the Nordic Countries, in order for the situation to not be covered by section 252, no agreement may have been made in the transport document that the port of discharge is or may be in a Nordic country and the transport document may not have been issued in a Hague-Visby Rule country.

With respect to cross-trade outside the Nordic countries, only such cases may be outside the scope of section 252 where the port of loading is in a non-Hague–Visby Rule country and where the transport documents are also issued in such a country. Hague Rule and Hamburg Rule countries qualify for this purpose. Under art. 2 of the Hamburg Rules, even these cases would be covered by the obligatory application of the Hamburg Rules.

In the cases mentioned which are not covered by section 252, it follows from the Rome Convention that the parties are free to make their own choice of law from any convention on carriage of goods by sea embodied in a national law or any other national law. If they have not done so, the court must apply the law to which there is the closest connection, subject to the presumption mentioned above 4.

The provision in section 252 is remarkable in several respects:

It is to a large extent based on art. 2 of the Hamburg Rules, despite the fact that Denmark has not ratified that Convention but has remained a party to the Hague-Visby Rules. That does not, however, give rise to any conflict with the Hague-Visby Rules since the scope of application rule in that Convention is one of minimum application and is complied with.

Further, it invalidates the choice of law by the parties in a considerable number of cases and replaces it with a law which, despite paying lip-service to the Hague–Visby Rules, is based in many respects upon the Hamburg Rules and in some respects even goes further.

Finally, and as opposed to the earlier legislation of 1937 and 1973, the substantive scope of application of section 252 is not limited to the provisions of the Maritime Code implementing the Hague-Visby Rules. The choice of law rules in section 252, including the lex fori rule, apply in respect of all provisions in the Code regulating carriage of general cargo by sea, regardless of whether or not they are within the scope of the Hague-Visby Rules. However, they do not apply to charterparties or to bills of lading issued under a charterparty, unless the bill of lading determines the relationship between the carrier and the holder of the bill of lading, i.e. after a transfer of the bill of lading.

According to its wording, section 252 is not restricted to applying to internationally mandatory or just mandatory provisions of the Danish Maritime Code. Section 254 specifies which provisions of the Code relating to general cargo are not mandatory. All other provisions are mandatory and, in view of the contents of section 252, must be regarded as internationally mandatory so that they may not be derogated from by agreement by the parties, even in international situations, cf. art. 7 of the Rome Convention on the law applicable to contractual obligations.

There is a serious risk that such a broad lex fori rule may lead to forum shopping. In earlier discussions about the possibility for parties to escape from the mandatory bill of lading legislation, it was never argued that any restrictions should be put on the parties right to choose the applicable law in respect of problems other than those regulated in the international conventions.

However, section 252 cannot be read to the effect that the parties cannot choose the application of a foreign law to matters regulated in the Code by non-mandatory provisions. Here, the general principles of private international law and of the Rome Convention must prevail.

As mentioned above, the protocol to the Rome Convention permitted Denmark to retain section 169 of the old Maritime Code and even to revise that provision without following the ordinary consultation procedure in art. 23 of the Rome Convention. Section 169 related solely to the application of the Hague-Visby Rules. It may be questioned whether the protocol really permits extending the provision to the degree done in the new Maritime Code, more or less abolishing any choice of law without following the usual consultation procedures. It might well be said that the old choice of law rule in section 169 on the application of Hague–Visby based law has been replaced by an internationally mandatory rule as regulated by art. 7 paragraph 2 of the Rome Convention covering the whole of the law of carriage of goods by sea. That, at least, was not what was in the minds of the drafters of the protocol.

7. Jurisdiction and Arbitration

As mentioned above, the Hague and Hague-Visby Rules do not contain any rules on jurisdiction, neither did the earlier Nordic legislation. The Hamburg Rules contain a provision on jurisdiction in article 21 and one on arbitration in article 22. Corresponding provisions are found in the new Nordic legislation in sections 310 and 311 of the Danish Maritime Code. These provisions should be seen in light of the discussion prior to the Hamburg Rules on the possibility of protecting the application of the mandatory provisions in the Hague and Hague-Visby Rules Conventions by setting aside any jurisdiction clauses which might lead to the application of less strict legislation in contravention of article 3 (8) of the Hague and Hague-Visby Rules. Under the earlier Nordic legislation, the position was not clear, but there was probably no basis for setting aside a jurisdiction clause for the reason that the result which would be reached under Danish law might not be reached under the law likely to be applied by the chosen forum.[3]

A jurisdiction clause may have two effects: it may confer jurisdiction upon a court which would not otherwise have jurisdiction or it may deprive a court which would otherwise have jurisdiction thereof or both.

Under article 21 of the Hamburg Rules, the plaintiff has an option to sue at certain places enumerated in the article and may not sue elsewhere. This option for the plaintiff may not be restricted by agreement between the parties until after a claim has arisen. The places where a plaintiff may sue are the defendant's principal place of business, the place where the contract was made (provided it was made through a place of business of the defendant situated there), the port of loading or discharge, and any additional agreed upon place. The article thus makes it possible to confer jurisdiction on courts which do not have it under the article. However, it does not permit the parties to deprive a court which would have jurisdiction under the article of that jurisdiction except after the claim has arisen and, thus, prevents the parties from gaining certainty about where the forum for any disputes is.

Article 21 also contains a provision on arrest jurisdiction and a provision limiting the possibility of suing in more than one place.

Section 310 of the new Danish Maritime Code builds upon article 21 with only minor changes. However, it does not apply unless the agreed port of loading or the agreed or actual port of discharge is in one of the Nordic countries. Nor does it apply if it would be contrary to the European Judgments Convention or, with respect to Sweden, Finland and Norway, to the Lugano Convention. This provision is necessary because the provisions of the two Conventions have priority over national legislation unless that legislation is based upon an international convention ratified by the member-countries. The Nordic countries have not, however, ratified the Hamburg Rules Convention. They are still parties to the Hague-Visby Rules which do not

---

[3] Cf generally about jurisdiction clauses Uffe Lind Rasmussen, *Jurisdiktionsklausuler og Voldgiftsklausuler i Søtransportkontrakter*, Marjus nr. 90, 1984 and Kristina Maria Siig, *Forum og Lovvalg vedrørende Transportansvaret*, nr. Marjus 215, 1995.

contain any jurisdiction rules, although they have adopted many provisions of the Hamburg Rules into their internal law.

Section 310 of the Maritime Code will be contrary to the Judgments Convention in the following situations:

Firstly, under the Judgments Convention, rules of jurisdiction are invalid if they extend or restrict the rules of jurisdiction in the Judgment Convention in respect of persons or companies having respectively their domicile or seat in a Contracting State. Unless, in the individual case, the port of loading or discharge is the place of performance or the place where a tort was committed, these ports would not be acceptable jurisdictions under the Judgments Convention. On the other hand, other heads of jurisdiction which exist under the Judgments Convention cannot be excluded by national legislation.

Secondly, if, under article 17 of the Judgments Convention parties have agreed to the jurisdiction of a court in a State Party to the Convention, that jurisdiction cannot be excluded and the jurisdiction of all other courts is accordingly excluded by the agreement.

It follows that section 310 is of limited interest. It does not apply if the defendant is domiciled (has its seat) in one of the EU or EFTA countries or if jurisdiction has been conferred upon a court in one of those countries. To put it differently, it applies only if the defendant is a shipowner or cargo owner living outside those countries and jurisdiction has not been conferred upon a court in one of them. In such cases it makes it possible for a Nordic cargo owner who receives cargo in a Nordic port or ships cargo from such a port to sue the shipowner there, even if the transport document contains a jurisdiction clause, e.g. providing for jurisdiction at the homeport of the vessel or the seat of the shipowner or some other non-European port. That, probably, is the only real effect of the rule.

Section 310 only applies to the carriage of general cargo. If the carriage is governed by a charterparty which contains jurisdiction clauses and bills of lading are issued and sold, section 310 applies if the purchaser does not know nor ought to know the charterparty and the bill of lading contains no express incorporation of the jurisdiction clause.

Section 311 on arbitration supplements the rule in section 310 restricting the possibility of adopting derogative jurisdiction clauses and builds upon the corresponding provision in article 22 of the Hamburg Rules.

Under section 311 the parties may agree on arbitration. However, if the agreed port of loading or the agreed or actual port of discharge is in one of the other Nordic countries, the parties are not free to determine the place of arbitration. That follows from the provision that it is for the claimant to choose the place of arbitration from among the places where he may sue in court under section 310, including any place agreed upon between the parties. This is an extraordinary provision in view of the significance ordinarily attached to the place of arbitration. It does, however, correspond to the provision of art. 22 of the Hamburg Rules which have much wider application.

Section 311, like article 22 of the Hamburg Rules, also contains a choice of law rule. It provides for the mandatory application by the Arbitration Tribunal of the provisions of the Danish Maritime Code on general cargo. This implies that, as with respect to cases before a Danish court, it is not even possible to apply the law of another country which is a party to the Hague-Visby Rules. The somewhat restrictive interpretation of the choice of law rule in section 252 explained above must also apply in respect of this rule. The scope of application of the choice of law rule is the same as for the rule relating to the choice of the place of arbitration.

Section 311 is very far reaching. It restricts the parties' free choice of the place of arbitration and it imposes a choice of law on them, at least as far as the applicable maritime law is concerned.

A restriction on the choice of place of arbitration is unusual elsewhere in the law of international arbitration, except in air law. The CMR Convention which contains a provision on jurisdiction in article 31 expressly permits, in article 33, arbitration provided the application of the Convention is stipulated in the contract.

A provision regulating the place of arbitration does not pursue the aims of legislation of carriage of goods by sea. The place of arbitration may be important in respect of the applicable law of arbitration, but it is difficult to see why that would be desirable to regulate. To obtain the object of the legislation, it ought to be sufficient to regulate the choice of law. On the contrary, it is preferable that the parties have freedom to choose the place of arbitration in order for it to be in a country with a well-developed law of arbitration and sufficient facilities and neutral surroundings for the purpose. In any event, it seems to be in both parties' interest to know in advance where an arbitration will take place. A system where the choice between several options is left to the claimant prevents that.

With respect to the choice of law provision, section 311 goes further than the Hamburg Rules and further than the jurisdiction rules can explain. The jurisdiction rules cannot prevent foreign law from being applied in foreign jurisdictions, even law which is not based upon the Hague Visby Rules or any other convention. The reasonable thing would have been to follow the example of the CMR Convention and require the application of the Convention or to go a step further and permit application of a law based upon the Hague Visby Rules. In practice, such a provision is only enforceable when the place of arbitration is in Denmark or when enforcement must take place there. The result is the creation of a lot of uncertainty for both parties without insurance that the aim is obtained.

When an award has been made which is not in accordance with the choice of law rule in section 311, it probably follows from article V 1(e) of the New York Convention on the recognition and enforcement of foreign arbitral awards that it may be set aside by the Danish courts and from article V 2(a) that it needs not be enforced in Denmark.

This is a different and much stricter position than the one recently taken by the US Supreme Court. In the Vimar v. M/V Sky Reefer case,[4] the Court decided that arbitration abroad was not in itself contrary to article 3 (8) of the US COGSA or to the Hague Rules on which it is based and that the risk that foreign arbitrators might not apply COGSA could not cause the invalidity of the arbitration clause, although if an award would lessen the liability under COGSA it might result in the award being set aside on the ground of public

---

[4] 63 U.S.L.W at 4617 (June 19, 1995).

policy. The Court again underlined the importance of taking a broad, non-nationalistic view of the law.

It might, perhaps, be doubtful whether the ordre public clause could be used by a Danish court in a corresponding situation, but as mentioned above, that is probably not necessary in order to obtain the same result.

SOME BRIEF REFLECTIONS ABOUT FEDERALISM IN THE EUROPEAN UNION AND IN THE UNITED STATES OF AMERICA

Carl Michael Quitzow

1. Introduction

The differences and similarities between the concept of American federalism and the European endeavours to create integration at different levels among the Member States may have given rise to discussions in the legal theory. Some comparative studies of major importance on this subject have been made by Europeans as well as American lawyers.[1] U.S. Constitutional Law, and case law of the U.S. Supreme Court, have also served as sources of inspiration for several other studies of EC-law.[2]

The scope of this short contribution to the above mentioned subject is to make some brief reflections about the ideas which have given character to federalism in the USA and the European integration process and which impact this might have for the future development of EC-Law. The purpose is thus not to in an exhaustive manner elaborate, or even evaulate the different ideas which can be

---

[1] See i.e. M. Cappelletti et al., Integration Through Law, Europe and the American Federal Experience, Berlin, New York, 1986, K. Lenaerts, Le Juge et la constitution aux Etats-Unis d'Amérique et dans l'ordre juridique européen, Bruxelles, 1988, W.H. Roth, Freier Warenverkehr und staatliche Regelungsgewalt in einem gemeinsamen Markt, München, 1977, T. Sandalow/E. Stein, Courts and Free Markets, Perspectives from the United States and Europe, Oxford, 1982. This study was completed in August, 1995.

[2] See i.e. J. Fejø, Monopolret og Marked, København, 1985, L. Gormley, Prohibiting Restrictions on Trade Within the EEC, Haag, 1985, C. Gulmann, Handelshindringer I EF-retten, København, 1980, C.M. Quitzow, Fria varurörelser i den Europeiska gemenskapen, Stockholm, 1995, H. Rasmussen, On Law and Policy in the European Court of Justice, Doordrecht, 1986, P.J. Slot, Technical and administrative obstacles to trade in the EEC, Leyden 1975.

derived through more in debt studies. The perspective lies on the issue which influence true federalism in the American sense might have in relation to the Inter-governmental conference between the Member States concerning Treaty-revision which was decided during the negotiations of the Maastrich Treaty and the future development of community law.

Federalism is a notion which may be defined in different ways. However, I will use the notion from the Meyers Konversations-Lexicon:

> "Neigung zur Bildung einer Föderation (s.d.), Vorliebe für das einer solchen zu Grunde liegende Prinzip, daß nämlich die verbundenen Staaten, bez. Länder in ihrer Vereinigung eine gegenseitige Stütze finden, doch auch nicht mehr als unumgänglich notwendig von ihrer Selbständigkeit einbüßen sollen."[3]

This notion shows that federalism is a very vague notion and that it may be given a different meaning in different contexts. One crucial issue for the analysis of federalism in different context seems to be what goals should be achieved by an inter-state co-operation. Another issue seems to be how much decision-making within the federation that shall take place at a supra-national level and how effective the supra-national decision making-processes shall be and how they shall be controlled. Furthermore, the question of division of powers and the settlement of conflicts of competence seems to be of crucial importance within federations.

According to the above-mentioned one can conclude that the American federal structure from its very beginning was aimed at creating a true statehood between the former British colonies in North-America. Thus, it was aimed to create a state-structure. The next question is why the federal structure was chosen and not any traditional European centralistic state-structure, as for example the French. The answer to that question seems to lie in the differences between the states involved in an economical as well as a religious and cultural sense. The ideas of the French revolution also had impact on the U.S. constitution. The link between the different states

---

[3] Fünfte Auflage, Sechster Band, Leipzig und Wien, 1897.

lies in the economic interaction. Thus economical means was the American way to achieve federalism.

Through a supranational parliament – the Congress –, federal authorities with executive competences and a constitutional court – the U.S. Supreme Court – the USA has developed to be a model for federalism, at least from a constitutional point of view.

European federalism differs very much from American federalism. It seems more or less to be statesmens' visions rather than political achievements and a political structure. Therefore European federalism has not been given a clear content. However, it seems that it is not aimed at creating a state structure like the American model of a federal state. Thus European federalism seems to be much less tangible than the American federalism. Its content must be analyzed together with the notion of integration.

2. Federalism and integration in the EU-context

Already before the negotiations of the ECSC-Treaty federal ideas were formulated for the shaping of a new Europe. These ideas, which mainly were formulated by Jean Monnet, were characterized by the American federal experience. At that time American political influence on the European economy was used in order to create a new political order within Europe.

In the ideas concerning European integration four main concepts can be identified: the functionalistic, the federalistic, the neofunctionalistic and the transactionalistic.[4]

The functionalistic school has as its aim to secure peace and to better satisfy the needs of the people through cooperation between states. The cooperation shall be carried out through the states transferring certain tasks of mainly technical character to international organizations. These, and their institutional structures, shall be designed according to the tasks, and led by unpolitical experts. Efficient solutions will result in more tasks being transferred to international organizations. Good results of the work of international organiza-

---

4 See further C. Gulmann, Handelshindringer i EF-retten, København, 1980, s. 88–92.

tions will lead to the transfer of loyalty from national level to supra-national level.

The federalists is a school which can trace its roots a long way back in history. The federalists mean that a European federal state is the right model of integration. The federal state shall be introduced through political decisions and constitutional documents. The America constitutional system serves as a model for the federalists.

The neofunctionalist is a mixture of the functionalists and the federalists. The final aim for integration is not exactly formulated by this school but the creation of some kind of statehood seems inevitabel according to representatives of this school. The main idea in this school is the self-fortifying effect of integration. Regulation at a supranational level will create solidarity over the national borders. This is called the "spill-over effect". Integration in one field creates integration in other fields. This theory seems however to have been modyfied due to among other things the development of the European integration process.

The transactionalists examine the elements which may create community of states and secure peaceful settlement of disputes. The representatives of this school mean that the creation of a feeling of solidarity between states and people is decisive. This feeling of solidarity can be measured by a high level of "transactions" between the states involved. The transactions can be trade, travels and exchange of students etc. The field of transactions or the number of transactions must grow and this fortifies the community of states. The representatives of this school are of the opinion that traditional forms of international co-operation of the opinion that traditional forms of international co-operation are enough and that institutionalization may be necessary but this is primarily not desirable.

The differences between the theories shall not be exaggerated. However, the most important difference seems to lie in the desirability to create supra-national institutions such as argued by the federalists and the neofunctionalists or just the creation of a socio-psychological community such as argued by the functionalists and the transactionalists. The differences are not absolute and may not be understood as incompatible amongst themselves.[5]

Furthermore, the theories related to the notion of integration are not verified by empirical examinations which may give rise to critisism and the actual development has not given any of them right.

However, the different schools have proven to be right on one point, trade and commercial transactions are important or even crucial for the achievement of integration. Trade can also create solidarity among people. Thus trade and economic progress resulting hereof can be argued to be one of the most important issues in European integration.

Due to the above-mentioned it can be concluded that integration is a vague notion which is very difficult to define and that trade through the establishment of a Common Market is the main feature in an integration process.

The Common Market is also a vague notion which is not defined in the EC Treaty. However, it is decisive for extensions of community competence according to Article 235 of the EC Treaty.

Kapteyn and Verloren van Themaat have – according to my opinion – made a successful attempt to define the notion of the Common Market.[6] In this connection they use the notions negative and positive integration. Negative integration is the abolishment of all barriers to free movement within the community. Negative integration is defined in Article 7a of the EC Treaty which deals with the establishment of the internal market. Positive integration is the introduction of new instruments to control the market and the creation of new institutions. An example of positive integration can be found in the merger-control regulation.[7]

Kapteyn and Verloren van Themaat define the Common Market as: "a market in which every participant of the Community in question is free to invest, produce, work, buy and sell, to supply or obtain services under conditions of competition which have not been artifi-

---

[5] C. Gulmann, ibid, s. 91.

[6] Introduction to the Law of the European Communities, 2nd Ed. Deventer/Boston, 1989, s. 78–79.

[7] Council Regulation (EEC) 4064/89, OJ 1990, L 257/13.

cially distorted wherever economic conditions are most favourable". According to this definition cross-border economic activites promote the achievement of the aims of the Treaty.

According to Kapteyn's and Verloren van Themaat's notions of positive and negative integration it can be concluded that the internal market only concerns liberalization of economic activities in the community and that the Common Market also includes regulation of the market which may affect competition relations and clear away distortions on competion created by liberalization. Thus liberalization and regulation of the market are important to create integration in the EC.

Thus the Treaty can be argued to be based upon a presumtion that the abolishment of barriers to cross-border economic activities leads to economic and social progress and creates solidarity among the peoples of Europe which are the fundament for an even closer union among them. This opinion is supported through the fact that the European Court of Justice (ECJ) uses the preamble and the principles of the Treaty in its teleological interpretations of the Treaty. It can thus be argued that European federalism is based upon economical visions. Accordingly, the Common Market is a central notion in European federalism.

However some Member States seem to be inclined to deepen the integration and to extend it to new areas such as foreign and security policy and home affairs. Other Member States are of a contrary opinion and oppose against a development of a European federal state. Since the mid 80's there has also been a struggle between regulation and deregulation within the community. This conflict was to be solved through the introduction of the subsidiarity principle in the EC Treaty.

4. The principle of subsidiarity

The principle of subsidiarity has developed from beeing a principle of catholic social philisophy to a rule to solve conflicts of competence in federal states such as the USA and Germany. The principle of subsidiarity is found in Amendment X of the U.S. Constitution and

Article 72 of the German Constitution. A federal principle has thus been introduced in the Community through Article 3b and the EC Treaty. One can put forward the question if this is compatible with the European integration which is based upon the Common Market.

Toth has argued that the principle of subsidiarity represents a breach of the system of the EC Treaty.[8] Boye-Jacobsen has however argued that the principle of subsidiarity has been in the background in the competence-structure of the community during long time.[9] I am inclined to give Boye-Jacobsen right. I do not think that the principle of subsidiarity will cause a revolution in community law.

Although the principle of subsidiarity represents federalistic structures, one must bear in mind that that the community legal system which frames the Common Market is based upon federalistic principles. This lies already in the original Treaty but became obvious after the coming into force of the Single European Act. To issue common rules with qualified majority through common institutions, in order to establish the internal market, is as such a supra-national decision making system, which is very close to a federal system. In this context, it may be argued that the principle of subsidiarity can clarify the division of powers between the Member States and the Community and be an instrument to solve conflicts related hereto. However, it may prove difficult to make this principle workable in a legal sence.[10] Thus, the principle of subsidiarity will probably have its greatest influence on the policy-making process in the Community.

The principle of subsidiarity is of a great interest for Swedish lawyers and has been studied intensely before the Swedish accession to the EU. One of the most extensive studies of this principle was made in a parliamentary investigation where Professor Lennart Pålsson was the legal expert.[11] As a Swedish pioneer of community

---

[8] See A.G. Toth, The Subsidiarity Principle in the Maastrich Treaty, Common Market Law Review 1992, p. 1081.

[9] See C. Boye-Jacobsen, Subsidiaritetsbegrebet i EF-retten, Ugeskrift for Retsvæsen 1992, s. 344 p.

[10] See P. Hallström, Några tankar omkring subsidiaritetsprincipens tillämpning i EG-rätten, Svensk Juristtidning 1992, s. 181 p.

[11] Statens Offentliga Utredningar 1994:12, Suveränitet och demokratin, Betänkande av EG-konsekvensutredningarna: subsidiaritet.

law, professor Pålsson participated in this study which gave important contribution to the debate that preceeded the Swedish referendum about EU-membership. The investigation also pointed out the difficulties in giving the principle of subsidiarity a legal content, but concludes that the ECJ probably will use its traditional legal methods in order to give this principle a juridical content. This may support the assumption that the principle of subidiarity is interpreted in line with the principle of proportionality and other principle of the Treaty as well as fundamental principles of law which will be of importance in cases concerning actions for annulment according to Article 173 of the Treaty.[12] This may give rise to discussions about other issues concerning actions for annulment such as for example the rather strict case law of the ECJ in relation to locus standi.[13] If the Court would widen the admissability to submit actions for annulments this could be regarded as a compensation for the democratic deficit of the community decision making process which can be of importance to get judicial review of legal acts issued by the Community where aspects concerning subsidiarity are relevant. This viewpoint may, however, be subject to criticism due to the fact that the ECJ could be overflowed with more or less substantial actions for annulment which could create chaos in the ECJ which already has a heavy work load.

According to the above.mentioned it can be concluded that the principle of subsidiarity will probably have a vitalizing effect on the future shaping of Community law and that it will impose restrictions on extension of Community competence, mainly through the use of Article 235 of the EC Treaty. It is, hovewer, unclear if this could lead to a more federalistic structure in the EC and the EU as a whole.

---

[12] See C. Boye-Jacobsen, Subsidiaritetsbegrepet i EF-retten, Ugeskrift for Retsvæsen 1992, s. 343.

[13] Concering locus standi, see further i.e. cases 25/62 Plaumann [1963] ECR 107, C-358 Extramet Industrie SA [1991] ECR I-2501 and C-309/89 Codornui v. Council, judgement of May 18th 1994.

5. The division of powers in the Community

The structure of the EU is rather peculiar from a constitutional point of view. It is a mixture of traditional state cooperation according to international public law and a quasi-federal structure concerning the Common Market, the EC, ECSC and the EURATOM.

The classic model concerning division of powers within a state, as formulated by Montesquieu, with a legislative, a judicial and a exec-utive power, is not present in the community structure. The Community institutions lack the exedutive authority which is necessary for the excercise of state competence. The Council of the European Union is the legislative power, the ECJ is the judicial power, but the Com-mission and the European Parliament do not fit in according to Montesquieus system of division of powers.

Thus, as long as the decision-making power concerning legislation lies in the Council of the European Union, the national governments and parliaments are responsible for the policies at the community level. However, if the Parliament's competence is extended, the EU gets more of a federal structure. The key to European federalism thus lies in the question about how much competence shall be transferred to the Parliament. A powerful Parliament would perhaps be compa-rable to the United States Congress. In this respect the existing treaty-structure leads to the conclusion that the issue concerning democratic deficit must be solved in other ways than increasing the powers of the Parliament if a larger extent of federalism is not wanted by the Member States. This could for example be done through higher transparency and openness in the community decision-making proc-ess.

Thus, European federalism seems to be of a limited nature. It is what could be called sectorial federalism.[14] As long as the European Council and the Council of the European Union are responsible for the political decision making in the EU, steps towards true federalism seem to be impossible. Only a development of the Parliament with

---

[14] See further P. Hallström, Europeisk Gemenskap och politisk union, Stockholm 1986, s. 51.

transferral of more important decision making functions to it can pave the way for creating a European federal state of a USA-model.

6. US federalism and European federalism compared

It follows from the above-mentioned that there are important differences between American fedralism and European federalism. Firstly, the constitutional structure and the refulatory instruments in the USA are quite different to those in the EU. In the USA there are also executive powers at a federal level. In the EU, in principle all executive powers lie within the competences of the Member States.[15] The Member States of the EU are also primarily responsible for the protection of fundamental rights, although the ECJ regards it as its task also to give protection to these rights within the context of the community treaties.

However, in the context of the Common Market the EC seems to have adopted the same federal principles which govern the American inter-state market. This argument is supported mainly on the basis of case law of the ECJ concerning free movement, especially goods, pre-emtion and competition law.[16] In the economic fields of integration in the EC almost the same principles apply as in the USA. This supports the opnion that there is already a kind of sectorial federalism within the EC, which was established by the ECJ already in 1961 in the Steenkolenijnen case.[17]

The economic federalism of the EC does not create a true federalism like in the USA. The political integration within Europe, e.g. in the fields of such political importance as criminal policy, immigration policy towards third countries, foreign policies and defence policy seems to be of a rather premature character. This character is not changes by the Maastricht Treaty. For common actions in the above

---

[15] On this issue see further, i.e. P. Hallström, Medlemsstaternas verkställande av EG-rätten, Juridisk Tidskrift, 1992–93, p. 59.

[16] Concerning the free movement of goods, see further C.M. Quitzow, Fria varurörelser i den Europeiska gemenskapen, Stockholm 1995.

[17] 30/59 Steenkolenmijnen, Slg 1961. S. 3.

mentioned areas traditional international cooperation has been chosen to create common European policies. This rather unique concept is defenitively not a step towards federalism in other fields than the economic ones. Even the realisation of a economic and monetary union with a common European currency, would assumably not change the character of the EU into a true federation of states. Although, it could be argued that increasing political integration will decrease the importance of free movement in the EU as an instrument to achieve a higher level of integration.

Due to the above-mentioned it can be concluded that the existing treaties do not give a basis for creating a true and overall federal state within Europe. This opinion is supported by the Maastricht Treaty which even limits federalism to only the economic aspects of European integration. Cooperation in foreign affairs and justice and home affairs shall be carried out through traditional international cooperation. The model chosen in the Maastricht Treaty seems to be supported by the existing Article 220 of the EC Treaty which presupposes the adoption of international conventions between the Member States concerning issues which are not affected by the competences transferred to the Community by the Member States and which thus primarily are to be regarded as national concerns.

The USA is a true federation where policy areas of typically national concern, such as foreign policy and defence policy, are covered by the federal competence. There are also federal executing authorites which can execute policy decisions taken at a federal level. The EU is however only a federation in an economic sense where all traditional national concerns outside economic areas and executing power lie within the competence of the Member States. This makes it, in fact, impossible to create a federal Europe according to the existing treaties framing the EU.

7. The solidarity principle of Article 5 of the EC Treaty and international public law

One of the most important provisions of the EC Treaty is the solidarity principle laid down in Article 5. This is the provision on which the

Court has based some of its extensive interpretations of community law. the ECJ has construed it in a manner which in different ways has enchanced the federal characteristics of the rules framing the Common Market, such as direct effect, primacy, indirect effect and preemption. The second section of this provision safeguards the aims of integration also in fields outside the field of application of the EC Treaty, which gives this article far-reaching effects. However, it must be borne in mind that the EC Treaty as well as the Maastricht Treaty, is an international treaty between sovereign states covered by international public law and is as such not a constitutional document. Thus, there are areas flanking to the Common Market, where the border line between EC-law and international public law is very diffuse and difficult to set.

According to this conflicts could arise between international public law and Article 5 of the EC Treaty extensions of federalism in Europe are based on the present treaties, since the applicability of international public law starts where the field of application of Article 5 ends.[18] Due to this it seems difficult to create a greater amount of federalism in Europe outside the area of the Common Market and other forms of ecenomic cooperation, without creating completely new and constitutional documents.

8. The future perspective

It is often said that the Treaty revision in the 1996 Inter-governmental conference which was decided in the negotiations about the Maastricht Treaty will give Europe more federal characteristics and pave the way for the accession of the reformed states of eastern Europe.[19] This seems, however, to be a contradiction. Is it possible to create a

---

[18] See P. Hallström, Europeisk Gemenskap och politisk union, Stockholm, 1985, p. 451.

[19] See further about the 1996 Treaty-revision conference, EU:s regeringskonferens, en nulägesrapport från EU 96 kommittén. This is a paper prepared by jur. kand. Magnus Rydén, legal advisor of the Swedish Ministry of Foreign Affairs, Department of Trade, Stockholm 1995. See also Report of the Court of Justice on Certain Aspects of the Application of the Treaty on European Union – Contribution of the Court of First Instance for the Purposes of the 1996 Intergovernmental Conference, Proceedings of the Court of Justice and Court of First Instance of the European Communities, Nr 15/95.

greater amount of federalism when new states with quite different traditions are to be new members? I think that a workable hypothesis is that the question to extend federalism within the EU, beyond the economic areas, must be dealt with after the accession of the new candidates for membership. One also faces the fact that the opinions of the different governments of the Member States differ very much and that it seems to be a very difficult project to unite these opinions in the treaty-revision conference. It may also be argued that the Inter-governmental conference will probably not lead to any revolutions. The results of that conference will perhaps be some minor adjustments in the existing treaties and some political statements about future policies of the EU, rather than steps toward higher degrees of federalism in new policy areas of primarily non-economic nature.

Accordingly, I do not think that the Inter-governmental conference will enhance federalism in Europe. Accession of new states seems to be more important in order to secure peace within the whole of Europe, which is the superior aim of the European Communities and the European Union.

There is a long way to go, if it is possible at all, to create a true federal state within Europe. The different languages and cultures makes it, in my opinion, hard to create a federal state within Europe. This makes it debatable whether to make changes in the legal structure of the Community such as extending the powers of the European Parliament. The issue of democratic deficit, a crucial issue which must be taken very seriously, must be solved by other measures, such as for example higher transparency and political responsibility in the decision-making processes at the Community level, rather than increasing the powers of the European Parliament and the use of clandestine methods to create quasi-federalism in areas which were not intended by the existing treaties to be exclusive community competences by the Member States.

The way to handle problems flanking to the original EC-competences through traditional international co-operation seems to be in line with the original ideas framing the EC Treaty in 1957. In areas not covered by the sectorial federalism which frames the Common Market, the Member States seem, according to the existing treaties, to be obliged to solve arising problems through traditional international cooperation. The way set forth in the Maastricht Treaty to shape cooperation between the Member States of the European Union in the fields of foreign affairs and justice and home affairs through traditional international cooperation seems to be the proper way to regulate cooperation between the Member States in those fields. This opinion is supported by the fact that already in the EC Treaty it is provided through Article 220, that certain flanking areas to the Common Market lying within the traditional state sovereignty, such as e.g. taxation and international private law, are foreseen to be regulated through international conventions.[20]

9. Conclusions

There are important differences between federalism in the European context and the American context. Such important issues for a federal state as foreign policy and defence policy are not covered by the supranational competence of the Communities. On the contrary, even after coming into force of the Maastricht Treaty, they are still mainly national competences.

The European federal ideas are primarily aimed at shaping economic federalism and to create economic interdependence in order to secure peace, and not to create a federal state. Thus, the enlargement of the Community in the East and European industrial policy should, in my opinion, be given priority in the coming treaty-revision conference. The strives to create a higher degree of federalism and to extend it into the EU-context in order to solve such problems as the democratic deficit in the decision-making process at Community level may create dangerous political situations and it also does not seem to be compatible with the structure and systems of the existing treaties. The creation of a true federation within Europe after a US model demands the shaping of new constitutional instruments which clear

---

[20] See also H. Rasmussen, EU-ret och EG-institutioner i kontekts, København 1994, p. 142–143.

away potential conflicts between Article 5 of the EC Treaty and international public law. The modelling of such documents may however take quite some time, but Rome was not built in one day. Progress in integration can not be extracted only through political ambitions. However, the superior aim of integration seems to be achieved. There has been peace between the Member States since 1945, the longest lasting peace between these states in our history. Perhaps federalism in other fields than the economic ones is unneccessary in order to achieve the goals for the European integration, even the creation of a citizen' Europe?

Bibliography

C. Boye-Jacobsen, Subsidiaritetsbegrepet i EF-retten, Ugeskrift for Retsvæsen 1992.

M. Cappelletti et al., Integration Through Law, Europe and the American Federal Experience, Berlin/New York, 1986, Walther de Gruyter.

J. Fejø, Monopolret og Marked, København, 1985, Juristforbundets Forlag.

L. Gormley, Prohibiting Restrictions on Trade Within the EEC, Haag, 1985, TMC Asser Instituut.

C. Gulmann, Handelshindringer i EF-retten, København, 1980, Juristforbundets Forlag.

P. Hallström, Europeisk Gemenskap och politisk union, Stockholm 1986.

P. Hallström, Medlemsstaternas verkställande av EG-rätten, Juridisk Tidskrift, 1992–93.

P. Hallström, Några tankar omkring subsidiaritetsprincipens tillämpning i EG-rätten, Svensk Juristtidning 1992.

P.J.G. Kapteyn/P. Verloren van Themaat, Introduction to the Law of the European Communities, 2nd Ed. Deventer/Boston, 1989, Kluwer.

K. Lenaerts, Le Juge et la constitution aux Etats-Unis d'Amerique et dans l'ordre juridique européen, Bruxelles, 1988, Bruylant.

Meyers Konversationslexicon, Fünfte Auflage, Sechster Band, Leipzig und Wien, 1897.

C.M. Quitzow, Fria varurörelser i den Europeiska gemenskapen, Stockholm, 1995, C.E. Fritzes Förlag.

H. Rasmussen, EU-ret og EU-institutioner i kontekst, København 1994, Karnovs Forlag.

H. Rasmussen, On Law and Policy in the European Court of Justice, Doordrecht, 1986, Martinus Nijhoff Publishers.

W.H. Roth, Freier Warenverkehr und staatliche Regelungsgewalt in einem gemeinsamen Markt, München, 1977, C.H. Beck'sche Verlagsbuchhandlung.

M. Rydén, EU:s regeringskonferens, en nulägesrapport från EU 96 kommittén. Utrikesdepartementets handelsavdelning, Stockholm 1995.

T. Sandalow/E. Stein, Courts and Free Markets, Perspectives from the United States and Europe, Oxford, 1982, Clarendon Press.

P.J. Slot, Technical and administrative obstacles to trade in the EEC, Leyden 1975, Martinus Nijhoff Publishers.

Statens Offentliga Utredningar 1994:12, Suveränitet och demokrati, Betänkande av EG-konsekvensutredningarna: subsidiaritet.

A.G. Toth, The Subsidiarity Principle in the Maastricht Treaty, Common Market Law Review 1992.

COMPARATIVE LAW AS A YARDSTICK FOR ACADEMIC LEGAL EDUCATION

Kurt Siehr

I. Dangerous Comparative Law

Comparative law is supposed to be not only a complicated subject matter but also a very dangerous one. This danger hardly seems to be fatal although comparative research has also been associated with physical risks. The hazards of comparative law are, rather, dangers of psychology and intellectual endeavours.

1. Teaching Comparative Law

Teaching comparative law may be dangerous for the lecturer's equilibrium because courses in comparative law, unless mandatory in the law school curriculum, do not attract many students. Most students abstain from foreign materials, concentrate their studies on domestic law and do not want to be made uncertain of the domestic solution of a universal problem. This intellectual lethargy or laziness of the majority is a chance for those lecturers who prefer small classes of devoted students who are willing to be exposed to the dangers inherent to comparative law.

2. Advocating Comparative Law

Whoever has taught comparative law has had to face another danger, one caused by his or her dear colleagues in faculty meetings, curriculum conferences or budget committees. "Why do we need courses in comparative law?" "Our students should concentrate on domestic law and have a firm grasp of domestic statutes, cases and other materials!" "Our tight library budget cannot cover the luxury of buying foreign law books which almost nobody reads and which take up space in overcrowded stacks."

As a teacher of comparative law, you realize very soon that you have to fight in several front lines. You do not only have to remove your students' ignorance, but you also have to convince your learned colleagues that some comparative law might be useful and even rewarding.

3. Making Use of Comparative Law

Last century Rudolph von Ihering wrote (in a modernized version):[1]

"Nobody will get from abroad what he has at home as well or even better, but only a fool will reject coffee because the coffee did not grow in his garden."

Yet there seem to be fools everywhere, since arguments based on comparative law research often meet considerable resistance.

Karl N. Llewellyn, Chief Reporter of the American Uniform Commercial Code, told Stefan A. Riesenfeld "never to reveal when [relying] on an idea coming from continental Europe, because that would be 'the kiss of death' ".[2] The same attitude prevails in many countries. The reason for this aversion to foreign experiences can hardly be explained. Whereas in natural sciences all novelties spread quickly, in social sciences every society, every country tries to reinvent the wheel and repeat bad experiences already suffered abroad. Apparently every community is so convinced of its uniqueness that there is supposedly no common ground with different communities. I shall come back to this sort of mainstreetism later.

4. Doing Research in Comparative Law

Ernst Rabel, one of the pioneers of comparative law, described another danger of comparative law research as follows: "Comparative

---

[1] R. von Ihering, *Geist des römischen Rechts auf den verschiedenen Stufen seiner Entwicklung*, vol. 1, 7th and 8th eds., 1924, pp. 8 and 9: "Niemand wird von der Ferne holen, was er daheim ebensogut oder besser hat, aber nur ein Narr wird die Chinarinde aus dem Grunde zurückweisen, weil sie nicht auf seinem Krautacker gewachsen ist."

[2] S.A. Riesenfeld, "Reminiscenses of Karl Llewellyn", in U. Drobnig & M. Rehbinder (eds.), *Rechtsrealismus, multikulturelle Gesellschaft und Handelsrecht. Karl N. Llewellyn und seine Bedeutung heute*, 1994, p. 14.

lawyers are used to penetrate unknown jungles and are prepared that in every bush a native with arrows is waiting".[3] This was written in 1951 and it is still true today. At the same time, however, it has to be added that comparative law research is by no means more complicated than any other ambitious research. Many problems are created by the fact that prejudices prevail and do not gradually collapse. Domestic niceties or sheer historical contingencies are built up into indigenous peculiarities of almost ethnological quality and interest. If a comparative lawyer is going to reveal such prejudices and reduce them to a common problem of a certain type of human society, such revelations will shatter the self-confidence of uncritical legal ethnologists. William Shakespeare may have had comparative lawyers in mind when, in Henry VI/2, butcher Dick said:

"The first thing we do, let's kill all the lawyers."[4]

Shakespeare should not, however, be taken too seriously – at least not with respect to comparative lawyers since they may be useful. Of course, comparative lawyers cannot reduce student numbers in over-crowded universities and they cannot abolish a chronic lack of money for academic education. What, however, they can do is cure academic legal education of an epidemic legal disease, of legal provincialism.

II. Legal Provincialism

1. Law as a National Subject of Studies

I do not know of any other subject of studies which is so narrow, so limited and nationally restricted as the subject of law. Whereas other branches of the humanities share the same language, the same methods and the same problems with all students and scholars engaged in the same field, law is a rather provincial subject matter. Since most civil law-countries and also common law-countries have codified

---

3 E. Rabel, "Deutsches und amerikanisches Recht", *Zeitschrift für auslndisches und internationales Privatrecht* 16 (1951), p. 340: "Rechtsvergleicher sind gewohnt, in fremde Dickichte einzudringen, und darauf gefaßt, daß unter jedem Busch ein Eingeborener mit Pfeilen lauert."

4 W. Shakespeare, *The Second Part of King Henry the Sixth*, Act IV, Scene II/86.

their law, either in comprehensive codes or in many statutes, the study of law tends to concentrate on these sources of national law. Is this inevitable?

2. Law as Part of the Humanities

The study of law need not become run-down as a matter of provincial importance only. Until at least the last century in many European countries, legal science was taught on a supra-provincial level based on Roman law and the Roman common law (Gemeines Recht) as developed in continental Europe and Latin America. Local niceties codified in regional codes or statutes were left aside or treated in subsidiary courses. Even research was supranational. Scholars exchanged books, periodicals and information about developments in foreign countries; arguments were discussed without distinguishing between local or foreign authors. Even in the United States scholars could still read foreign languages, including Latin, and make use of foreign ideas and experiences. This open-mindedness vanished to a large extent as soon as comprehensive codes of national law gave up the unwritten bases of common legal problems. Law became a national or provincial subject matter and the study of it was reduced to an exegetic and analytical treatment of local codes.

Maybe this deterioration was inevitable in times of national codifications, national political unification and in an atmosphere which was quite nationalistic. Circumstances have changed in the meantime. European law, whether unified or harmonized, is emerging;[5] a new European common law has been privately formulated in the laws of contracts[6] and civil procedure.[7] Students and professors have become mobile by a program initiated by the European Union. They study abroad as was done in former times and get some flavour of an international and supranational legal science. At home, we should also abandon nationalistic provincialism and turn to a more compre-

---

[5] Cp. P. Hommelhoff & E. Jayme (eds.), *Europäisches Privatrecht. Textausgabe*, 1993.

[6] Cp. O. Lando & H. Beale (eds.), *Principles of European Contract Law. Part I: Performance, Non-performance and Remedies*, 1995; A.S. Hartkamp & others (eds.), *Towards a European Civil Code*, 1994.

[7] M. Storme (ed.), *Approximation of Judiciary Law in the European Union*, 1994.

hensive legal education based on comparative law and take advantage of some glances "out of the cave".[8]

III. Advantages of Comparative Law

Up to now I have dealt only with the dangers connected to comparative law. We have to face them and be aware of them, but at the same time we have to apply comparative law, making use of its advantages and broadening our perspective. Is this endeavour worthwhile? Let me give you two examples.

1. The Indian Temple as a Plaintiff in English Courts

An antique Indian bronze sculpture representing the Hindu god Siva was stolen in India and brought to England. The London police seized the sculpture from the plaintiff, the Bumper Development Corporation, which claims to have bought the artifact in good faith from an art dealer. The Bumper Corporation brought an action against the Commissioner of Police of the Metropolis of London claiming recovery of the sculpture. The Indian temple from which the Siva sculpture was stolen intervened as an interpleader and sued for the recovery of the sculpture. One might expect that the Court of Appeal[9] had to answer difficult questions about the return of stolen cultural property and the bona fide purchase of movables. This was not the case. The main problem was whether the Indian temple had a standing to sue in English courts. The English court qualified this problem as a procedural one to be decided under the lex fori. As in English law not every foreign legal person can be a party to proceedings in English courts, a conflict arose because under Indian law the temple is recognized as a legal entity capable of holding title to an object and of suing or being sued in respect thereof in Indian courts. Finally, the Court of Appeal held "that the temple is acceptable as a

---

8 Cp. H.E. Yntema, "Comparative Legal Research. Some Remarks on 'Looking Out of the Cave' ", *Michigan Law Review* 54 (1956), p. 899.

9 Bumper Development Corporation v. Commissioner of Police of the Metropolis, [1991] 1 W.L.R. 1362 (C.A.).

party to the proceedings and that it is as such entitled to sue for the recovery of the [sculpture]".[10]

Interesting are the reasons for this conclusion. In many continental European legal systems the arguments would be like this: The standing to sue, although a notion of procedural law, is the procedural aspect of the general ability to be recognized as a legal person. This conclusion is drawn from general reflections on the nature of legal entities and their recognition in local courts. Whether a foreign legal person will be recognized is a matter of conflict of laws to be decided either by the principle of incorporation (Switzerland, England, USA) *or* by the principle of factual place of principal administration (Austria, Germany). If the forum State adheres to the principle of incorporation and the foreign country of incorporation recognizes the plaintiff as a legal person, this quality should also be recognized by the forum State unless prohibited by some special forum policies (e.g. foreign corporation acts). The English Court of Appeal did not follow this line. It admitted the Indian temple as an interpleader as a matter of comity, that is, by a general principle hardly connected with the real issues.

My objection is not that the Court of Appeal did not make use of comparative law to find the correct specific principle for the very issue to be decided by the court. My point is rather that comparative law has to start in law school and more emphasis should be laid on general principles of law, general ideas and their interaction in various fields of law.

In many continental European universities, students are compelled to pursue such general studies not in courses of jurisprudence but in normal courses of private, criminal or public law. The explanation is as follows: Many civil codes or similar codifications of other subject matters comprise "general parts" with basic notions and principles valid for the entire codification. Even if this is not the case, a long tradition of legal research dating back to the 17th century and even further has developed several general ideas – arguments based

---

[10] Bumper (last note) at p. 1373 (at E).

on logic, the nature of things and interrelations between problems which may be used in many different fields of law.

These general parts have been ridiculed or, to phrase it better, there is a continental European habit of boiling down special problems to the essential general idea and applying, in future cases, this general idea and the special rules emanating from them. There is no cause for this ridicule since dogmatism has been given up in favour of a functional approach and also simple logic may sometimes even be a very useful argument. Because of this treasure of general ideas, principles and notions, some continental European systems have been more flexible and adjustable to modern social needs than some jurisdictions normally qualified as being pragmatic and extremely flexible.

2. Mistake with Regard to Future Events

Some jurisdictions are very generous in permitting the avoidance of contracts because of mistake. This is especially true of Germany and Switzerland.[11] Based on theories of bygone ages, these jurisdictions want to make sure that the correct intentions of the parties are fulfilled without taking into account that a unilateral mistake, and because of this mistake an avoidance, must inevitably work at the expense of the other party. Therefore, such an attitude has correctly been described as being "mistaken on mistakes".[12]

Some evidence might be useful. In Switzerland, parties agreed to sell and buy a piece of land which, it was assumed by the seller, would be opened up for building in the future. When this anticipation did not materialize, the seller tried to avoid the contract on the basis of mistake. The Swiss Federal Court,[13] applying Swiss law, had to answer a general question: Can there be any legally relevant error with regard to future events? The Swiss Code of Obligations does not

---

[11] Cp. § 119 German Civil Code and Article 24 Swiss Code of Obligations.

[12] K. Zweigert, "Irrtum über den Irrtum. Rechtsvergleichende Bemerkungen zur Irrtumslehre", *Zeitschrift für Rechtsvergleichung* 7 (1966), pp. 12–22.

[13] Bundesgericht 7 June 1983, Entscheidungen des Schweizerischen Bundesgerichts 109 II p. 105 (Rüttimann v. Gemeinde Aclens).

deal with this problem and therefore some comparative law and even economic studies would have been very useful. The Austrian General Civil Code of 1811,[14] English law[15] as well as the recently published Principles of International Commercial Contracts[16] are rather reluctant in permitting the avoidance of a contract because of unilateral mistake. The general idea of a fair distribution of risks prevails in these systems. In general, mistakes are only relevant if the other party can be blamed for any misrepresentation or if the avoidance does not work at the expense of the other party.

Another lesson could have been learned from other legal systems and from economics. As soon as you include the future as a relevant factor for the conclusion of a contract and as soon as present facts and future expectations are treated alike, the law of contracts and business transactions is being undermined.[17] This can easily be explained: Many contracts are part of more comprehensive transactions. In many cases cirumstances will change and the future will not live up to personal wishes or expectations. If all those future circumstances and the disappointment caused by them would allow the avoidance of a single contract, almost every contract would be condemned to avoidance by one or the other party. If you do not realize this, you are missing the whole idea of contracting. Unless contracts are stipulated and performed on the spot, executory contracts are concluded to try to fix certain conditions because the future is uncertain and the contracting parties want to avoid this uncertainty or the daily conclusion of executed contracts. Therefore, contracts have to be relieved from any danger of being avoided by parties who are disappointed prophets.

---

[14] Cp. § 871 Austrian General Civil Code.

[15] Misrepresentation Act 1967 (c. 7).

[16] Cp. Article 3.5 (Relevant Mistake) in: UNIDROIT (ed.), *Principles of International Commercial Contracts*, 1994, p. 69.

[17] Cp. M. Adams, "Der Irrtum über 'künftige Sachverhalte' – Anwendungsbeispiel und Einführung in die ökonomische Analyse des Rechts", *recht* 1986, pp. 14–23.

IV. Comparative Law as a Yardstick

Examples of the advantages of comparative law and comparative studies could be added and discussed in greater detail. There is, however, no need for such a list of additional examples. The advantages of comparative law are obvious and can hardly be contested. What I should like to do is draw some conclusions for academic legal education.

1. Introduction to Foreign Legal Systems

Comparative law presupposes a solid knowledge of foreign legal systems. Therefore it is necessary to offer academic courses on such systems and some collateral courses on the legal terminology of foreign legal systems. Such courses should be mandatory and should try to repeat and consolidate the problems already known from courses on domestic law. This way, every course on a foreign legal system starts to become a course on comparative law proper.

2. Domestic Law and Foreign Solutions

Teaching domestic law may become boring – at least for the lecturer – if not accompanied by remarks about comparative law. Not only this, but in many cases the characteristics of a domestic solution can only be explained by giving some solutions found in foreign legal systems.

There is another advantage of such a mixture of domestic and foreign law. From my experience, students respond to foreign cases, solutions and theories very vividly. Their imaginations are stimulated and they start to ask questions about the utility and correctness of domestic law. Thereby, they mature for academic learning which should not be based on positivistic studies of domestic law. Also, domestic solutions are not so important. What really counts is the problem itself and the discussions of existing or hypothetical answers. Our academic legal education urgently needs some inspiration from comparative law.

3. Comparative Law Research

Comparative law is more than some knowledge about foreign legal systems and foreign solutions to universal problems. Comparative law is a difficult and dangerous though extremely useful method for solving problems. This should be taught in seminars offered to senior students and doctorate candidates. Yet, only in small groups can the very skills of comparison be conveyed. It is a burdensome process of trial and error, but eventually the students get some firm ability to try comparative law on their own.

V. Conclusions

1. Every national legal system is often venerated at home as being close to eternal wisdom and as emanating from ethnological uniqueness.

2.- In fact, national legal systems are in most cases no more than local attempts to solve universally known problems.

3. In order to know your own national legal system, you should learn something about foreign legal systems.

4. Positivistic studies should be left for cram schools.

5. Academic legal education should concentrate on legal problems.

6. To solve these problems both domestic and foreign law should be applied.

7. Therefore, foreign law should be part of the normal curriculum.

8. Domestic law should be taught more openly by including comparative law aspects.

9. Comparative law should be offered to senior students in seminars or small classes.

10. In short: Comparative law should be a yardstick for a decent and open-minded academic legal education.

Bibliography

Adams, Michael, Der Irrtum über "künftige Sachverhalte" – Anwendungsbeispiel und Einführung in die ökonomische Analyse des Rechts, in: recht 1986, pp. 14–23.

Hartkamp, Arthur S. & others (eds.), Towards a European Civil Code, Nijmegen-Dordrecht-Boston-London 1994: Ars Aequi Libri/Martinus Nijhoff Publishers.

Hommelhoff, Peter & Erik Jayme (eds.), Europäisches Privatrecht. Textausgabe, Munich 1993: Beck Verlag.

Ihering, Rudolph von: Geist des römischen Rechts auf den verschiedenen Stufen seiner Entwicklung, vol. 1, 7th and 8th eds., Leipzig 1924: Verlag Breitkopf & Härtel.

Lando, Ole & Hugh Beale (eds.), Principles of European Contract Law. Part I: Performance, Non-performance and Remedies, Dordrecht-Boston-London 1995: Martinus Nijhoff Publishers.

Rabel Ernst: Deutsches und amerikanisches Recht, in: Zeitschrift für ausländisches und internationales Privatrecht 16 (1951), p. 340.

Riesenfeld, Stefan A.: Reminiscenses of Karl Llewellyn, in: Ulrich Drobnig & Manfred Rehbinder (eds.), Rechtsrealismus, multikulturelle Gesellschaft und Handelsrecht. Karl N. Llewellyn und seine Bedeutung heute, Berlin 1994: Duncker & Humblot.

Shakespeare, William, The Second Part of King Henry the Sixth.

Storme, Marcel (ed.), Approximation of Judiciary Law in the European Union, Dordrecht-Boston-London 1994: Martinus Nijhoff Publishers.

UNIDROIT (ed.), Principles of International Commercial Contracts, Rome 1994: UNIDROIT.

Yntema, Hessel E., Comparative Legal Research. Some Remarks on "Looking Out of the Cave", in: Michigan Law Review 54 (1956), p. 899.

Zweigert, Konrad, Irrtum über den Irrtum. Rechtsvergleichende Bemerkungen zur Irrtumslehre, in: Zeitschrift für Rechtsvergleichung 7 (1966), pp. 12–22.

SOCIAL ASSISTANCE AND MIGRANT WORKERS – REGULATION NO 1612/68 FROM A SWEDISH PERSPECTIVE

Lotta Westerhäll

1. Questions at issue

The achievement of a common labour market is the primary goal within the field of free movement for persons. In a common labour market, the workers have the right to travel freely to another member country, and stay there to look for a job, take an employment or pursue a trade. Employees shall be treated equally regardless of nationality. Free movement applies to family members and certain other relatives of an employee, as well as to self-employed persons. The EC rules also favours the free movement of students and pensioners, even if these persons are not economically active.

This article will deal with the question whether a migrant person coming to Sweden with the purpose to work or study, has a possibility to receive social support if she/he is not capable of supporting herself/himself. In order to be able to answer this question, the legal prerequisites for free movement of different categories of persons have to be penetrated. The right to free movement includes the principle of non-discrimination, which means that the migrant person must have the same rights and duties as the country's own citizens. The consequences of this principle for migrant jobseekers will be examined here on the basis of the right to social assistance. The questions arisen from such an examination are not readily answered, since the Swedish Foreigners' Act stipulates an ability to support oneself in order to get a residence permit. It appears that the Swedish and the EC rules contradict one another. In certain aspects, the EC rules themselves are not very easy to interpret. Even though the EC rules about free movement also applies to job-seekers, it is not as evident that the principle of equality of treatment shall be valid in such cases. Neither is it clear what the role shall be of the national regulations in such circumstances. This article is an attempt to answer the posed question, taking into consideration both EC and national legislation.

2. Free movement of persons

2.1 Background

Below, I will discuss the legislation on free movement in relation to certain categories, namely employees and private entrepreneurs in possession of a job, jobseeking employees and private entrepreneurs, persons remaining in a contry after the cessation of an employment, family members of employees and private entrepreneurs, students, pensioners, and certain other cathegories of economically inactive persons. There is a number of legal sources determining the possibilities for free movement of these persons. The basic regulations are to be found in primary legislation, but there are also a number of important secondary legal acts in the forms of regulations and directives. The latter part of this section will deal with restrictions of the free movement. Restrictions of the free movement according to EC legislation will be compared to restrictions caused by national legislation, such as rules on residence permits.

2.2 The concept of free movement

The basic rules about the free movement of persons are to be found in arts 48 and 52 in the Treaty of Rome. They are concerned with employees and establishment, respectively. These regulations have, after a transition period, been given a direct effect within the EU, and can thus be called upon by private persons at national courts.

According to art 48 in the Treaty of Rome, a citizen of an EU country has the right to accept an employment in another EU country, to move there, and to move freely within the territories of the concerned countries, only being restricted by consideration to order, security and health. A person is also allowed to stay in a country in accordance with laws and regulations in this country in order to fulfill an employment there. A former employee has the right to stay also after the cessation of the employment.

The free movement of persons is, as has been stated above, dealt with in a number of secondary lawsuits. The basic regulations about migrant workers are to be found in Regulation No 1612/68 from the 15 October 1968.

2.3 The persons concerned

2.3.1 Employees

The question of who is to be considered as an employee, and therefore has the right to go to and stay in another country, has been investigated by the Court of Justice. It found that the concepts of "employee" and "employment" have a special legislative implication within the EU, and national legislation is therefore subordinate.[1] An employee is somebody who gets paid to do favours for somebody else under somebody else's guidance.[2] In principle, the employee concept therefore comprises all persons performing work for somebody else and according to this person's directions, against payment.

The extent of the work that the employee makes is of no importance. This implies that, apart from "ordinary workers", also practitioners, apprentices and persons working in somebody else's home, e.g. au pairs, are considered as employees. Part-time workers have been caracterized as employees in a couple of EC cases. It is, however, a minimal prerequisite that the business is "efficient and genuine", and not of such a small extent that it could be considered as purely marginal and subordinate.[3] Furthermore, a certain amount of eco-

---

[1] See 53/81 Levin (ECR/1982/1035); from a Swedish legislative point of view, see the final report from the Commission on Social Insurances and the EEC (State Public Commission Series, SOU 1993:115), Social Security and the EEA (Social trygghet och EES), p. 104–116.

[2] See 66/85 Lawrie-Blum (ECR/1986/2121).

[3] See 197/86 Brown (ECR/1988/3205), 357/89 Raulin (ECR/1992/1027) and 3/90 Bernini (ECR/1992/1071).

nomic activity is required. A part-time worker is considered as an employee also when the income from the part-time employment is not enough to support her/him, but she/he has to live on e.g. the yield of a fortune or support from the public.[4] The Court has found that gainful employment in the sense of the treaty is at hand also when a person performs work without getting a proper payment, but is instead supported through the organisation for which she/he works.[5] In a case concerning the application of the Treaty of Rome, the Court has stated that the question of a sport's organization's discrimination of a few competition motor cyclists fell outside the frames of the treaty, since it had no economic consequences.[6] Other activities, which can give the performer a certain compensation, but where the primare purpose is not financial, have, on the same grounds, not been referred to as work in the sense which I am discussing here. According to the Court, business within the frames of a drug abuse treatment paid by the state, is not to be considered as financial activities.[7] The principle which this case expresses has, however, not been applied to general "protected work".

There is a general and uniform concept of employees within the EC as far as migrant workers are concerned. This concept is imperative, which means that it cannot be interpreted differently in different countries. The Court has given the concept an extensive practise.

2.3.2 Self-employed persons

There are no rules in Regulation No 1612/68 concerning the free movement of self-employed persons. Such persons are instead directly subordinated the Treaty of Rome, the arts 52–58 about the right to establishment and 59–66 about the right to offer services being of particular importance. There is no big difference between the right to free establishment and the right to offer services. Both concern trade or business which is performed against payment. The first right implies the right to start a business in another member country. This

---

[4] See 53/81 Levin (ECR/1982/1035) and 139/85 Kempf (ECR/1986/1741).

[5] See 196/87 Steymann (ECR/1988/6159).

[6] See 36/74 Walrave & Koch (ECR/1974/1405).

[7] See 344/887 Battray (ECR/1989/1621).

to live together with the employed person is, however, that she/he has a domicile for her/his family which can be considered as normal for the country's employees in the region where she/he is employed.

The right for a spouse to stay in an EU country together with the employee is given only as long as the marriage exists, but it is independent of whether the spouses live together or not. If the marriage is dissolved according to a legal act or alike, the right for the spouse ceases according to art 10 in Regulation No 1612/68.[13] If the employee dies, those members of her/his family who used to stay with her/him, has the right to remain in the country under prerequisites which are described in art 3 in Regulation No 1251/70.

According to art 11 in the Regulation No 1612/68, the spouse and children of an EU citizen who has an employment in a member state other than her/his own, has the right to take an employment in that country even though they are not citizens of that state.

There are no rights for a cohabitant corresponding to the rights of a spouse. However, when a Swede living in Sweden has a cohabitant, who is a citizen of another EU country, and this cohabitant is given the right to stay in Sweden, the same right has to be given to the cohabitant of a person from another EU country, e.g. Great Britain, but who is living in Sweden.[14]

2.3.6 Students, pensioners and certain economically inactive people

According to the Council's directives 90/364/EEC, 90/365/EEC and 90/366/EEC, the right to free movement of persons also covers certain people who are economically inactive, students and pensioners, under the condition that they are EU citizens. It also applies to the family members of these people, regardless of citizenship. As a basic prerequisite, these categories of people have to have a full sickness insurance valid in the country where they are staying, and they have to be able to show that they have enough resources to support themselves, so that they will not burden their host country's social system. Students have the right to residence permits for the

---

[13] See 267/83 Diatta (ECR/1983/591).
[14] See 59/85 Reed (ECR/1986/1283).

whole duration of the studies, though it can be decided that the permit has to be renewed each year. Other categories are usually given residence permits to last for a period of five years. All the mentioned legal acts give further prerequisites for the right to stay.

2.4 Limitations of the free movement of persons

According to the Council's directive 64/221/EEC, the member states are allowed to break the rules concerning the free movement of persons only with regard to public order, security or health. This directive applies to all measures that have been agreed upon by the member states about entering a country, the issuing or renewal of residence permits, or expulsion from the country. The reasons mentioned may not be called upon for economic purposes (art 2). According to art 3 in the directive, measures taken with regard to general order or security, must be founded upon the behaviour of the concerned person. Previous crime sentences shall not in themself be a reason for taking such measures. As follows from art 4, only diseases and disabilities mentioned in an appendix to the directive, serve as reasons to refuse a person to enter the country, or to issue a first residence permit. The diseases named in the appendix are on one hand diseases that could jeopardize public health, and on the other diseases and disabilities that could threaten general order and security. To the first group belongs diseases that require quarantine according to the WHO International Declaration of Health (no 2 from the 25 May 1951), respiratory tuberculosis which is active, or shows signs of developing, syphilis, and other infectious diseases or contagious parasitic illnesses if comprised in regulations about protection of the host country's citizens. The latter group comprises narcotic drug abuse and deep mental disorders, obvious psycotic conditions with excitement, delirium, hallucinations or confusion.

The limitations mentioned above shall be given a narrow interpretation. The Court has stated that only a realistic and serious threat can motivate limitations in the free movement.[15] It should also

---

[15] See 67/74 Bonsignore (ECR/1975/297).

be noted that the Public Service is not covered by the regulations on free movement, and that activities concerned with public power can be reserved for the country's own citizens. In practise, this exception is, however, limited to employments which require solidarity with the State.

2.5 EEC rules on residence permits

The EEC rules on residence are to be found in the Council's directives 68/360/EEC, 73/148/EEC, 90/364/EEC, 90/365/EEC and 90/366/EEC. From these follows that an EU citizen getting an employment in another country shall, as a rule, be given a residence permit lasting for five years, as shall also her/his family members. The permit shall thereafter be renewed without further trial for at least twelve months. The residence permit may not be withdrawn if the holder gets sick or unvoluntarily unemployed. The duration of a prolonged residence permit can, however, be limited if the unemployment has lasted for more than a year. There are special rules for people who work for a period of less than three months, commute between countries or are seasonal workers. In such cases, a residence permit is not required, but these people are instead submitted to an obligation of notification. There are also special rules for people who retire, or cannot continue gainful employment for other reasons, and their families.

No working permit is needed for a person using the free movement to work in an EU country other than his own, and the host country has no possibilities of raising such a demand.

The right to enter another EU country only requires a valid passport or document of identification. An EU citizen working in another country cannot be expelled from this other country only because certain formalities are not fulfilled. The Court's practise gives that, for persons fulfilling the conditions for EC legislation, an issued residence permit is only a matter of proof, and not a prerequisite to be able to stay in another EU country.[16] The rules also give that an employee or a self-employed person shall be able to start working in

---

[16] See 48/75 Royer (ECR/1976/497) and 357/89 Raulin (ECR/1992/1027).

another member state before residence permits have been granted to her/him and her/his family. The formalities concerning the permit may not delay the starting of the work. Pensioneers, students etc have corresponding rights.

A residence permit may not be withdrawn because a person, against her/his wish, loses his job, or because she/he becomes unable to work due to sickness or injury.[17] The Court has decided that a person who becomes unemployed does not lose the benefits of free movement. If a person, after becoming unemployed, stays in the country to look for a new job, and she/he can be said to have reasonable possibilities of finding one, she/he cannot be asked to leave her/his country of residency, even if her/his residence permit is no longer valid.[18]

2.6 Swedish national rules on residence permits

The EU-directives mentioned above, have been implemented in Sweden through changes in the Foreigners' Act (1989:529) and the Foreigners' Regulation (1989:547).

In the Foreigners' Act, rules are given for the rights of foreign citizens to enter, stay, and get an employment in Sweden. It holds a condition for residence permit and working permit for non-Nordic citizens. In the Foreigners' Act 2:4, regulations on the cases when a foreign citizen may be given a residence permit on other grounds than that she/he is entitled to asylum here, are to be found. The government may prescribe that a residence permit is to be issued also in other cases than those mentioned in this paragraph. With support from this right, the government has declared in the Foreigners' Regulation 3:5a and b, that residence permits are to be issued for EU-citizens on showing up a valid passport or other identification document.

Employees and self-employed persons are to be given residence permits lasting for five years on showing up an employment certif-

---

[17] Directive 68/360/EEC.
[18] See 292/89 Antonissen (ECR/1991/745).

icate or a document showing the person's enterprise position, respectively. These residence permits shall be possible to renew.

A person who offers or is given services, a permit shall be given for the duration of these services, as told in a document strengthening the situation.

A pensioner, who is not covered by the rules which gives the right to stay in an EU country after the cessation of the employment, shall be given a five-year residence permit on condition that she/he has a pension which secures her/his living. If she/he is not, or will not, be covered by the Swedish Social Insurance, she/he also has to have a full-covering sickness insurance valid in Sweden. This kind of residence permit shall be possible to renew, but it can, however, be re-tried after the first two years.

Students shall be given residence permits lasting the entire education. If the education is longer than one year, the permit can be issued for one year at a time, and shall be possible to renew. The student has to be registered at a recognized school, and she/he has to be able to show that she/he has enough money for her/his own living. Just like the pensioners, a student has to have a full-covering sickness insurance valid in Sweden, if is not, or will not, be covered by the Swedish social insurance system.

For other categories of EU-citizens, a five-year residence permit is to be given, provided that they are able to secure their own living, and that they have a valid, full-covering sickness insurance if not covered by the Swedish legislation. The permit shall be possible to renew, but can be re-tried after two years. An interruption of the stay in Sweden exceeding six months, or absence due to military service, shall not affect the permit's validity.

For an employee as mentioned above, the residence permit may not be withdrawn only because she/he is temporarily incapable of working, due to sickness or injury, or that she/he is involuntarily unemployed, if this can be strengthened by the employment exchange. When the permit is renewed for the first time, its duration can be restricted, however, to not less than twelve months if the worker has been unemployed for more than twelve months in a row.

Family members of an EU citizen shall, regardless of their own citizenship, be given residence permits to the same extent as the EU citizen herself/himself, on condition that they can show a valid passport or identity card, a family certificate, or a document showing that they are dependent on the EU citizen.

As a conclusion, it can be stated that an EU citizen shall be able to seek, get and start a job in Sweden before a residence permit is granted, and without being delayed by formalities performed by national authorities (the Foreigners' Regulation 3:7a).

In the Foreigners' Act 2:11, the third paragraph, the government is authorized to determine conditions for the withdrawal of given residence permits, other than those already described in the law. With the support of this paragraph, it is stated in the Foreigners' Regulation 3:5c that there is a right to withdraw the residence permit of an EU citizen who does not properly earn her/his living here, or in other ways lacks fundings for her/his own support. If an EU citizen has been given a residence permit because she/he has an employment here, and then leaves this employment without seeking a new job, and does not have other ways to support herself/himself in Sweden, her/his residence permit might have to be withdrawn. However, one must be allowed to seek another employment, and a certain period of unemployment in between has to be accepted. In this situation, the person is a job-seeker, and is thus covered by the EC rules about the protection of such persons. Thus, an intervention shall only take place in the case of "obvious disproportions".[19]

A foreign citizen can be expelled according to the Foreigners' Act 4:2, the first paragraph, if she/he lacks sufficient fundings for her/his stay in this or another Nordic country, or for her/his journey home. The Danish Foreigners' Act 28 §, holds a corresponding regulation, but with the addition that a foreigner covered by EC rules cannot be expelled on these grounds.[20] This exception has been added because the formulation of the former law was critizised by the EC Commission. The Commission asserted that the demand for documentation of sufficient financial fundings is in violation with the second paragraph in the directive 64/221/EEC, according to which the consid-

---

[19] SOU 1993:120, Appendix 5.

[20] The Danish Foreigners' Act 2 §.

eration for general order, security or health, that can serve as grounds for the expulsion of this group of foreign citizens, cannot be called upon due to financial conditions.

The regulation on expulsion in Swedish legislation is entirely founded on a presumption about the foreigner's financial situation. Consideration to general order, security or health cannot be founded on financial conditions. Thus, there may not be any restriction as to the free movement of persons covered by the EEA agreement with support from the mentioned regulation.

3. Equality of treatment

3.1 Background

The principle of equality of treatment, or the non-discrimination principle, is fundamental for the concept of free movement for persons. It is essential within both primary and secondary legislation. it has been tried in a large number of cases in the Court, and there are few issues concerning free movement for persons which have been penetrated so carefully. The concept shall be briefly described below, according to the rules in the Treaty of Rome, and the Court's application of these rules, whereafter the different fields where the rules are applicable shall be established with help from both primary and secondary legislation. Then the principle will be applicated on the groups of persons that can come into question, namely employees, private entrepreneurs, job-seekers, persons remaining in a country after the cessation of their employment, family members and students.

3.2 The concept of equality of treatment

The central regulation about equal treatment is found in the Treaty of Rome, art 6. It expresses a general prohibition of discrimination due to nationality. A fundamental part in the establishment of the internal market is namely that all discrimination due to a person's nationality shall be abolished. This concerns a number of situations, such as occupation, salary, and other employment- and working conditions primarily related to an employed person. Legal practice show that the principle of equality of treatment prohibits hidden as well as open, indirect as well as direct, discrimination. The Court has established that the prohibition is not only applicable on disfavouring due to nationality, but also on circumstances that can lead to the same result, such as demand for residency within the country, or residency for a certain period of time before one is entitled to a benefit, unless the same conditions are required for the country's own citizens as well.[21] In fact, the demand for a certain period of residency, which is required also for the country's own citizens, has been proved to be unlawful due to the fact that it is generally easier for the country's own citizens to fulfill this prerequisite than it is for non-citizens.[22] The right to benefits can thus not be dependent on permanent residency,[23] or minimal duration of staying in the country.[24] Neither can a certain amount of gainful employment in the country be demanded.[25]

3.3 Fields where the principle is applicable

As stated above, the principle of equality of treatment is important in a number of different aspects and in several areas. Below, I will focus on the area of social protection in a vast sense. Social protection is regulated by special regulations in both primary and secondary legislation. Art 48 in the Treaty of Rome concerns equality of treatment for social protection in the form of both social insurance and social support.

As is stated in art 7.2 in Regulation No 1612/68, the principle of equality of treatment is valid for social advantages. It is prescribed that an employed person, who is a citizen of one EU state, shall be entitled to the same benefis as the citizens of another member state during time that she/he spends in this other state. The article can be

---

[21] See 152/73 Sotgiu (ECR/1974/162) and 249/83 Hoeckx (ECR/1985/973).

[22] See 111/91 The Commission v Luxembourg (ECR/1993/817).

[23] See 175/88 Biehl (ECR/1990/1779).

[24] See 197/86 Brown (ECR/1988/3205).

[25] See 157/84 Frascogna (ECR/1985/1739) and 39/86 Lair (ECR/1988/3161).

said to express the general idea that a migrant worker shall be integrated in the host-country's society, and be treated on the same conditions as the citizens of that country.

The Court has, in several cases, tried the question of what is to be comprised in the concept of social benefits. In practise, the concept has been given a vast interpretation, and it has become evident that it concerns not only legislative rights, but also rights that are given on more random basis.[26] The Court has found that the concept covers all social benefits given to national employees, based either on these persons' status as employees, or on the fact that they reside within the territory of the state. It does not matter whether or not the benefits are connected to any kind of employment. Among social benefits are not only social insurance benefits, but also public social or medical care, such as e.g. social assistance from the municipality where the worker stays. All measures, financial or not, which can help incorporating the worker into the host-country's society, are comprised in the concept, as long as they are part of the competence of the EC according to the Treaty of Rome.[27]

It may seem to be of minor importance to distinguish between social insurance benefits and social assistance, since both are comprised in the concept of social benefits. This is, however, not the case. Regulation No 1408/71 contains several rules on social security for migrant workers. Social security primarily means such benefits that are covered by the member countries' social insurance systems. A description of what parts of the social security systems that are covered by the regulation can be found in art 4. The purpose is to coordinate the social security systems of the different EU states. The principle of

---

[26] See 32/75 Cristini (ECR/1975/1085), 63/76 Inzirillo (ECR/1976/2057), 207/78 Even (ECR/1979/2019), 249/83 Hoeckx (ECR/1985/973) and 157/84 Frascogna (ECR/1985/1739).

[27] Among benefits that have been found to be comprised in art 7.2 in Regulation No 1612/68 can be mentioned measures to help handicapped persons to regain their working ability, train ticket reductions for large families, loans free of interest to newly become mothers, financial support to women at the time of birth, work support to young persons, and retirement pension with the purpose to ensure a minimal benefit, see 76/72 Michel (ECR/1973/457), 65/81 Reina (ECR/1982/33), 111/91 The Commission v Luxembourg (ECR/1993/817), 94/84 Deak (ECR/1985/1873) and 261/83 Castelli (ECR/1984/3199).

equality of treatment is expressed in art 3 in Regulation No 1408/71. The rule gives persons residing in one member state the same rights and obligations concerning social security as that country's own citizens. So shall e.g. Swedish citizens covered by German legislation, be entitled to the same benefits according to German legislation, and on the same conditions, as German citizens. Consequently, demands for citizenship for the right to benefits in a country's national legislation, are not valid for persons covered by the Regulation. Neither can there be demands for a certain period of residency for other than the country's own citizens.

As has been stated above, the Treaty of Rome comprises both social insurances and social assistance; Regulation No 1408/71 only social insurances (social security); and Regulation No 1612/68 all kinds of social advantages. The latter concept is wider than social insurances and social assistance put together. One can see that the borderline between social insurances, social assistance, and benefits, that fall outside these concepts, is not at all clear. This has caused problems in the application of the legislation as to different kinds of benefits which are not financed on charges. By the restriction to benefits that can be covered by the concept of social security, benefits belonging to e.g. the social assistance systems, are excluded. The demand for distinguishing between these different kinds of benefits when applying Regulation No 1408/71 has given rise to a number of cases where the Court has developed principles on which to found the delimitation.

It can generally be said that the development of the welfare systems has made it difficult to draw a straight line. Concrete needs is a characteristic criterion for the rules on social assistance, and its purpose is to guarantee a minimum standard of living, independent of employment, insurance, period of residency or payment of charges. Social security rules, on the other hand, are legislative rights connected to one of the branches of social security as described in art 4.1; they are based on association with e.g. a certain insurance system, and their conditions are clearly described, thus giving the persons concerned a well defined legal position.

The enumeration in art 4.1 serves to give a careful description of what branches of the social security field that are covered by Regulation No 1408/71, and to determine and define this area. There must thus be a connection between the benefit in question and one of the cases mentioned in the article for the regulation to be applicable. If this prerequisite is not fulfilled, it is not a benefit for social security in the sense of the regulation.[28]

As a conclusion, it can be said that benefits for social assistance are not covered by Regulation No 1408/71, but are instead regulated by the rules on social advantages in Regulation No 1612/68. Benefits in the kind of social security fall under both of the mentioned regulations. The concept of social assistance is not defined in any of the regulations. I can, however, be concluded that, according to the Court's legal practise, social assistance means support given to cover a person's basic needs after an individual trial. In the Swedish legal system, questions of this kind are referred to the legislation on Social Services.

3.4 The persons concerned

As has been stated above, the rules in art 7.2 in Regulation No 1612/68 concerns *employed persons*. An employed person, who loses her/his job involuntarily, does not lose her/his status as an employed person, or her/his rights to benefits according to the regulation. This is true also if she/he begins an education, if this education is somehow connected to her/his former work.[29] However, if a person leaves her/his employment voluntarily and starts studying, this can lead her/him losing the status as an employed person, unless there is a connection between the studies and the former employment.[30]

Legal practise states that, when it comes to social benefits, the principle of equality of treatment only applies to persons who have an actual employment, and not for persons staying in a member state other than their own to seek a job.[31]

In the case 316/85 Lebon, it is stated that it is important to note

---

[28] See 249/83 Hoeckx (ECR/1985/973) and 122/84 Scrivner (ECR/1985/1027).

[29] See 39/86 Lair (ECR/1988/3161) and 357/89 Raulin (ECR/1992/1027).

[30] See 3/90 Bernini (ECR/1992/1071), 293/83 Gravier (ECR/1985/593), 197/86 Brown (ECR/1988/3205) and 308/89 Di Leo (ECR/1990/4185).

[31] See 316/85 Lebon (ECR/1987/2811).

that the wording of art 7 of Regulation No 1612/68 refers to the actual pursuit of an activity. It is significant in any event that wherever in Title I to that regulation, a *person seeking work* is referred to, it is made clear and the expression "worker" is not used. It is also appropriate to mention the fact that in the description of the nature of the right to freedom of movement in art 48 of the Treaty of Rome, there is at most reference to offers of employment, but it is nowhere stated that persons seeking work are to be treated as workers for the purposes of that provision. In order to enter the territory of another member state, a national of a member state who intends to acquire the status of worker, does not need to produce an offer of employment; she/he must, however, prove the seriousness of her/his intention. To establish a right to residence, with which a claim to equality of treatment as a worker is associated, serious and genuine efforts to find employment are not sufficient; the pursuit of an activity as a worker is necessary.

The Court concludes that equal treatment with regard to social and tax advantages which is laid down by art 7.2 of Regulation No 1612/68, operates only for the benefit of workers, and does not apply to nationals of other member states, who move in search of employment.

The right to equality of treatment for workers is valid only as long as they have a right to stay in the host country. In this context it should be noted, however, that art 7 in Regulation No 1251/70 states that the right to equality of treatment as described in Regulation No 1612/68, shall apply also to persons covered by Regulation No 1251/70. As has been briefly described above, if certain conditions are fulfilled, the latter regulation gives e.g. employed persons a right to stay in a foreign member state after the cessation of the employment due to e.g. retirement.

The right to equality of treatment for social benefits given to employed persons by art 7.2 in Regulation No 1612/68 can, according to the Court, also apply to *family members* and relatives described in art 10, if they have used the possibilities to free movement as given to them in that article.[32] This right is, however, only indirect, and is a part of the social benefits given to the employed person herself/himself, that is, they can be given to the family member only if it can be seen as a benefit for the employed person in the sense that the family member is dependent on her/him for support. If this is the case, it is not important whether, in the national legislation, the benefit is described as a right for the employed person or e.g. for her/his child.[33] Under certain conditions, the family members of a deceased employee, who have lived together with this person in another member state, have the right to remain in the country. For such family members, the principle of equality of treatment should be applicable, also if the benefit is applied for after the death of the employed person.[34]

4. Concluding analysis

Social benefits that are not comprised in Regulation No 1408/71 can, in several cases, be considered as social benefits according to Regulation No 1612/68. In Sweden, this ought to be the case for e.g. great parts of the social services. This means that an EU citizen who works here, is entitled to equality of treatment in the field of social services for as long as she/he is settled here. Social benefits in this context means economic support, such as social assistance, as well as other kinds of support, such as home aid, transport aid, personal aid etc.

The idea behind free movement of persons is that EU citizens shall be allowed to reside anywhere within the area. A person who wishes to work in another country, shall have the possibility to go to this country to look for a job. She/he keeps the right to unemployment benefit from her/his home country for a maximum of three months.

---

[32] Several cases ruled by the Court show that the principle of equality of treatment in the Treaty of Rome, and the rules in Regulation No 1612/68 are not applicable on purely national conditions, that is, in situations without any EEC legislative element, or crossing of frontiers. It is e.g. stated that the regulation gives no right to benefits for non-EU-members who are, at the same time family members of an EU citizen, unless the latter has used his right to free movement, and works and lives in an EU state other than his own.

[33] See 316/85 Lebon (ECR/1987/2811) and 3/90 Bernini (ECR/1992/1071).

[34] See 32/75 Cristini (ECR/1975/1085).

However, what will happen if a person comes to Sweden to look for a job, and the unemployment benefit that she/he gets from the home country is not enough? Is she/he entitled to social support (social assistance) already before she/he has found herself/himself a job?

As has been made clear above, this issue has been tried by the Court.[35] It was found that there is a clear distinction between workers and job-seekers, and only the former category can demand to be treated in the same way as the country's ordinary citizens. According to the EC regulations, there is thus no right to social assistance in situations as the one described. A job-seeker who does not have enough fundings, is supposed to return to her/his own country. However, three months as the maximal time she/he is allowed to spend in the other country can be doubled, at least if it is clear that her/his job-seeking is serious. The lack of economic fundings is not in itself a ground for expelling a person. A residence permit may only be withdrawn on such reasons due to obviously bad behaviour.

What will happen if the same question is tried according to Swedish legislation?

A person working in Sweden who, against her/his will, loses job, is counted as an employee, and has the right to stay here to find a new employment. The same applies to a person whose employment ceases in accordance with her/his own will, as long as she/he is serious in the search for a new job. In the cases mentioned, as well as when a person who has a job, but still has difficulties supporting herself/himself and her/his family, EC legislation gives that these persons shall be treated equally with the country's own citizens. No discrimination is allowed. Somebody residing and working in Sweden with reference to the EC rules is thus entitled to full social support.

But the regulations in the Social Services Act pay attention to neither whether the person has a job in Sweden, nor if she/he is a Swedish resident. As a general rule, a municipality has the ultimate responsibility for every person who stays there and lacks economic means for her/his own support. This means that, according to a

---

[35] See 316/85 Lebon (ECR/1987/2811).

literal interpretation of Swedish legislation, the money-short job-seeker mentioned above should be entitled to social assistance.

The issue of whether the stay in itself implies a right to support to EU citizens, also comprises the question of the extent of such support. Since this has not yet been tried by the Swedish courts, it is uncertain how far the responsibility of the municipalities goes during the first three months in Sweden (and during the following months if the person in question is still looking for job). The municipalities have, in other contexts, interpreted the law as if it does not mean that a person who temporarily stays in Sweden shall be treated in the same way as a permanent Swedish resident. In practise, such a person usually has her/his request for social assistance turned down with reference to that her/his needs can be fulfilled in another way, namely by returning to her/his home country. It happens, however, that a person is given financial support for rent and travel expenses.

The governmental Social Services Commission has stated in the report "The Social Services in an EU Perspective" (SOU 1994:139), that the municipalities, just like today, must judge from case to case to what extent assistance is to be given in such a case. The practise applied for Nordic citizens coming to Sweden to look for work should, according to the Commission, be applicable also for EU citizens, meaning that the person in question would normally fiind her/his request refused with the motivation that her/his needs can be fulfilled if she/he returns to her/his own country.

I doubt this interpretation of 6 § in the Swedish Social Services Act to be correct. As mentioned above this section says that the municipality has responsibility for every person staying within its boundary and who lacks economic resources. That EC regulations give an EU citizen the right to stay in Sweden does not mean that the country's own legislation can be used in a discriminating way towards the EU citizen, even though she/he does not have the right to be treated equally with the country's own citizens in matters of social assistance due to EC rules. However, if the national regulations do not require citizenship or residency, but only temporary staying, this cannot be interpreted in another way for persons who are only staying temporarily in Sweden, than for Swedish citizens, who are only staying temporarily in one municipality that is not the home-municipality, and thereby giving the requisite "fulfillment of needs in another way" another meaning for foreign citizens. This practise is not justified by the fact that it came into use before Sweden joined the EU. In the case of a person who comes from a country with higher unemployment and smaller possibilities for social assistance than Sweden, a rejection with the mentioned motivation is not acceptable.

The Social Services Commission has also stated that if a person has not succeeded in getting a job after three months in Sseden, her/his right to stay here with reference to EC legislation would normally be forfeit. She/he then ought to get her/his request for a prolonged residence permit rejected. But as has been made clear above, there is no three-months rule for job-seeking in another EU country. This, in turn, means that the Swedish rules concerning the right to social assistance are still applicable.

Finally, the Social Services Commission has pointed out that there are reasons to follow the consequences for the free movement closely during the coming years. If it turns out that foreign citizens, covered by EC legislation, to a large extent claim social assistance, it may be time to revise the Swedish legislation. The measure which would then seem closest at hand, would, according to the Commission, be to consider creating a rule which makes it possible for the Social Services Boards to report to authorities responsible for questions about rejection and withdrawal of residence permits, without breaking confidentiality rules.[36]

This would, however, not be a good way of decreasing the possibilities for migrating EU citizens to get social assistance, which, of course would be the intention of the Swedish legislation. As has been made clear above, EC rules do not consider difficulties to support oneself as a reason for expelling, rejecting or withdrawal of a residence permit, no matter what the Swedish legislation says about it. Swedish rules and their interpretation may not be in disagreement with EC legislation. If one wants to make it impossible for job-seeking EU citizens to get Swedish social assistance, one has to change the concept of temporary staying. Such a measure would, on one hand,

---

[36] See SOU 1934:139, p. 574.

not be in violation with EC legislation, since the principle of equality of treatment does not apply to job-seekers, but, on the other hand, it could not be considered as being compatible with the basic EC principle of free movement. Interpreting rules or changing rules with the purpose to make a hindrance for free movements cannot be in accordance with art 6 in the Treaty of rome. This fundamental prohibition of discrimination due to nationality is interpreted as a true safeguard against more or less heavy attacks to abolish the principle of free movements and it can also be used in this context as a fundament for free movement of job-seekers.[37]

---

[37] See Ruth Nielsen, Arbejdsgiverens ledelsesret i EF-retlig belysning (The Managerial Prerogatives of the Employer in the Light of Community Law), p. 93–123.

LIST OF PUBLICATIONS 1960–1996
BY LENNART PÅLSSON

Edited by Olle Serin

The list of publications does not claim to be complete. Compendiums and expert's opinion reports are not included. The bibliography is in chronological order, containing own works, collaborations with other authors, anthologies, articles and official reports. Reprints are not included.

Abbreviations

JT   Juridisk tidskrift vid Stockholms universitet
RabelsZ   Rabels Zeitschrift für ausländisches und internationales Privatrecht
SvJT   Svensk juristtidning
TfR   Tidsskrift for rettsvitenskap

1960
Några frågor rörande arvsrättspreskription
    SvJT 1960 p. 541–545

1966
Haltande äktenskap och skilsmässor : komparativa studier över internationellt-privaträttsliga problem beträffande äktenskap och skilsmässor med territoriellt begränsad giltighet. – Stockholm : Norstedt, 1966. – 623 p. – Dissertation, Lund univ.

1967
Institutet litispendens i den internationella civilprocessrätten
    TfR 80 (1967) p. 537–586

1968

Bibliografisk introduktion til fremmed og komparativ ret – Bibliografisk introduktion till utländsk och komparativ rätt / Lennart Pålsson og Ole Lando. – København : Erhvervsøkonomisk forl., 1968. – 309 p.

Om innebörden av erkännande och icke-erkännande av utländska familjerättsliga statusavgöranden
　　TfR 81(1968) p. 145–192

1969

Review of Kristian Dorenberg: Hinkende Rechtsverhältnisse im internationalen Familienrecht. – Berlin, 1968
　　RabelsZ 33(1969) p. 577–580

1970

EEC-rätt. – Lund : Studentlitt., 1970. – 150 p.

Internationellt privaträttsliga rättsfall. – 2. uppl. / sammanställd av Åke Lögdberg och Lennart Pålsson. – Lund : Juridiska föreningen, 1970. – 177 p.

The Institute of *Lis Pendens* in international civil procedure
　　Scandinavian studies in law 1970 p. 59–108

Review of Sten Niklasson: Rätt och beslut i EEC. – Lund, 1969
　　SvJT 1970 p. 314–317

Review of Ulf Bernitz: Europeisk marknadsrätt. – Stockholm, 1969
　　SvJT 1970 p. 389–391

Review of Ole Lando: Udenrigshandelens kontrakter. Udenrigshandelsret I: Skandinavisk, vesteuropaeisk og amerikansk ret om kontraktforhold i almindelighed samt om køb, agentur og eneforhandling. – København, 1969
　　SvJT 1970 p. 473–476

1971

Internationellt privaträttsliga rättsfall. – 3. uppl. / sammanställda av Åke Lögdberg och Lennart Pålsson. – Lund : Juridiska föreningen, 1971. – 221 p.

1972

Internationellt privaträttsliga rättsfall. – 4. uppl. / sammanställda av Åke Lögdberg och Lennart Pålsson. – Lund : Juridiska föreningen, 1972. – 229 p.

1973

Konventionssamling i internationell privaträtt / utg. av Eric W. Essén och Lennart Pålsson. – Lund : Studentlitt., 1973. – 207 p.

Review of Torben Svenné Schmidt: International skilsmisse- og separationsret. – Århus, 1972
SvJT 1973 p. 406–410

1974

Marriage and divorce in comparative conflict of laws. – Leiden : Nijthoff, 1974. – lxxxviii, 345 p.

Författningssamling i internationell privaträtt. – Lund : Juridiska föreningen, 1974. – 260 p.

1975

Review of István Szászy: Conflict of laws in the western, socialist and developing countries. – Leiden, 1974
SvJT 1975 p. 216–218

1976

Författningssamling i internationell privaträtt. – Lund : Studentlitt., 1976. – 301 p.

EG-rätt. – Lund : Studentlitt., 1976. – 359 p.

Review of Hjalte Rasmussen: Domstolen i EF. – København, 1975
SvJT 1976 p. 303–304

1977

Rättsfalls- och övningsmaterial i internationell privaträtt. – Lund : Juridiska föreningen, 1977. – 349 p.

Review of Internationales Privatrecht / hrsg. von Paolo Picone und Wilhelm Wengler. – Darmstadt, 1974
SvJT 1977 p. 218–219

1978

Marriage and divorce

International encyclopedia of comparative law. – Tübingen : Mohr, 1971-. – Vol. 3 : Private international law : chapter 16. – 175 p.

Review of Allan Philip: Dansk international privat- og procesret. – 3. udg. – København, 1976
TfR 91(1978) p. 577–585

Review of Ralph Lansky: Handbuch der Bibliographien zum Recht der Entwicklungsländer : Entwurf
TfR 91 (1978) p. 726–728

1980

Författningssamling i internationell privaträtt. – 2. uppl. – Lund : Studentlitt., 1980. – 337 p.

EG:s domskonvention
SvJT 1980 p. 497–530

Utkast till EG-konvention om tillämplig lag på kontraktsrättsliga förpliktelser : värdering från svensk synpunkt
Nordisk tidsskrift för international ret 49 (1980) p. 152–171

1981

Marriage in comparative conflict of laws : substansive conditions. – The Hague : Martinus Nijhoff, 1981. – lxxvi, 388 p.

Rättsfalls- och övningsmaterial i internationell privaträtt. – 2. uppl. – Lund : Studentlitt., 1981. – 358 p.

Konventionssamling i internationell privaträtt / utg. av Eric W. Essén, Lennart Pålsson. – 2., omarb. uppl. – Lund : Studentlitt., 1981. – 237 p.

1982

Svensk rättspraxis : internationell privat- och processrätt 1976–1980
SvJT 1982 p. 214–251

1983

Författningssamling i internationell privaträtt. – 3. uppl. – Lund : Studentlitt., 1983. – 332 p.

Internationella faderskapsfrågor : betänkande av utredningen om internationella faderskapsfrågor. – Stockholm : Liber/Allmänna förl., 1983. – 223 p. – (Statens offentliga utredningar ; 1983:25)

1984

Rättsfall- och övningsmaterial i internationell privaträtt. – 3. uppl. – Lund : Studentlitt., 1984. – 331 p.

Utvecklingslinjer och aktuella problem i svensk internationell privaträtt

   SvJT 1984 p. 841–860

1986

Svensk rättspraxis i internationell familje- och arvsrätt. – Stockholm : Norstedt, 1986. – 217 p.

Rules, problems and trends in family conflict of laws : especially in Sweden

   Recueil des cours de l'Académie de droit international de la Haye. T. 199 (1986-IV) p. 313–413

Review of Karnovs EF-samling (EF-Karnov) : 1978–84. Supplement til 1978-udgaven / Claus Gulmann ... – København, 1984

   SvJT 1986 p. 362–363

1987

Rättsfalls- och övningsmaterial i internationell privaträtt. – 4. uppl. – Lund : Studentlitt., 1987. – 339 p.

Suède – filiation paternelle – droit international privé

   Revue critique de droit international privé 1987 p. 198–201

Svensk rättspraxis : internationell privat- och processrätt 1981–1985
SvJT 1987 p. 331–368

Internationella familjerättsfrågor : slutbetänkande av familjelagssakkunniga. – Stockholm : Allmänna förl., 1987. – 365 p. – (Statens
offentliga utredningar ; 1987:18)

Internationella förmynderskapsfrågor : betänkande av förmynderskapsutredningen. – Stockholm : Allmänna förl., 1987. – 192 p. –
(Statens offentliga utredningar ; 1987:73)

1988
Konventionssamling i internationell privaträtt / [utg. av] Eric W.
Essén och Lennart Pålsson. – 3., omarb. uppl. – Lund : Studentlitt.,
1988. – 271 p.

Författningssamling i internationell privaträtt. – 4. uppl. – Lund :
Studentlitt., 1988. – 354 p.

1989
Svensk rättspraxis i internationell processrätt. – Stockholm : Norstedt, 1989. – 241 p.

Adoptionsfrågor : slutbetänkande av förmynderskapsutredningen. –
Stockholm : Allmänna förl., 1989. – 291 p. – (Statens offentliga utredningar ; 1989:100)

1990
Vårdnad och umgängesrätt i svensk internationell privaträtt
Festskrift till Lars Hjerner : studies in international law. – Stock-
holm : Norstedt, 1990. – p. 485–512

Luganokonventionen
SvJT 1990 p. 441–470

1991
Författningssamling i internationell privaträtt. – 5. uppl. – Lund :
Studentlitt., 1991. – 332 p.

Rättsfallssamling i internationell privaträtt. – 5. uppl. – Lund : Studentlitt., 1991. – 303 p.

Forum solutionis i Luganokonventionen
Festskrift till Ulla Jacobsson. – Stockholm : Norstedts juridik, 1991.
– p. 175–189

Review of Dieter Henrich: Internationales Familienrecht. – Frankfurt
a.M., 1989
RabelsZ 55 (1991) p. 173–175

1992
Luganokonventionen. – Stockholm : Norstedts juridik, 1992. – 312 p.

Luganokonvensjonen. – Oslo : TANO, 1992. – 347 p.

Konventionssamling i internationell privaträtt / [utg. av] Eric W.
Essén, Lennart Pålsson. – 4., omarb. uppl. – Lund : Studentlitt., 1992.
– 270 p.

Svensk rättspraxis : internationell privat- och processrätt 1986–1990
SvJT 1992 p. 475–503

Schweden (Länderbericht)
Der internationale Rechtsverkehr in Zivil- und Handelssachen /
Arthur Bülow . . . – Bd 3. – München : Beck, 1983-14. Ergänzung-
slieferung 1992. – 12 p.

1993
Författningssamling i internationell privaträtt. – 6. rev. uppl. – Lund :
Studentlitt., 1993. – 313 p.

Produktansvaret och Luganokonventionen
JT 4 (1992/93) p. 853–864

Nya lagvalsregler för försäkringsavtal
SvJT 1993 p. 43–63

Underhållsfrågor och internationell privaträtt
SvJT 1993 p. 613–633

1994
Skiljeförfarande och Bryssel/Luganokonventionerna
SvJT 1994 p. 1–22

Nyare rättspraxis till Bryssel- och Luganokonventionerna
SvJT 1994 p. 593–615

Utländska kärandes skyldighet att ställa säkerhet för rättegångskostnader, särskilt inom EU/EFTA-området
JT 6 (1994/95) p. 464–475

Suveränitet och demokrati : betänkande av EG-konsekvensutredningarna: subsidiaritet. – Stockholm : Fritze, 1994. – 245 p. + bil. 343 p. – (Statens offentliga utredningar ; 1994:12)

1995
Bryssel- och Luganokonventionerna. – Stockholm : Fritze, 1995. – 337 p.

Författningssamling i internationell privaträtt. – 7. rev. uppl. – Lund : Studentlitt., 1995. – 329 p.

1996
Säkerhetsåtgärder och andra interimistiska åtgärder i internationella tvister
SvJT 1996 p. 385–413

Svensk rättspraxis : internationell privat- och processrätt 1991–1995
SvJT 1996 p. 593–634

Lag (1992.794) med anledning av Sveriges tillträde till Luganokonventionen / [kommenterad] av Thorsten Cars, Lennart Pålsson
Karnov : svensk lagsamling med kommentarer / huvudredaktörer Birgitta Blom ... – Stockholm, 1996. – D. 3. -p. 2650–2678

NOTES ON THE CONTRIBUTORS

Michael Bogdan, b. 1946. Professor of comparative and private international law. Has written on various subjects in the fields of conflict of laws, private law, international law and comparative law.

Ole Due, b. 1931. Honorary professor, University of Copenhagen. Jur. dr. h.c. Stockholm university. Former president of the Court of Justice of the European Communities. Has written on problems of EC-law, international private law and administrative law.

Jens Fejø, b. 1942. Professor, LL.D., of EU Competition Law, Copenhagen Business School, Law Department. Has written on various subjects mostly in relation to EC/EU Competition Law and in relation to Intellectual Property Rights. Expert member of the Board of Appeal dealing with tenders for building and construction works and purchases within The European Communities. Member of The Danish Competition Appeals Tribunal. Expert Member of The Commission for revision of the Danish Competition Act 1993–95. Board member of the Danish Association of European Law. Board Member of the Danish Energy Law Assembly.

Ulf Göranson, b. 1947. Chief Librarian of Uppsala University Library. Former professor of comparative and international private law, Uppsala university. Has written on property and contract law, conflict of laws and comparative law.

Maarit Jänterä-Jareborg, b. 1954. Associate professor of private international law; legal adviser in private international law at the Swedish Ministry of Justice. Has written on, i.a., conflict of laws and international procedural law.

Ole Lando, b. 1922. Professor emeritus, Copenhagen Business School, dr. jur., dr. oecon. h.c. (Stockholm School of Economics), dr. jur. h.c. (Osnabrück). President of the Commission on European Contract Law. Member of the International Academy of Comparative Law. Has published books and articles on private international law, EU law and comparative law.

Hans Henrik Lidgard, b. 1946. Former member of the Swedish Bar Association. Since 1984 in managing positions in the pharmaceutical industry. Has written on various subjects relating to European competition law and other trade related aspects.

Göran Melander, b. 1938. Received a law degree from the University of Lund, Sweden in 1964 (LL.M.). He became assistant professor of international law at the same university in 1976 and professor of international law in 1995. He is the director of the Raoul Wallenberg Institute of Human Rights and Humanitarian Law since 1984, when the Institute was founded.

Allan Philip, b. 1927. Former professor of private international law, University of Copenhagen. Partner Philip & Partners, Copenhagen. Member of Institut de Droit International. Has written on private and public international law and maritime law, and practices in international commercial law and EU law.

Carl Michael Quitzow, b. 1962. Associate professor of EC-law, LL.D., Lund university. Has written on various subjects of EC-law, mainly on free movement, competition law and the interpretation of Article 5 EC-Treaty.

Kurt Siehr, b. 1935. Professor of private law, private international law and comparative law, Zürich University. Has written on various subjects of private law, private international law, law of cultural property, uniform law and comparative law.

Lotta Westerhäll, b. 1944. Professor of public law and social law, School of Economics and Commercial Law, Göteborg University. Has written on various subjects in the fields of social security law, medical law, social welfare law, administrative law and constitutional law.